RETHINKING TRANSITIONAL JUSTICE FOR THE TWENTY-FIRST CENTURY

Transitional justice is the dominant lens through which the world grapples with legacies of mass atrocity, and yet it has rarely reflected the diversity of peace and justice traditions around the world. Hewing to a largely Western and legalist script, truth commissions and war crimes tribunals have become the default means of "doing justice." *Rethinking Transitional Justice for the Twenty-First Century* puts the blind spots and assumptions of transitional justice under the microscope and asks whether the field might be reimagined to better suit the diversity and realities of the twenty-first century. At the core of this reimagining is an examination of the broader field of postconflict peacebuilding and associated critical theory, from which both caution and inspiration can be drawn. By using this lens, Dustin N. Sharp shows how we might begin to generate a more cosmopolitan and mosaic theory and imagine more creative and context-sensitive approaches to building peace with justice.

Dustin N. Sharp is an associate professor at the Joan B. Kroc School of Peace Studies at the University of San Diego. Prior to teaching, he covered Francophone West Africa for Human Rights Watch.

Preface

What does it mean to "do justice" in the wake of massive human rights violations? Justice for what, exactly? Justice for whom? And justice to what ends?[1] Such questions have aroused fierce debate from antiquity[2] up through the present day. They are profoundly political, ideological, ethical, philosophical, religious, and, yes, legal questions. Over the brief course of the last thirty years, these questions have become inseparable from the field of "transitional justice," the "globally dominant lens"[3] through which we now grapple with legacies of violence and mass atrocity. Today, this field has come to provide something of a blueprint for postconflict justice around the world. Its various mechanisms – ranging from trials and truth commissions to reparations and reconciliation initiatives – increasingly follow in war's wake, even though many outside of the field have never even heard the term *transitional justice*. Arguments for the necessity of some form of transitional justice are often grounded in notions of atrocity prevention and deterrence ("never again"), nation building (building or restoring democracy and the "rule of law"), and moral necessity (just deserts).[4]

Since the initial explosion of transitional justice practice in the 1980s, the programs and institutions associated with it have in some respects moved from the exception to the norm, embraced by the United Nations (UN) and major international donors alike. We now take it for granted that a permanent International

---

[1] I have drawn these three questions from Rosemary Nagy and her influential article "Transitional Justice as Global Project: Critical Reflections," *Third World Quarterly* 29, no. 2 (2008): 276.
[2] See generally Jon Elster, *Closing the Books: Transitional Justice in Historical Perspective* (Cambridge: Cambridge University Press, 2004).
[3] Paul Gready and Simon Robins, "From Transition to Transformative Justice: A New Agenda for Practice," *International Journal of Transitional Justice* 8, no. 3 (2014): 339.
[4] See Christine Bell, "Transitional Justice, Interdisciplinarity and the State of the 'Field' or 'Non-Field,'" *International Journal of Transitional Justice* 3, no. 1 (2009): 13 (discussing the different overlapping conceptions of the field of transitional justice).

Criminal Court exists, that donors routinely help fund truth commissions in post-conflict scenarios, and that human rights abusers, including even former heads of state, are increasingly put on trial in a range of tribunals, at national, regional, and international levels. Yet these are developments that would have been unthinkable as early as the 1970s, and that is a startling change in the blink of a historical eye.

Despite this trajectory, the fundamental questions of justice at stake in the wake of large-scale repression and violence have not become easier with the passage of time. Whether it is genocide in Rwanda or the mass atrocities unfolding in Syria today, the question of how to grapple with the unfathomable and unspeakable continues to strain the moral imagination.[5] True, international law plays an increasingly important role in international policy making and interventions around the world, providing a limited degree of guidance. Concepts such as genocide and crimes against humanity are now well defined – we are not making it up after the fact, as seemed to be the case with the post–World War II Nuremburg tribunal. And yet "justice" remains a messy, elusive, and essentially contested concept often deeply rooted in context-specific history and culture. At times, the proliferation of postconflict justice institutions and initiatives might seem to suggest a greater base of knowledge and consensus about such matters than actually exists. If the questions I posed at the outset are not therefore new, this book is premised in part on the notion that there is value to be found in occasionally returning to first principles and asking foundational questions – as if for the first time – with a view to taking stock and looking forward.

Transitional justice was born out of the euphoria, triumphalism, and, perhaps, arrogance of the "end of history," a time in the 1980s and 1990s when some believed, in a sort of democratic domino theory, that the world was inevitably converging, or at least normatively *should* be converging, upon Western liberal market democracy as the only plausible form of governance.[6] It was in the forge of the ideology and intellectual ebullience of this era that the "dominant script" of transitional justice

---

[5] John Paul Lederach, *The Moral Imagination: The Art and Soul of Building Peace* (Oxford: Oxford University Press, 2005).

[6] The phrase "the end of history" was made famous by political scientist Francis Fukuyama and his influential book *The End of History and the Last Man* (New York: Avon Books, 1992). For Fukuyama's critics in particular, the concept of "the end of history" has come to stand for a sort of arrogant, *fin-de-siècle* triumphalism. Fukuyama's book however is far more nuanced than is often remembered. While Fukuyama certainly thought humans could do no better than liberal market democracy, he did not see liberal market democracy as perfect, and he acknowledged the very real possibility that democracies could fall back into other forms of governance. In other words, liberal market democracy might be normatively desirable, but Fukuyama did not see it as inevitable that it would be attained or maintained. One could always slide back into the darker side of human history. Throughout this book I will use the phrase "the end of history" not with the plenitude of Fukuyama's nuance in mind, but as a shorthand for the arrogance and triumphalism with which it has become associated in the popular imagination, and which otherwise so aptly characterized the zeitgeist of the times.

was created, a script premised on a core liberal-legalist narrative.[7] With the fall of the Berlin Wall and the emergence of dozens of countries in Eastern Europe and Latin America from periods of Cold War repression, many asserted, embracing this narrative, that countries in transition from authoritarianism could help to expedite and consolidate momentum toward liberal democracy by grappling with dark histories of human rights abuses via mechanisms such as trials and truth commissions. Behind the activist impetus for accountability and calls of "never again" lay a faith in the redemptive power of law and human rights to help postconflict societies move beyond their troubled pasts and take an evolutionary leap forward into the end of history. The law, it seemed – through a focus on civil and political rights and atrocity justice – might serve as liberalizing handmaiden to a new democracy that was imagined to be almost postideological and postpolitical.

Of course, to say that transitional justice is a "liberal" project and has a "legalist" orientation might seem obvious to many, and these concepts are not in and of themselves suggested here as inherently pejorative or problematic as at times seems to be the case in some of the critical studies literature. However, a key argument in this book is that while transitional justice can be associated with liberalism writ large and its many variants, it has been particularly shaped by a narrower form of *neoliberalism* – a turbocharged liberal capitalist ideology – which has in turn fostered and cemented rather reductive and minimalist understandings of violence, justice, and human rights at the core of the field. These limited and pinched understandings have been tightly woven into the dominant script, not only helping to shape initial thinking about what it meant to "do justice" in times of transition but also casting a long shadow over transitional justice thinking, policy, and practice up though the present day. In other words, debates about some of the field's most vexing questions – justice for what, for whom, and to what ends – cannot be understood without reference to that (dominant, neoliberal) script. It has effectively come to shape the field's core and periphery, what is emphasized and what is marginalized.

This book puts the dominant script of liberal-legalist transitional justice under the microscope, looking at its underlying ideology, politics, blind spots, and assumptions. I argue that if that script has at times provided a compelling narrative for the mobilization of activists, NGOs, and international organizations, it has also had the effect of narrowing the policy horizon of national actors working to build peace, justice, and reconciliation and has come to undergird a rather top-down, interventionist, and cookie-cutter transitional justice template, imagined to be somehow apolitical. In terms of more specific anxieties arising from the dominant script, one could point to the field's narrow conceptions of violence and justice, asking why

---

[7] I have borrowed the phrase "dominant script" from James Cavallaro and Sebastián Albuja. See "The Lost Agenda: Economic Crimes and Truth Commissions in Latin America and Beyond," in *Transitional Justice from Below, Grassroots Activism and the Struggle for Change*, ed. Kieran McEvoy and Lorna McGregor (Oxford: Hart, 2008), 125.

questions of economic violence, economic justice, and other structural drivers of conflict have been largely excluded from the ambit of historical transitional justice concern. Others have questioned the field's reliance on largely Western cultural modalities of justice (often coming as imposed, top-down solutions) as a means of grappling with the past, arguing that local, traditional, or otherwise non-Western and perhaps nonliberal forms of justice need to be given greater pride of place if transitional justice is to become more of a truly global project that does not spark local resistance and backlash. And still others point out that transitional justice practices have for some time been applied to a range of contexts (both transitional and nontransitional, democratic and less democratic) and seem as likely to help consolidate the power base of illiberal regimes as they are to foster liberal democracy, significantly undermining a core teleological premise of the dominant script.

It is therefore clear that transitional justice is a contested project from both within and without. At present, many of these voices are centrifugal, seeking to push outward and through the historical boundaries of the field to enlarge the subjects of its embrace and concern. At the same time, while the dominant script has not remained entirely static amid all of this normative ferment and contestation, there are also strong centripetal forces at work as the field is increasingly normalized and mainstreamed into the practice and programming of NGOs, international organizations, and bilateral donors. Many of the field's historically core features and tenets – especially a faith in the power of law and retributive justice to mediate social change and foster democracy – have been assimilated into a sort of deep-seated professional cosmovision, even if often less explicitly articulated than in earlier decades. Transitional justice programs and policies increasingly tip their hats to conceivably radical concepts like economic justice and local ownership, and yet the day-to-day practice of transitional justice remains little changed.

Meanwhile, we live in a post–post–Cold War world – it has been nearly thirty years since the fall of the Berlin Wall. The optimism of the "end of history" that animated a nascent field seems today premature, naïve, or simply a distant memory. Headlines today suggest an explosion of religious extremism and the resurgence of nationalism, spheres of influence, and muscular authoritarianism.[8] The most recent wave of "transitions" in the Middle East and North Africa were all but aborted, turning out, in most cases save Tunisia, to usher in more disaster than democracy. It seems that history has returned with a vengeance, if it ever went away to begin with. At the same time, transitional justice, though seemingly ascendant, is said to be in a state of "crisis," owing to deep questions about the effectiveness and perceived legitimacy of programs and initiatives around the world.[9] A 2015 call for papers for

---

[8] Walter Russell Mead, "The Return of Geopolitics; the Revenge of Revisionist Powers," *Foreign Affairs* (May/June 2014).
[9] See Vasuki Nesiah, "Transitional Justice Practice: Looking Back, Moving Forward," Scoping Study, Impunity Watch, May 2016, 5.

the *International Journal of Transitional Justice*, the leading academic journal in the field, provocatively asked whether the field has a future.[10]

Against this backdrop, one would do well to ask hard questions about the continued relevance of the field of transitional justice as a global project. Might a field shaped by intellectual currents of the late twentieth century be reimagined to better serve the realities of the twenty-first? Might there be a new and better script on which the field might be modeled? What might a more cosmopolitan, heterogeneous, and mosaic theory and practice befitting of a true global project look like? How might concerns about legitimacy and effectiveness best be addressed? These are among the central questions this book investigates.

While largely critical of much the field as it has evolved, I will argue that the narrow understandings at the heart of the dominant script are not inevitable or hardwired into transitional justice or liberalism itself. Indeed, there are broader aspects of the liberal tradition that might lead to more extended conceptions of violence, justice, and human rights, and a more context-sensitive approach to questions of transitional justice. Inspiration for a renewed transitional justice practice can also be found in concepts from the critical studies literature of peacebuilding and development. Part of this book is therefore about what liberal societies that have championed transitional justice around the word can learn from themselves when it comes to developing transitional justice practice that benefits from a greater sense of local legitimacy and ownership, and that might quite possibly be more effective when it comes tackling potential drivers of future mass atrocities. I argue that we need to recover alternative liberalisms and principles that can help reshape transitional justice going forward into a more flexible, needs-sensitive project grounded in principles such as pluralism, subsidiarity, inclusion, participation, autonomy, and self-determination. In short, it may not be necessary to throw the liberal baby out with the bathwater in trying to imagine more emancipatory forms of transitional justice. To contest some of the liberal ideological assumptions of transitional justice is not therefore to jettison liberalism itself.

STRUCTURE OF THE BOOK

Before advancing this line of argument further, it is necessary to explore transitional justice foundations in greater detail, which I do in Chapter 1. It is by examining and dissecting core narratives and assumptions that the deeper politics of the transitional justice project can be laid bare for careful scrutiny. This in turn will serve as a prelude to exploring, in Part I of this book, what I call transitional justice "peripheries" – those aspects of transitional justice policy and practice that have historically been pushed to the margins as a result of the dominant script. By asking and interrogating

---

[10] See International Journal of Transitional Justice, "Transitional Justice: Does It Have a Future?," www.oxfordjournals.org/our_journals/ijtj/call_for_papers_2015.html.

the questions with which I began – justice for what, for whom, and to what ends – I hope to both elucidate the dynamics of the dominant script and engage with critical questions as to what transitional justice might become going forward. Part I consists of three chapters.

In Chapter 2, I ask the question of "justice for what" by exploring the ways in which the (neo)liberal frames at the heart of the field have served to limit our sense of what the "justice" of transitional justice should reasonably be expected to cover. I argue that while there is increasing momentum behind the notion that the tools of transitional justice should be marshaled in response to large-scale human rights atrocities and physical violence – including murder, rape, torture, disappearances, and other crimes against humanity – the proper role of transitional justice with respect to economic violence – including violations of economic and social rights, corruption, and plunder of natural resources – is far less certain. Historically, if mass atrocities and physical violence have been placed in the transitional justice spotlight, issues of equally devastating economic and social justice have received little attention. The marginalization of the economic within the transitional justice agenda serves to distort our understanding of conflict, and the policies thought to be necessary in the wake of conflict. Key to reimagining transitional justice practice going forward then will be an embrace of more extended conceptions of violence and justice.

In Chapter 3, I ask the question of "justice for whom" by exploring the frictions and contractions generated by the interface point between a largely liberal internationalist transitional justice enterprise and dimensions of "the local" (local ownership, local values, local practices, etc.). Relatedly, this chapter looks at the "how" of dominant transitional justice practice. I argue that the dominance of law, legalism, liberalism, and Western conceptions of justice associated with the field has occasionally fostered a rather clumsy and tense engagement with questions of nonconventional (i.e., non-Western) justice, resulting in a loss of legitimacy and effectiveness. While this is widely recognized, the question of how to avoid such problems going forward is far less clear. Ultimately, I argue that while the local is as problematic as it is promising, making transitional justice into more of a true global project – where *global* is not simply a byword for *Northern* or *Western* – will require an at times uncomfortable degree of legal pluralism for many Western human rights lawyers with a large margin of appreciation, even if that pluralism is still best managed within the values of a loosely liberal system.

In Chapter 4, I ask the question "justice to what ends" by exploring the continued relevance of viewing transitional justice as a vehicle for the promotion of liberal democracy. One could also think of this as questioning the "why" of liberal-legalist transitional justice. While the field undoubtedly has its roots in the paradigmatic transitions to liberal democracy in places like Argentina and Chile, I argue that transitional justice practice has for some time been applied to a range of contexts, and can be leveraged to serve both liberal and illiberal means. This suggests that transitional justice practice is not a one-way ratchet of liberal betterment, but depends in large measure on the context in which it is deployed and the motivations of its architects. Accordingly, I call for a more open-ended transitional justice project, seeking to understand how practice works in a range of contexts, from paradigmatic transitions, to nontransitions, to consolidated democracies. I will also review case studies and the empirical literature looking at the long-term effects of transitional justice practice.

In Part II of this book, having probed some of the central blind spots of transitional justice as a form of liberal postconflict governance associated with the globalization of human rights and market democracy, I then turn to focus on the question of possible alternative paradigms or groundings for the field, and specifically to the interface between transitional justice and postconflict peacebuilding. The departure point for this inquiry is an observation that the central narrative of transitional justice is beginning to change. While the idea of transitional justice as handmaiden to liberal democratic political transitions remains a deeply embedded narrative, the more overt preoccupation with transition as transition to democracy has receded since the birth of the field in the 1980s and 1990s. Increasingly, transitional justice is associated with nation building and peacebuilding in the postconflict context more generally. In some respects, this is a striking development insofar as, historically, transitional justice has at times been seen as being in competition with the demands of peace, and not as a potentially important component of peacebuilding itself. We can then ask whether "transitional justice as peacebuilding" as an alternative frame to "transitional justice as liberal democracy building" might prove useful when it comes to addressing some of the blind spots of the dominant script. How could or would it differ from what came before?

To the extent that "peace" invokes more holistic sets of objectives than the narrower goals associated with facilitating liberal political transitions, the turn to peacebuilding might be seen to represent a broadening and a loosening of earlier paradigms and moorings, making this a significant moment in the normative evolution of the field. Yet with few exceptions, there has thus far been little scrutiny as to what "transitional justice as peacebuilding" might actually mean, how it might be different than "transitional justice as liberal democracy building," or how transitional justice can and should relate to existing components of the postconflict peacebuilding recipe-book (including efforts to disarm previously warring parties, reintegrate former soldiers into society, demine and destroy weapons, reform the formal "security sector," repatriate or resettle refugees, and various forms of democracy, governance, and rule-of-law assistance, including monitoring elections). Part II consists of three chapters.

I set the stage for my inquiry in Chapter 5 by exploring the emergence and trajectory of the concept of postconflict peacebuilding, from a 1991 report by UN Secretary-General Boutros Boutros-Ghali, to the more recent notion of "sustaining peace." In particular, I will examine the concept of peacebuilding as a facet of liberal postconflict governance. Together with development, human rights, and transitional justice, peacebuilding has become a global project, the invocation of which often serves to prize open the door of sovereignty for liberal state-building interventions. I pay particular attention to the role of concepts of law and justice as they have been played through the peacebuilding prism.

In Chapter 6, I focus in detail on the parallels between transitional justice and what has become known as "liberal international peacebuilding." I observe that the growing sense of shared space between transitional justice and postconflict peacebuilding initiatives has sparked new interest in sounding out potential connections between both fields. If transitional justice has its own "toolbox," one might then ask whether it cannot simply be subsumed into the larger postconflict peacebuilding template. However, while the pursuit of synergies is a worthwhile goal, I argue that in developing these connections, we must also be attentive to mutual shortcomings. Transitional justice and postconflict peacebuilding have historically proceeded on separate tracks, yet there has been a remarkable similarity in the critiques and concerns that have been leveled against both fields. Considered together, there is reason to worry that better integration and coordination between peacebuilding and transitional justice might exacerbate some of the tendencies that have given rise to these parallel critiques rather than alleviate them. I therefore argue that to the extent that we seek to promote coordination or even synthesis, we should seek synergies with thorough cognizance of the historic concerns and critiques leveled against both fields, and this may in turn serve as one technique of resistance to the tendencies that gave rise to the critiques in the first place.

Given some of the problems evoked in the preceding chapters, in Chapter 7, I ask whether it might be possible to develop a more emancipatory "transitional-justice-as-peacebuilding" narrative. I argue that the central problem being analyzed is not that human rights, the rule of law, good governance, democracy, or other key liberal goods are themselves undesirable or unworthy goals of the transitional justice enterprise. Indeed, many of the critiques leveled against both peacebuilding and transitional justice are based on decidedly liberal principles. Much of the critique leveled therefore stems from the reductionism, chauvinism, and arrogance of a particularly narrow liberal form of transitional justice that tends to privilege certain forms of expertise and knowledge, promote reductionist "justice" over broader forms of justice irrespective of context, which has too often been associated with exogenous imposition, and which has not adequately questioned its own assumptions and checkered history. I contend that the recovery of alternative liberalisms and associated concepts is a necessary prelude to imagining what an emancipatory "transitional-justice-as-peacebuilding" narrative might look like, offering several concepts from critical peacebuilding theory – including the "everyday," "popular peace," and "hybridity" – that might serve as useful correctives to historically narrow assumptions. Taken together, I argue, critical reflection along these lines can help to lay the groundwork for a transitional-justice-as-peacebuilding paradigm that reflects a commitment to human rights ideals and the consolidation of a more open-textured, contextually relevant, and genuine positive peace.

This book concludes in Chapter 8 with a look at some of the potential policy implications that flow from the critiques presented in Chapters 1 to 7. Though the chapter does not constitute a detailed road map, I present five broad policy arcs for change that, if taken to heart, would prove transformative for transitional justice practice in the twenty-first century.

Acknowledgments

This is a work of long gestation. I have experimented with many of the ideas and arguments presented here in previously published work. Accordingly, this book contains excerpts from:

"Development, Human Rights and Transitional Justice: Global Projects for Global Governance," *International Journal of Transitional Justice* 9, no. 3 (2015): 517–26.

"Emancipating Transitional Justice from the Bonds of the Paradigmatic Transition," *International Journal of Transitional Justice* 9, no. 1 (2015): 150–69.

"Addressing Dilemmas of the Global and the Local in Transitional Justice," *Emory International Law Review* 29 (2014): 71–117.

"Beyond the Post-Conflict Checklist: Linking Peacebuilding and Transitional Justice through the Lens of Critique," *Chicago Journal of International Law* 14 (2013): 165–96.

"Interrogating the Peripheries: The Preoccupations of Fourth Generation Transitional Justice," *Harvard Human Rights Journal* 26 (2013): 149–78.

"Addressing Economic Violence in Times of Transition: Toward a Positive-Peace Paradigm for Transitional Justice," *Fordham International Law Journal* 35 (2012): 780–814.

1

Introduction

Transitional Justice Foundations

HISTORICAL AND IDEOLOGICAL ORIGINS OF TRANSITIONAL JUSTICE AS A GLOBAL PROJECT

Definitions of transitional justice vary and have evolved and broadened over time,[1] yet the field can be broadly conceived of as a set of moral, legal, and political dilemmas involving how best to respond to mass atrocities and other forms of profound injustice in the wake of periods of conflict and repression.[2] It is often defined in part by reference to a set of practices now associated with responses to widespread human rights violations. According to a widely cited United Nations (UN) definition, transitional justice comprises

> the full range of processes and mechanisms associated with a society's attempts to come to terms with a legacy of large-scale past abuses, in order to ensure accountability, serve justice and achieve reconciliation. These may include both judicial and non-judicial mechanisms, with differing levels of international involvement (or none at all) and individual prosecutions, reparations, truth-seeking, institutional reform, vetting and dismissals, or a combination thereof.[3]

---

[1] Many of these definitions have been quite narrow and legalistic. For example, Ruti Teitel defines transitional justice as "the conception of justice associated with periods of political change, characterized by legal responses to confront the wrongdoings of repressive predecessor regimes." Ruti G. Teitel, "Transitional Justice Genealogy," *Harvard Human Rights Journal* 16 (2003): 69. For a review of how some of these definitions have broadened over time, see Rosemary Nagy, "Transitional Justice as a Global Project: Critical Reflections," *Third World Quarterly* 29, no. 2 (2008): 277–78.

[2] Chandra Lekha Sriram, "Justice as Peace? Liberal Peacebuilding and Strategies of Transitional Justice," *Global Society* 21, no. 4 (2007): 582–83. For a review of how definitions of transitional justice have evolved over time, see Nagy, "Transitional Justice as a Global Project," 277–78; see also Paige Arthur, "How 'Transitions' Reshaped Human Rights: A Conceptual History of Transitional Justice," *Human Rights Quarterly* 31, no. 2 (2009): 329–32 (tracing the history of the use of the term "transitional justice").

[3] UN Secretary-General, "The Rule of Law and Transitional Justice in Post-conflict Societies," UN Doc. S/2004/616 (August 23, 2004), ¶ 8.

The use of many such practices can be traced back to antiquity.[4] More recently, however, one could see the Nuremburg Military Tribunals that began shortly after World War II, set up by the victorious Allied powers in order to prosecute high-ranking Nazi officials for war crimes and crimes against humanity, as the first "generation" of modern-day transitional justice.[5] While the importance of this tribunal's legacy should not be underestimated, the Nuremburg moment itself was short-lived, as the emergence of the Cold War soon closed down many of the possibilities for interstate cooperation needed to support further justice initiatives.[6] But whatever the historical antecedents, most agree that the origins of the modern field of what has come to be known as "transitional justice" have firm roots in the 1980s and 1990s and the attempts of nascent democracies to grapple with historical legacies of repression and widespread human rights abuses.[7] Political scientist Samuel Huntington referred to this as the "third wave," a period of global democratization beginning in the mid-1970s that touched more than sixty countries in Europe, Latin America, Asia, and Africa.[8]

If this was a tumultuous time for societies experiencing "third-wave" transitions, it was an especially heady and euphoric era in the liberal West. It was not just that the Cold War had been won. Rather, consonant with Francis Fukuyama's sense of the "end of history,"[9] it was the notion that with the collapse of communism, there really was no viable political or economic alternative to Western liberal market democracy. Free-market capitalism had won. Liberal democracy had won. The "choice" was clear because there was no other plausible choice. Accordingly, the best and most benevolent thing the West could do for the rest would be to help accelerate the inevitable path to global convergence. Recognition of the long and imperfect road that democracy and concepts like the "rule of law" have followed in the liberal West (together with their less-than-perfect state in even their supposed modern-day paragons such as the United States) might seem to call for a certain humility. And yet the projects of this era were animated with a sort of proselytizing and liberalizing zeal premised on the assumption not only that history tends toward

---

[4] See generally Jon Elster, *Closing the Books: Transitional Justice in Historical Perspective* (Cambridge: Cambridge University Press, 2004) (reviewing historic practices now associated with the modern field of transitional justice).

[5] Teitel, "Transitional Justice Genealogy," 70.

[6] See John Dugard, "Obstacles in the Way of an International Criminal Court," *Cambridge Law Journal* 56 (1997): 329 (noting that "[t]he enthusiasm generated by Nuremberg and Tokyo for a permanent court in the immediate post war period was ... abandoned during the Cold War"). Between 1949 and 1954, the International Law Commission prepared several draft statutes that would have led to the creation of a permanent international criminal court, but consensus proved impossible.

[7] See Arthur, "How 'Transitions' Reshaped Human Rights," 325–26. The definitive source that captures the thinking and spirit of the period is Neil Kritz's seminal three-volume work. See generally Neil Kritz, ed., *Transitional Justice: How Emerging Democracies Reckon with Former Regimes*, 3 vols. (Washington, DC: USIP, 1995).

[8] See generally Samuel Huntington, *The Third Wave: Democratization in the Late Twentieth Century* (Norman: University of Oklahoma Press, 1991).

[9] See generally Francis Fukuyama, *The End of History and the Last Man* (New York: Avon Books, 1992).

definitive ends but also that the historical sequence followed by the West might be both reengineered and compressed, even in regions with radically different histories and cultures.[10]

With the ascendency of Reaganism and Thatcherism, the political climate and policyscape that came to shape these efforts to remake the world in the image of the West were positively neoliberal ones. Thus, in the development sphere, countries around the world were told that growth would only come with "good governance" reforms inspired by the "Washington Consensus," making deregulation, privatization, elimination of subsidies, free trade, and so forth into near-biblical injunctions to be imposed on developing and postcommunist countries via loan conditionalities. Rule-of-law projects funded by institutions such as the World Bank were largely geared toward commercial and market reforms, making domestic laws more friendly to international investors, all in the name of alleviating poverty. In the human rights arena, Western governments and even major global nongovernmental organizations (NGOs) emphasized the importance of civil and political rights, with scant attention paid to economic, social, and cultural rights (when these same rights were not being affirmatively denied as "real rights" or otherwise derided). International peacekeeping missions of the era emphasized the need for quick elections as the surest path to peace, leading to shallow procedural democracy at best, but often with more calamitous results.[11] While it is true that these spheres of activity were not quite as monolithic as this broad-brush overview might suggest, the symmetry of their common thrust was clear, and they generally shared a common faith that human welfare could be increased, and "the good" brought one step closer to attainment, through a process of social, political, and economic (neo)liberalization.

In keeping with this same zeitgeist, when it first took the global stage in the 1980s and 1990s, transitional justice was largely thought of as a vehicle for helping to deliver important liberal goods in postconflict and postauthoritarian societies, including democracy and the rule of law. Thus, the "transition" at stake was understood as an explicitly political one involving "the move from less to more democratic regimes."[12] If it was hoped that transitional justice mechanisms could help to strengthen transitions to Western liberal democracy, such efforts were also seen by some as bound up with an imperative to provide an effective *legal*[13] remedy for a very narrow (if not egregious) band of international human rights and international humanitarian law violations.[14] Thus, for example, in Argentina, the truth

---

[10] Linn Hammergren, *Justice Reform and Development: Rethinking Donor Assistance to Developing and Transitional Countries* (New York: Routledge 2014), 179.

[11] See generally Roland Paris, *At War's End: Building Peace after Civil Conflict* (Cambridge: Cambridge University Press, 2004).

[12] Ruti G. Teitel, *Transitional Justice* (New York: Oxford University Press, 2000), 5.

[13] Ruit Teitel defined once defined transitional justice as "the conception of justice associated with periods of political change, characterized by legal responses to confront the wrongdoings of repressive predecessor regimes." Teitel, "Transitional Justice Genealogy," 69.

[14] All violations of international human rights law entail legal consequences, including the right to redress and compensation – a fact that has without doubt given impetus to the field of transitional

commission looked solely at forced disappearances, despite a much broader range of physical and economic crimes that the armed forces had committed. Commissions in Chile, Uruguay, and South Africa offered similarly thin conceptions of justice. In short, in many contexts, "transitional justice" came to stand for a sort of "atrocity justice," where accountability was often seen as synonymous with individual criminal accountability for extreme acts of physical violence, and where broader questions of structural, economic, and quotidian violence and justice were either invisible or treated as mere context.

Implicit in the twin impulses of transitional justice – democratization and atrocity justice – was a progressive view of history in which countries evolve, through the redemptive power of law, from barbarism, communism, and authoritarianism to Western liberal democracy. But if the law was a key vector for liberalizing change, it was also important to consider the role of political elites. In analyzing the chances for successfully transitioning to the pinnacle of this evolutionary sequence, influential scholars from the period attempted to predict to what extent the scope of transitional justice would be determined by a set of bargains between the various elite groups facilitating the democratic transition, with more or less justice possible depending on the extent to which previous elites retained a grip on the levers of power.[15] The (clean, good) power of the law to foster liberalizing change might therefore be limited by the (grubby, bad) power of illiberal local politics. Taken together, such work tended to situate the origins of democracy in choices by elite groups and legal-institutional reforms and initiatives rather than being the product of social conditions or some more "bottom-up" process, which had been the more typical way of viewing things in the earlier democratization literature. This top-down

---

justice. Theo van Boven has noted that the "United Nations Principles and Guidelines on the Right to a Remedy" were developed in the shadow of expanding transitional justice practice. See Theo van Boven, "Basic Principles and Guidelines on the Right to a Remedy for Victims of Gross Violations of International Human Rights Law and Serious Violations of International Humanitarian Law," Introductory Note, December 16, 2005, http://legal.un.org/avl/ha/ga_60-147/ga_60-147.html. Today, the "normative framework supporting transitional justice [includes] the right to justice, truth and guarantees of non-recurrence." See UN Secretary-General, "The Rule of Law," ¶ 8. Yet it is also true that the bulk of international institutional capital has been invested in examining and articulating remedies for "gross" violations, a category heavily associated with genocide, torture, crimes against humanity, disappearances, and other extremely serious violations of physical integrity, and civil and political rights more generally. See van Boven, Introductory Note, 2–3. Many early transitional justice scholars had these sorts of violations in mind when they analyzed the intersection between international legal duties and transitional justice policy, particularly as regarding duty to prosecute. See generally Diane Orentlicher, "Settling Accounts: The Duty to Prosecute Human Rights Violations of a Prior Regime," *Yale Law Journal* 100, no. 8 (1991): 2537. As I discuss in Chapter 2, the narrow legalism and focus of transitional justice on physical integrity and civil and political rights violations is increasingly questioned, and the conceptualization of rights violations as either "gross" or "simple" must itself be interrogated as a political and ideological construct.

[15] Samuel P. Huntington, "The Third Wave: Democratization in the Late Twentieth Century," in Kritz, *Transitional Justice*, 54–81; Guillermo O'Donnell and Philippe Schmitter, "Transitions from Authoritarian Rule: Tentative Conclusions about Uncertain Democracies," ibid., 57–64.

theory of change would implicitly shape many of the transitional justice initiatives in the decades to come.

The conceptualization of the field as an expression of these twin aims and its subsequent global dissemination can thus be linked to the broader globalization of international human rights and Western governance ideals, especially those civil and political rights norms strongly associated with liberalism and neoliberalism.[16] Together with postconflict peacebuilding, development, and human rights, transitional justice has, since the end of the Cold War, been an important feature of liberal postconflict governance, a means by which Western liberal values are pushed from core to periphery.[17] Some three decades after the Latin American and Eastern European democratic transitions associated with the field's naissance, the idea of transitional justice as handmaiden to liberal political transitions – the "paradigmatic transition" of transitional justice – remains a deeply embedded narrative.[18]

Examined closely, therefore, the core narratives of the field contain something of a contradiction. Transitional justice is at times imagined as a postpolitical and postideological enterprise, part of the "end of history," and yet is also heavily associated with liberal democratic political transitions, has been dominated by largely Western conceptions and modalities of justice, and has significant implications for the distribution of power in the postconflict context. In this way, viewing transitional justice as an apolitical "toolbox," a notion implicit in UN and other definitions,[19] fails to account for the important historical and ideological underpinnings of the field. While transitional justice is dynamic and evolving, these origins remain key to understanding some of its modern conceptual boundaries, assumptions, and blind spots, shaped as they have been by a particular faith in the ability of key liberal goods, including the rule of law, democracy, and human rights, to create peace.[20]

FROM THE EXCEPTION TO THE MAINSTREAM

Though the term was arguably coined in the 1991,[21] transitional justice probably did not emerge as a distinct field until at least 2000.[22] Despite being a very new

---

[16] Paul Gready and Simon Robins, "From Transition to Transformative Justice: A New Agenda for Practice," *International Journal of Transitional Justice* 8, no. 3 (2014): 341.

[17] Philip Cunliffe, "Still the Spectre at the Feast: Comparisons between Peacekeeping and Imperialism in Peacekeeping Studies Today," *International Peacekeeping* 19, no. 4 (2012): 428.

[18] See generally Arthur, "How 'Transitions' Reshaped Human Rights."

[19] See, e.g., UN Secretary-General, *The Rule of Law*, ¶ 8.

[20] Sririam, "Justice as Peace?," 579. On the dominance of law and legalism in transitional justice, see generally Kieran McEvoy, "Beyond Legalism: Towards a Thicker Understanding of Transitional Justice," *Journal of Law and Society* 34, no. 4 (2007): 412.

[21] Ruti G. Teitel, "Transitional Justice Globalized," *International Journal of Transitional Justice* 2, no. 1 (2008): 1.

[22] See Arthur, "How 'Transitions' Reshaped Human Rights," 329–32 (tracing the history of the use of the term "transitional justice"); Christine Bell, "Transitional Justice, Interdisciplinarity and the State of

field, transitional justice has become ever more prominent in the years that have followed. The voyage the field has taken from the exception to the mainstream is an important one for understanding policy and practice today.

At the outset, transitional justice mechanisms and interventions were premised on a notion of a special "window of opportunity," a period of rupture in which some kind of extraordinary justice might be carried out, involving both prosecutions and amnesties that might not be possible during ordinary, nontransitional times. While the duration of the transitional opportunity was not entirely clear, wisdom at the time held that one had to strike while the proverbial iron was hot and the political context made some kind of justice possible.[23] The sense was that transitional justice was an extraordinary justice for exceptional times, an opportunity that might not come again. The exceptionality of transitional justice was exemplified in part through a greater willingness to accept some form of amnesty as a necessary compromise even if this deviated from the rule-of-law ideal.[24] As examples of this phenomenon, one might consider the amnesty offered to military officials in Argentina after an initial wave of prosecutions led to unrest and instability.[25] In South Africa, very few prosecutions took place at all, because impunity and preservation of the economic status quo were seen as necessary to ensuring a peaceful transition.[26] Perhaps reflecting this pragmatic balancing act, key concerns from this early period – including whether there is a duty to punish egregious human rights violations under international law – spawned sharp debates in academic and policy circles relating to pardons and amnesties (peace vs. justice), and to whether a truth commission could replace prosecutions as a viable form of justice (truth vs. justice).[27]

In the decades that have followed, transitional justice practices have become increasingly widespread. Priscilla Hayner, for example, has documented the existence of some forty modern-day truth commissions.[28] Starting with the Sábato Commission (Comisión Nacional sobre la Desaparición de Personas, CONADEP)

---

the 'Field' or 'Non-Field,'" *International Journal of Transitional Justice* 3, no. 5 (2009): 7 (arguing that transitional justice did not emerge as a distinct field until after 2000).

[23] Samuel P. Huntington, "The Third Wave: Democratization in the Late Twentieth Century," in Kritz, *Transitional Justice*, 74–75.

[24] Teitel, "Transitional Justice Genealogy," 76.

[25] See Carlos Santiago Nino, *Radical Evil on Trial* (New Haven, CT: Yale University Press, 1998).

[26] See Bell, "Interdisciplinarity," 14.

[27] See Diane F. Orentlicher, "Settling Accounts: The Duty to Prosecute Human Rights Violations of a Prior Regime," *Yale Law Journal* 100 (1991): 2537 (arguing for the existence of a duty to prosecute some violations of physical integrity under international law). For a general exploration of the "truth versus justice" debate, see Miriam Aukerman, "Extraordinary Evil, Ordinary Crimes: A Framework for Understanding Transitional Justice," *Harvard Human Rights Journal* 15 (2002): 94–97; Reed Brody, "Justice: The First Casualty of Truth?," *Nation*, April 30, 2001, 25.

[28] Prisilla Hayner, *Unspeakable Truths: Confronting State Terror and Atrocity* (New York: Routledge, 2011), 256–62.

in Argentina and its best-selling report, *Nunca Más* (Never Again), the truth commission has become a worldwide phenomenon.[29] Exported to South Africa where the postapartheid drama and the charisma of Nelson Mandela and Desmond Tutu riveted international attention, new commissions now spring up almost as a matter of course in postconflict scenarios. Beyond the truth commission phenomenon, Kathryn Sikkink has documented an increasing crescendo of human rights prosecutions taking place at national and international levels, leading, she argues, to the emergence of a new global norm of accountability, at least for certain harms.[30] Though the rich and powerful often evade accountability, a former president from Liberia sits in a jail cell in the United Kingdom for crimes he abetted in Sierra Leone, a former president of Chad has been convicted by a special court in Senegal, and a former president of Côte d'Ivoire now stands trial before the International Criminal Court in the Hague. Legal theorist Ruti Teitel has posited that such developments reflect a "steady state" transitional justice, a time in which we see transitional justice as a sort of default option, a normalized response to postconflict atrocity.[31]

The sense that the field had moved from the periphery to the core of international attention and policy making was cemented with the publication of a landmark 2004 report by the UN Secretary-General reflecting an official, if rhetorical, institutional endorsement of transitional justice.[32] While the UN's embrace of transitional justice has not always been translated into consistent practice,[33] it has nevertheless come to possess a deep repository of transitional justice experience ranging from the ad hoc tribunals for the former Yugoslavia and Rwanda to hybrid tribunals in Sierra Leone, East Timor, and Cambodia. Today, the UN agency with the primary responsibility for transitional justice issues is the Office of the High Commissioner for Human Rights (OHCHR), which has supported transitional justice programs in more than twenty countries.[34] As part of the "new normal," the UN holds that peace and justice go hand in hand, rhetoric that tries to smooth over frictions arising out of the peace versus justice debates of the previous decades, even if it cannot eliminate them entirely.[35] Paralleling these developments at the UN, transitional justice is now, in

---

[29] *Nunca Más, Report of the Argentine National Commission on the Disappeared* (New York: Farar, Straus, and Giroux, 1986).
[30] See Kathryn Sikkink, *The Justice Cascade: How Human Rights Prosecutions Are Changing World Politics* (New York: W. W. Norton, 2011), 21.
[31] See Teitel, "Transitional Justice Genealogy," 89.   [32] See UN Secretary-General, *The Rule of Law*.
[33] See Padraig McAuliffe, "The Marginality of Transitional Justice within Liberal Peacebuilding: Causes and Consequences," *Journal of Human Rights Practice* 9, no. 1 (2017).
[34] See UN High Commissioner for Human Rights, Message by Ms. Navanethem Pillay at the Special Summit of the African Union (October 22, 2009), www.unhchr.ch/huricane/huricane.nsf/o/110E705F1034E048C1257657005814CE?opendocument.
[35] See UN Secretary-General, *The Rule of Law*, 1 (arguing that "[j]ustice, peace and democracy are not mutually exclusive objectives, but rather mutually reinforcing imperatives").

a sense, its own industry, with dedicated NGOs and an army of consultants and experts deployed all over the world.[36]

In a relatively brief span of history, therefore, transitional justice has gone mainstream, embraced by the UN and bilateral donors, together with activists and NGOs. In the postconflict context, the question no longer seems to be *whether* there will be some kind of transitional justice, but *what* particular interventions will be deployed, and what their scope and sequencing might look like.[37] Given that the default option as recently as the 1970s was a gilded exile for most architects of mass atrocity, the emergence this "new normal" is nothing short of extraordinary. This is not to say that mass murderers do not continue to benefit from enormous impunity but, Sikkink argues, there has been a shift in terms of our expectations about what *should* happen.[38] This shift has been both pushed and pulled by the legalization of transitional justice, with amnesties for certain crimes increasingly seen as intolerable if not illegal, a development both symbolized and foretold by the UN's refusal in 1999 to endorse the blanket amnesty provisions of a Sierra Leone peace agreement.[39]

Not surprisingly, for the activist concerned with questions of accountability and impunity for atrocity crimes, the normalization of transitional justice is often seen as a good thing. To others, however, the mainstreaming, together with the increasing legalization and internationalization of transitional justice that has come with it or perhaps because of it, is a more ambiguous development in the sense that it represents yet one more way in which the postconflict context has become enmeshed in and colonized by both law and international actors. When combined with good governance, rule of law, and other justice-sector reforms, the mobilization of the law – seen as distinct from politics and political choices – may have the effect of justifying intrusive interventions and limiting sovereign policy autonomy under the guise of apolitical technocratic assistance. This raises concerns resonant with arguments made by Abdullahi An-Na'im, who has suggested that the historical and ideological underpinnings of the field include an implicit neocolonial logic that places dominant conceptions of transitional justice within "the grand 'modernizing' mission of North Atlantic societies."[40]

But whatever their effects or implicit logic, the spread of transitional justice ideas around the world and the field's journey from exception to the mainstream, has

---

[36] See, e.g., International Center for Transitional Justice, www.ictj.org.
[37] See Nagy, "Transitional Justice as a Global Project," 276; see also McEvoy, "Beyond Legalism," 412.
[38] See generally Sikkink, *The Justice Cascade*.
[39] See generally Priscilla Hayner, *Negotiating Peace in Sierra Leone: Confronting the Justice Challenge* (Center for Humanitarian Dialogue/International Center for Transitional Justice, December 2007 Report).
[40] See Abdullahi Ahmed An-Na'im, "Editorial Note: From the Neocolonial 'Transition' to Indigenous Formations of Justice," *International Journal of Transitional Justice* 7, no. 2 (2013): 197.

been less part of some grand conscious and intentional conspiracy on the part of transitional justice actors to place a colonial yoke on the Global South than the often prosaic day-to-day work of transitional justice "experts," professionals and epistemic communities operating with the best of intentions. After all, it is commonly thought: *Impunity for mass murderers is unacceptable and justice of one kind or another must be done. How should we address these problems if not through the mechanisms of transitional justice?* As David Kennedy has argued, it is increasingly difficult to understand the workings of global governance without understanding the quotidian choices, values, and sensibilities of such experts.[41]

From the outset, such experts and advocates played a critical role, both in creating a shared collective sense of a new and common field and in disseminating the field's norms, practices, and institutional parameters around the world. Paige Arthur, for example, has documented the critical role that a 1988 conference held at the Aspen Institute funded by the Ford Foundation played in generating an initial sense of the emergence of a new field with shared sets of concerns, approaches, and practices.[42] By furnishing the vocabulary, central concepts, binaries, and debates, together with the institutions, mechanisms and "best practices" that key actors around the world turn to when they engage thorny questions of postconflict justice, the shared mental map that these experts came to generate has in turn shaped the real-world post-conflict policyscape for millions. Albuja and Cavallero have emphasized that such shared mental maps often go on to be replicated again and again not because they are particularly well suited to a range of contexts, but through a process of "acculturation" that takes place through "repeated information exchanges and consultations with prior [truth] commission members and a cadre of international scholars and practitioners in the area."[43] As this process continued, the field has, over time, become increasingly internationalized as seasoned scholars and experts fluidly navigate between the academy, NGOs, and international organizations, themselves strongly internationalized social worlds.[44] In tandem, the field has been increasingly professionalized as salaried employees have replaced volunteers.[45] No longer the sole province of activists and the aggrieved, transitional justice work is now often carried out by liberal legal professionals, many of them trained and socialized in a handful of elite Western universities. Taken together, all of these developments help

---

[41] See generally David Kennedy, "Challenging Expert Rule: The Politics of Global Governance," *Sydney Law Review* 27 (2005).

[42] See Arthur, "How 'Transitions' Reshaped Human Rights," 325.

[43] James Cavallaro and Sebastián Albuja, "The Lost Agenda: Economic Crimes and Truth Commissions in Latin America and Beyond," in *Transitional Justice from Below, Grassroots Activism and the Struggle for Change*, ed. Kieran McEvoy and Lorna McGregor (Oxford: Hart, 2008), 125.

[44] Sandrine Lefranc and Frederic Vairel, "The Emergence of Transitional Justice as a Professional International Practice," in *Dealing with Wars and Dictatorships: Legal Concepts and Categories in Action*, ed. Liora Israël and Guillaume Mouralis (New York: Springer, 2013), 237–41.

[45] Ibid., 246.

to explain the overall mainstreaming and normalization of the field of transitional justice.[46]

PROFESSIONAL SENSIBILITIES AND THE PREDISPOSITIONS IN THE FIELD

It turns out that who these experts and professionals are has much to do with the origins of the field as well as what it has become, and so understanding the dominance of certain disciplines, approaches, and professional sensibilities is key. In the abstract, the question of how best to respond to mass atrocities is one well suited to a range of disciplines, including philosophy, history, religion, anthropology, and psychology, yet in practice the field has for the most part been dominated by lawyers and, to a far lesser extent, political scientists.[47] Given the dominance of lawyers, it is perhaps not surprising that mass atrocities have been largely analogized as a form of mass crime,[48] and that the tools that have been marshaled in response have had a heavily legal character, often focusing more on retributive justice via formal courts and tribunals rather than other forms of justice.[49] As the saying goes, if you only have a hammer, everything looks like a nail. This "prosecution preference," under which anything short of Western-style courtroom justice is often seen as comprised justice, is seemingly hardwired into the DNA of mainstream transitional justice.[50] It has been and continues to be persistent source of debate and the global-local frictions that will be discussed in greater detail in Chapter 3.[51]

As a thought experiment, Paige Arthur observes, one might consider the possible orientation of theory and praxis if the intellectual origins of transitional justice had been rooted in paradigmatic transitions to socialism and the dominant disciplines

---

[46] For a helpful synthesis of the role of internationalization, professionalization, and legalization in the gradual normalization of transitional justice, see Line Engbo Gissel, "Contemporary Transitional Justice: Normalising a Politics of Exception," *Global Society* 31, no. 3 (2016): 353–69.

[47] See Arthur, "How 'Transitions' Reshaped Human Rights," 333.

[48] Miriam Aukerman, "Extraordinary Evil, Ordinary Crimes: A Framework for Understanding Transitional Justice," *Harvard Human Rights Journal* 15 (2002): 94–97.

[49] Rama Mani stands as an early exception to this trend, arguing for a more balanced approach to postconflict reconstruction that would include three dimensions of justice: retributive, rectificatory, and distributive. See Rama Mani, *Beyond Retribution: Seeking Justice in the Shadows of War* (Malden: Blackwell, 2002).

[50] Aukerman, "Extraordinary Evil," 39–44 (describing the "prosecution preference").

[51] The prosecution preference can be seen in debates that raged in the late 1990s concerning whether a truth commission alone could constitute an adequate form of justice. See, e.g., Brody, "Justice: The First Casualty of Truth?," 25 (arguing that truth commissions can serve as "a soft option for avoiding justice.") More recently, one can look to controversies sparked by ICC indictments of leaders of the Lord's Resistance Army rebel group in Uganda where some members of the Acholi community in Northern Uganda would prefer to forgo prosecutions in favor of *Mato Oput*, a local ritual that emphasizes reconciliation and reintegration rather than simple retribution. See generally Adam Branch, "Uganda's Civil War and the Politics of ICC Intervention," *Ethics and International Affairs* 21, no. 2 (2007): 179.

had been history and developmental economics.[52] While it is impossible to say for sure, it seems likely that the perceived dilemmas and preoccupations, together with the tools marshaled to address them would look considerably different. As an example that will be explored in greater depth in Chapter 2, one could note the historic preoccupation of transitional justice with civil and political rights rather than economic and social rights, with acts of egregious physical violence such as murder, torture, and rape, rather than equally devastating acts and policies of economic and structural violence. Greater attention to questions of distributive justice in transition – something that might have come more naturally if the field had different historical, ideological, and professional grounding – might well have entailed a focus on prosecutions for corruption and other economic crimes, together with a push for policies involving redistributive taxation or land-tenure reform in the wake of conflict. Yet as the field has evolved, these issues have been largely pushed to the margins.[53] Thus, the Western (neo)liberal roots of transitional justice together with the professional orientations of those who have dominated the field helped to shape conceptions of both problems and solutions.

While the historical, ideological and professional origins of transitional justice may have predisposed the field to privilege certain forms of harm and certain ways of responding to those harms, it can be argued that the field's roots in Western (neo)liberalism and legalism do not necessarily dictate internationally imposed solutions, "top-down" responses, or the more general marginalization of local and non-Western voices that has featured in many transitional justice interventions over time, and which will be discussed in greater detail in Chapter 3.[54] At the same time, the historic association between transitional justice and largely Western and law-centered responses to mass atrocity, when coupled with the field's grounding in international law and international human rights more generally, has served to privilege international institutions, norms, practices, knowledge, and expertise.[55] Criminal justice approaches to mass atrocity tend to privilege comparatively elite, expertise-driven, top-down approaches to the problem of mass atrocities. The dominance of lawyers and legalism may therefore help to explain in part that component of the field's DNA that has tended to view social change as a function of elite bargaining and top-down legal-institutional reforms.[56] The result is an emphasis on a constrained yet institutionally and professionally demanding understanding of

---

[52] See Arthur, "How 'Transitions' Reshaped Human Rights," 359.
[53] See generally Zinaida Miller, "Effects of Invisibility: In Search of the 'Economic' in Transitional Justice," *International Journal of Transitional Justice* 2, no. 3 (2008): 266.
[54] Roland Paris has made this point with respect to similar critiques that have been leveled against the broader field of postconflict peacebuilding. See Roland Paris, "Saving Liberal Peacebuilding," *Review of International Studies* 36, no. 2 (2010): 363. I outline these critiques in more detail below.
[55] See generally Sharp, "Interrogating the Peripheries; The Preoccupations of Fourth Generation Transitional Justice," *Harvard Human Rights Journal* 26 (2013): 149–79.
[56] See Sandra Rubli, *Transitional Justice: Justice by Bureaucratic Means?* (Geneva: Swiss Peace Working Paper 4, 2012), 11.

justice that some have argued is not consistent with the quality and capacity of state institutions in many postconflict countries, to say nothing of cultural congruence.[57]

Against this backdrop, the felt need for prosecutions and truth commissions "in conformity with... international standards"[58] often leads to the involvement of international donors, NGOs, and experts and consultants, placing a further thumb on the scales favoring the primacy global rather than local professionals and expertise. Indigenous or homespun solutions come to appear rough around the edges, second-best approaches to questions of how to do justice in times of transition.[59] Mirroring the savages-victims-saviors paradigm at the heart of some human rights advocacy, these dynamics produce a situation where the locals (savages) need to be assisted by international lawyer-experts and institutions (saviors) not just from the abuses they have committed against victims during the conflict, but from the "mistakes" locals would make in attempting to devise their own postconflict solutions as well.[60] Internationally constructed categories of "perpetrator" and "victim" are essential to justifying such interventions. (Who after all will defend the rights of "victims" if not members of the "international community"?)[61] The international assistance offered in such a context is projected as apolitical and technocratic, yet it carries with it heavy implications for the distribution of power (political, legal, social, etc.) in the postconflict context.[62]

Of course, origins are not destiny, and the biases and blind spots of the early years of transitional justice need not necessarily be those of tomorrow. Thus, in seeking to understand contemporary challenges, unduly rigid notions of path dependency must be avoided. As will be discussed in subsequent chapters, there are signs of limited but increasing openness to more diverse and culturally grounded approaches to

---

[57] See Lydiah Bosire, "Overpromised, Underdelivered: Transitional Justice in Sub-Saharan Africa," *Sur International Journal on Human Rights* 5, no. 5 (2006): 72.

[58] UN Secretary-General, *The Rule of Law*, ¶ 36.

[59] See An-Na'im, "Editorial Note," 197 (observing that "preference is given to a standard of justice that is mandated by the international community over indigenous or 'traditional' practices.")

[60] See generally Makau Mutua, "Savages, Victims, and Saviors: The Metaphor of Human Rights," *Harvard International Law Journal* 42 (2001): 201.

[61] For a useful deconstruction of the problematic term "international community," see generally Berit Bliesemann de Guevara and Florian Kuhn, "'The International Community Needs to Act': Loose Use and Empty Signaling of a Hackneyed Concept," *International Peacekeeping* 18, no. 2 (2011): 135.

[62] See Patricia Lundy and Mark McGovern, "Whose Justice? Rethinking Transitional Justice from the Bottom Up," *Journal of Law and Society* 35, no. 2 (2008): 276–77 (noting that "wider geo-political and economic interests too often shape what tend to be represented as politically and economically neutral post-conflict and transitional justice initiatives"); Bronwyn Anne Leebaw, "The Irreconcilable Goals of Transitional Justice," *Human Rights Quarterly* 30, no. 1 (2008): 98–106 (arguing that a superficial consensus as to the goals of transitional justice can serve to mask a deeper level of politicization and debate, and that assessment of the tensions, trade-offs, and dilemmas associated with transitional justice has become difficult to the extent that they have been conceptualized in apolitical terms); Sriram, "Justice as Peace?," 587–88 (discussing the ways in which postconflict institutional reform strategies relating to the judiciary, constitution, and security forces may be seen by key protagonists as permanently cementing new power arrangements and therefore not as neutral or apolitical processes).

justice and a growing reconsideration of the need to address questions of economic justice. The field is also increasingly being shaped by perspectives from disciplines other than law. Yet it is also true that once sets of practices and assumptions come to dominate a field, more than superficial change can prove difficult and slow going. As Cavallaro and Albuja have observed, the dominant script produced during the early years of transitional justice has often gone on to be replicated irrespective of how suited it has been to some new contexts, and there is no reason to expect that this will change overnight.[63]

CRACKS IN THE FOUNDATION: CONTESTED PERIPHERIES OF THE FIELD

Though efforts are increasing to close the gaps, for much of its brief history, transitional justice as a field has been both underempiricized[64] and undertheorized. This is not to say that critique has been absent. Indeed, transitional justice practices and policies have often been criticized on normative grounds, and the literature is replete with arguments that transitional justice is "top-down," that it has failed to be inclusive or participatory, that a particular transitional justice initiative was a failure due to poor implementation, lack of coordination, and so on. Yet the articulation of more robust theoretical constructs and paradigms that might help to provide deeper context and substance to these specific critiques has been largely lacking.[65] Efforts to link specific critiques of transitional justice practice with the deeper undercurrents of transitional justice ideology and assumptions – exploring the ways in which transitional justice practice might even legitimate or obfuscate forms of injustice while legitimating other political and ideological purposes – have also not been

---

[63] Cavallaro and Albuja, "The Lost Agenda," 125. The problem of set templates and formulaic paths is of course not unique to transitional justice but has dogged the broader work of postconflict peacebuilding as well. See Ole Sending, *Why Peacebuilders Fail to Secure Ownership and Be Sensitive to Context*, Security in Practice, NUPI Working Paper 755 (2009), 7. It is important to note, however, that even established and dominant scripts can and do change (as evident in the growing work of certain African truth commissions on questions of economic justice), even if it typically involves a very slow and uneven process. See generally Dustin Sharp, "Economic Violence in the Practice of African Truth Commissions and Beyond?," in *Justice and Economic Violence in Transition*, ed. Dustin Sharp (New York: Springer, 2014), 79.

[64] For efforts on the empirical front, see, e.g., Tricia Olsen, Leigh Payne, and Andrew Reiter, *Transitional Justice in Balance: Comparing Processes, Weighing Efficiency* (Washington, DC: USIP, 2010); Oskar Thoms et al., "State-Level Effects of Transitional Justice: What Do We Know?," *International Journal of Transitional Justice* 4, no. 3 (2010): 332; Hugo van der Merwe, Victoria Baxter, and Audrey Chapman, eds., *Assessing the Impact of Transitional Justice* (Washington, DC: USIP, 2009); Phuong Pham and Patrick Vinck, "Empirical Research and the Development and Assessment of Transitional Justice Mechanisms," *International Journal of Transitional Justice* 1, no. 2 (2007): 231.

[65] Perhaps it is not so surprising, then, that Eric Posner and Adrian Vermeule's 2003 assertion the so-called dilemmas of transitional justice are no different – theoretically or empirically – from the dilemmas of domestic (nontransitional) justice has gone largely unanswered. See generally "Transitional Justice as Ordinary Justice," *Harvard Law Review* 117, no. 3 (2003): 761.

as plentiful as they could be. If transitional justice is often "good,"[66] might it also occasionally be "part of the problem"?[67] This question has not received as much attention as it deserves.

This book is largely written in a critical studies tradition, resonant with both the "critical legal studies" movement of the late twentieth century and so-called Third World Approaches to International Law (TWAIL) scholarship. Taken together, this critical theory approach attempts to do for transitional justice what scholars such as Duncan Kennedy and others once did for domestic private law: to bring to the surface the politics and ideological assumptions of regimes and practices that are often presented as technocratic, apolitical, and nonideological, and to examine the implicit trade-offs and distributional consequences that often go undiscussed.[68] The hope is to stimulate new thinking by attempting to deconstruct aspects of the transitional justice, and thereby *strip it of its sense of naturalness and inevitably*. This book is part of a small but growing literature written in this vein.[69]

Far from being an armchair exercise, such work is sorely needed if the field is to better confront its many challenges. To date, empirical evidence of many of the magic-making claims of transitional justice – that it can promote democracy, respect for human rights, reconciliation, and so on – is equivocal.[70] In other words, there is still much to be tried and learned when it comes to promoting peace and justice in the aftermath of mass atrocity. Meanwhile, the field is beset by a collective sense of crisis owing to persistent concerns about the effectiveness and perceived legitimacy of transitional justice initiatives.[71] Taken together, all of this suggests that the dominant script can and should be carefully examined with a view to reshaping the field for the twenty-first century.

At one level, the simultaneous sense of normalization and crisis seems paradoxical. After all, if Sikkink is correct that there is an emerging global norm of accountability – and newspaper headlines increasingly reflect the march of international justice – why isn't crisis giving way to a sense of confidence and (tentative) victory?[72]

---

[66] Thomas Obel Hansen, "Transitional Justice: Toward a Differentiated Theory," *Oregon Review of International Law* 13 (2011): 17; see also Siphiwe Ignatius Dube, "Transitional Justice beyond the Normative: Towards a Literary Theory of Political Transitions," *International Journal of Transitional Justice* 5, no. 2 (2011): 181.
[67] See, e.g., David Kennedy, "The International Human Rights Movement: Part of the Problem?," *Harvard Human Rights Journal* 15 (2002): 101.
[68] See, e.g., Duncan Kennedy, "Form and Substance in Private Law Adjudication," *Harvard Law Review* 89 (1976): 1685.
[69] For an example of recent efforts to close the theoretical gap in the literature, see, e.g., Susanne Buckley-Zistel et al. (eds.), *Transitional Justice Theories* (New York: Routledge, 2014); Nicola Palmer, Phil Clark, and Danielle Granville (eds.), *Critical Perspectives in Transitional Justice* (Antwerp: Intersentia, 2012).
[70] Thoms et al., "State-Level Effects," 332.
[71] See Vasuki Nesiah, *Transitional Justice Practice: Looking Back, Moving Forward*, Scoping Study, Impunity Watch, May 2016, 5.
[72] See, e.g., Dionne Searcey, "Hissène Habré, Ex-President of Chad, Is Convicted of War Crimes," *New York Times*, May 30, 2016.

On the other hand, one might say that it is precisely at the moment when transitional justice is no longer considered to be a "frail child" that academics and activists, once afraid of airing dirty laundry in public, might have the confidence to engage in more searching public critique, exploring the field's deeper limitations and contradictions. In this sense, it is perhaps not surprising that even as transitional justice has become institutionalized and mainstreamed, there has been an increasing willingness to interrogate some of the boundaries and blind spots of the field. One might even say that it is precisely *because* the field has been pushed to the nerve centers of international policy making that other voices push outward, questioning dominant liberal scripts, templates, and toolboxes. Such efforts therefore likely represent a new phase of maturity. And while these opposing centripetal and centrifugal forces may generate tensions, they may also ultimately prove to be a source of creativity and dynamism that helps the field resist the slide to over-standardization.

These dynamics are reflected in part by an increased willingness to explore what I call the "peripheries" of the field, those concerns that have been either historically dominant or historically marginalized by the liberal-legalist dominant script of transitional justice:

Set in the Foreground	Set in the Background[73]
the global, the Western	the local, the non-Western "other"
the modern, the secular	the traditional, the religious
the legal	the political
civil and political rights	economic and social rights
physical violence	economic and structural violence
extraordinary violence	ordinary, quotidian violence
the state, the individual	the community, the group
formal, institutional, "top-down" change	informal, cultural, social, "bottom-up" change

Part I of this book will be largely dedicated to exploring some of these peripheries. The goal of this inquiry is to call into question the reasons for the historic privileging of certain items over others, to examine what this emphasis might say about transitional justice as a political and ideological project, and to disturb the sense of normalcy that has accrued around the field's many mental maps. Such a shaking-up may then make possible a more clear-eyed and context-specific inquiry into the needs of particular postconflict scenarios, in addition to providing an important perspective for reimaging the field and its dominant script going forward more generally.

---

[73] Chart adapted from Dustin Sharp, "Addressing Economic Violence in Times of Transition: Toward a Positive-Peace Paradigm for Transitional Justice," *Fordham International Law Journal* 35, no. 3 (2012): 799.

Seen from this "beginner's mind" perspective,[74] if the historic foreground remains important to the work of transitional justice, neither is it obvious that peace and justice are always best advanced by heavily privileging those items while pushing others to the margins. In certain times and places, for example, local communities may wish to place a stronger emphasis on economic and social rights than has historically been the case in mainstream transitional justice practice; yet in other contexts this may make little sense. While potentially messier and more time consuming, such open-ended efforts, may pave the way for approaches to questions of justice in transition that are more holistic and balanced, reflecting fundamental commitments to local needs, deliberation, and autonomy. Ultimately, to paraphrase Sally Engle Merry's suggestion, this may allow for the sort of "transnational consensus building" emerging "out of specific local interests and concerns"[75] that will be as important to Sikkink's "justice cascade" as any domestic courtroom or international tribunal. In this sense, interrogating the peripheries is fundamentally about the democratization of a field born out of a commitment to fostering democracy, and a potential means of confronting the crisis of legitimacy that has at times dogged transitional justice initiatives across the globe.

[74] Shunryu Suzuki, *Zen Mind, Beginner's Mind* (Boston: Shambhala, 2011).
[75] Sally Engle Merry, "Human Rights and Global Legal Pluralism: Reciprocity and Disjuncture," in *Mobile People, Mobile Law: Expanding Legal Relations in a Contracting World*, ed. F. von Benda-Beckmann, K. von Benda-Beckmann, and A. Griffiths (Aldershot: Ashgate, 2005), 217.

PART I

Transitional Justice Peripheries

2

Justice for What?

With the birth of the field and the explosion of practice in recent decades, an increasing consensus has arisen that the various mechanisms of transitional justice should be mobilized as part of a response to violent conflict.[1] More than ever, the question is not whether there will be some kind of transitional justice, but what mechanisms from the transitional justice "toolbox" – including trials, truth commissions, vetting and lustration, reparations, and broader institutional reform – will be put in place.[2] Viewed from a historical perspective, the emergence of this transitional justice consensus some twenty-five years after the term was coined is nothing short of remarkable.

At the same time, this seeming consensus masks a deeper politicization and debate at the heart of the field.[3] For despite the increasingly shared sense that one must "do something" and the proliferation of transitional justice institutions and initiatives that make it possible for that "something" to be done, the increasingly privileged place of justice in international affairs and postconflict reconstruction begs the question of exactly what kind of "justice" transitional justice should be. It is therefore worth asking anew: *In the postconflict context, what specifically are we indignant about? What exactly are those acts or conditions of injustice that demand some sort of intervention? Why justice for this and not for that?*

To many, and perhaps lawyers in particular, it might seem rather obvious and natural that it is the killings, the sexual violence, the torture, and so on, that call out for justice. When human rights activists condemn "impunity," it is often precisely the

---

[1] See Ruti G. Teitel, "Transitional Justice in a New Era," *Fordham International Law Journal* 26, no. 4 (2002): 894 (noting the emergence of a "steady state" phase of transitional justice in which "the post-conflict dimension of transitional justice is moving from the exception to the norm").

[2] See Rosemary Nagy, "Transitional Justice as a Global Project: Critical Reflections," *Third World Quarterly* 29, no. 2 (2008): 276 (noting the standardization of transitional justice).

[3] See generally Bronwyn Anne Leebaw, "The Irreconcilable Goals of Transitional Justice," *Human Rights Quarterly* 30, no. 1 (2008): 95.

lack of punishment for these sorts of harms that they have in mind. And when political scientist Kathryn Sikkink talks about a "justice cascade," an emerging global norm of accountability, it is a norm entwined exclusively with such harms. Not surprisingly then, the dominant script of transitional justice has historically tended to focus heavily on the need to respond to egregious acts of "physical violence" – a category I use to cover murder, rape, torture, disappearances, and other physical integrity rights falling under the broader umbrella of civil and political rights.

With practice and time, a sense of naturalness has accrued around this rather narrow conception of physical integrity atrocity justice. Surely, it is thought, if it means anything then "justice" must involve accountability for perpetrators who commit unspeakable acts of physical violence. If we try to wipe the mental slate clean for a moment, however, it is not self-evident that these particular violations of international law and these particular forms of violence should constitute the beginning and the end of transitional justice concern. It is worth recalling that the human rights violations prohibited under international law go well beyond violations of bodily integrity, and include both civil and political as well as economic and social rights.[4] And as Evelyne Schmidt has made clear, serious violations of economic and social rights can in fact rise to the level of war crimes.[5]

Similarly, there are more extended concepts of violence that go beyond the acts of direct physical violence that have tended to occupy the foreground transitional justice concern. For example, peace theorist Johan Galtung famously spoke of "structural violence," which he understood to comprise those social structures that harm people and keep them from meeting basic needs through, for example, institutionalized racism, or sexism.[6] Galtung distinguished structural violence from what he called "direct violence" (and my notion of "physical violence" would fit into this latter category). In practice, however, the two categories are highly interdependent and mutually reinforcing. For example, from apartheid South Africa to the modern-day United States, we have seen a tight nexus between institutionalized racism and police brutality against blacks. Galtung also proposed the concept of "cultural violence," which he conceptualized as those aspects of culture that tend to support, normalize, and legitimize direct or structural violence.[7] The various dimensions of cultural violence are part of what allows perpetrators to commit unconscionable acts

---

[4] Beyond the International Covenant on Economic, Social, and Cultural Rights, economic, social, and cultural rights have the status of binding law in a number of international human rights treaties. Examples include the Convention on the Elimination of All Forms of Discrimination against Women; the International Convention on the Protection of the Rights of All Migrant Workers and Members of Their Families; the Convention on the Rights of Persons with Disabilities; the Additional Protocol to the American Convention on Human Rights in the Area of Economic, Social and Cultural Rights; the European Social Charter; and the African Charter on Human and Peoples Rights.

[5] See Evelyne Schmid, "War Crimes Related to Violations of Economic, Social and Cultural Rights," *Heidelberg Journal of International Law* 71, no. 3 (2011): 3, 5, 9–17.

[6] See Johan Galtung, "Violence, Peace, and Peace Research," *Peace Research* 6, no. 3 (1969): 170–73.

[7] Johan Galtung, "Cultural Violence," *Journal of Peace Research* 27, no. 3 (1991): 291–305.

firm in the belief that they are upholding the greater good, protecting the innocent, and so on.

Adding to this taxonomy, I have invoked the concept of "economic violence" – a concept that includes violations of economic and social rights, corruption, plunder of natural resources, and other economic crimes. The phrase "economic violence" has resonance with and might easily be confused with Galtung's concept of structural violence.[8] However, while Galtung's structural violence is conceived of as being less "personal," "direct," and "intentional" than physical violence, many acts of economic violence, cannot be so characterized. After all, for example, stealing money intended for the health care and education of AIDS orphans and placing it in the proverbial Swiss bank account is no accident and can do serious physical harm. Preventing food aid from reaching certain areas resulting in widespread starvation is a deliberate act. In that sense, acts of economic violence often share much in common with direct physical violence. Economic violence is often reinforced by physical violence, together with dimensions of structural and cultural violence.

Both physical violence and economic violence are clearly conceptual oversimplifications. Not all violations of civil and political rights involve direct physical violence, and many violations of economic and social rights – hunger and starvation, for example – are arguably a form of physical violence. While most physical violence constitutes a violation of civil and political rights under international law, the concept of economic violence includes, but is broader than, violations of economic and social rights under international law. Nevertheless, as a form of binary shorthand, both terms constitute loose categories that are useful to a discussion of the historical emphasis and blind spots of the field of transitional justice.

With this vocabulary in mind, it is worth pausing briefly to consider what we mean by the "justice" of transitional justice. Considered most expansively, "justice" could be understood as a broad social project and a condition in society. To "do justice" with such a conception in mind would likely involve a wide spectrum of efforts involving components of retributive, restorative, and distributive justice.[9] Yet this holistic view of justice stands in contrast to a narrower human rights legalism often associated with transitional justice that has often tended to see "justice" and "accountability" as synonymous with retributive justice and individual criminal accountability. While great strides have been made to expand the parameters of the field beyond lawyerly thinking and discourse, the field remains heavily anchored in a cosmovision that holds courtroom justice as the "gold standard." This is not to say that highly legalized approaches to transitional justice focusing on individual criminal responsibility are not valuable. Yet to conflate such approaches with what it

---

[8] See generally Dustin Sharp, *Justice and Economic Violence in Transition* (New York: Springer, 2014).
[9] See Rama Mani, *Beyond Retribution: Seeking Justice in the Shadows of War* (Cambridge: Blackwell, 2002), 5.

means to "do justice" in times of transition without examining their potential blind spots and limitations would be highly problematic.

Such an examination would be incomplete without considering the "what" of this particular form of highly legalized justice. For while there is an increasing consensus that the tools of transitional justice must be marshaled in response to egregious acts of physical violence, the proper role of transitional justice with respect to economic violence is far less certain. Indeed, historically, economic violence and economic justice have sat at the periphery of transitional justice work.[10] As Zinaida Miller notes, to the extent that transitional justice has dealt with economic issues, these concerns have been treated as little more than useful context in which to understand the perpetration of physical violence.[11] Despite some increasing attention to the issue on the part of the United Nations (UN), a handful of truth commissions and academics, questions of economic violence and economic justice remain largely marginal concerns for mainstream transitional justice today. The continuing invisibility of the economic suggests that despite several decades of evolution, the field of transitional justice has not moved far from its origins in which the "transition" in question was assumed to be a transition to a Western-style (neo)liberal market democracy with a package of interventions tailored to suit.

As the field of transitional justice moves beyond its historic origins in the wave of democratic transitions in Eastern Europe and Latin America in the 1980s and 1990s, and away from its roots in law and legalism, to a UN-sanctioned global phenomena tied to conflict prevention more generally, the almost exclusive emphasis on civil and political rights and justice for physical violence appears increasingly untenable. It is untenable first because this emphasis provides a distorted narrative of conflict premised on the notion that economics and conflict can be neatly separated.[12] When seen through this lens, conflicts become one-dimensional, when in reality they are a messy mix of political, social, economic, and cultural factors. Second, relegating economic issues to the background of transitional justice limits and biases the range of policies imagined to be necessary in the wake of conflict. Because poverty and economic violence can be associated with the onset of conflict, exacerbated by conflict, and continue afterward as a legacy of conflict, failure to strike a better balance between a range of justice concerns in transition is unlikely to generate policies and interventions that respond to "root causes" and may serve to obfuscate and legitimate very serious human rights abuses.[13] Physical violence and economic violence

---

[10] See Louise Arbour, "Economic and Social Justice for Societies in Transition," *New York University Journal of International Law and Politics* 40, no. 1 (2007): 4 (discussing why "economic, social, and cultural rights have not traditionally been a central part of transitional justice initiatives").

[11] See Zinaida Miller, "Effects of Invisibility: In Search of the 'Economic' in Transitional Justice," *International Journal of Transitional Justice* 2, no. 3 (2008): 275–76.

[12] See Miller, "Effects of Invisibility," 268.

[13] See Paul Collier et al., *Breaking the Conflict Trap: Civil War and Development Policy* (Washington, DC: World Bank and Oxford University Press, 2003), 22 (arguing that civil wars are more likely in

are intertwined and mutually reinforcing, and the language of "never again" has little meaning if the self-imposed blind spots of the field distort our understanding of the conflict and limit the range of possible solutions.

While greater inclusion of economic issues within the transitional justice agenda therefore seems necessary, and would constitute a significant modification of the dominant script, it also raises difficult questions that have yet to be fully worked out at the level of theory, policy, and practice. In particular, some have argued that the inclusion of economic concerns will overburden and overstretch transitional justice institutions, raising expectations that cannot possibly be fulfilled, while diluting the quality of any work that is done. To such critics, addressing questions of corruption or unjust economic systems more generally, while important, should it be left to the work of "development" and longer-term political and social processes. As I will argue in this chapter, however, the challenges posed, though real, are more pragmatic and methodological than fundamental.

I begin this chapter by first looking at why it is important to include economic violence within the core of transitional justice concern if the field is to foster more peaceful societies over the long term. After examining some of the historic reasons for the "constructed invisibility" of the economic, I will then address some of the concerns raised by critics and examine potential ways of rendering the inclusion of questions of economic violence more manageable. I will also review developments in policy and practice, which suggest that recognition of the need for greater engagement with the economic is gaining momentum.

THE INVISIBILITY OF THE ECONOMIC IN TRANSITIONAL JUSTICE

As the Cold War recedes in time, conflicts across the globe are increasingly intrastate in nature, less fueled by a grand global ideological battle between East and West than by local struggles for resources and control of government.[14] The majority of these modern conflicts now take place in some of the poorest countries on earth. As the reports of media, human rights, and conflict resolution organizations vividly illustrate, societies emerging from civil war and other forms of conflict are often completely devastated: civilians are killed and traumatized; infrastructure – from roads and the electric grid to schools and hospitals – are destroyed; and key institutions of governance are hollowed out by years of conflict, corruption, and mismanagement. Despite the best efforts of local and international communities to build peace in the wake of conflict, a significant number of these conflicts will reignite in the years following their apparent settlement.[15]

---

low-income countries, have disastrous effects on poverty rates, and have negative effects that persist well after formal cessation of hostilities).

[14] Of course, this is not to negate the legacies of colonialism and Cold War politics, whose ripple effects can still be felt.

[15] Paul Collier et al., *Breaking the Conflict Trap*, 155.

Transitional justice and international prosecutions are, of course, global phenomena. Nevertheless, for a number of reasons, both political and economic, it seems likely that much of their application in the coming years will be in the poorer countries of the Global South, particularly sub-Saharan Africa.[16] Given the role of the modern-day scramble for resources in shaping many conflicts in the developing world, together with the role of the Global North in fueling the arms trade, and in facilitating corruption, money laundering, and other forms of economic violence, this emphasis is deeply problematic. Sadly, there has been a persistent failure of transitional justice mechanisms to account for the effects of "outside actors" on the course of conflict, and this seems unlikely to change in the near term.[17] Although countries such as China, Israel, Russia, and the United States would likely benefit from the application of transitional justice practices, great-power politics, and Security Council vetoes continue to make this appear less likely than in the smaller, poorer countries of the world.

The causes of the conflicts that lead to calls for the application of transitional justice are multiple and complex. While poverty and economic violence are only pieces of this larger conflict resolution puzzle, they remain important ones, central to conflict dynamics in many countries.[18] This fact has been recognized by several truth commissions. For example, a Sierra Leone truth commission concluded that "the central cause of the war was endemic greed, corruption, and nepotism that deprived the nation of its dignity that reduced most people to a state of poverty."[19] Similarly, a Liberian truth commission identified as among the "root causes of the conflict," factors such as poverty, an "entrenched political and social system founded on privilege, patronage... and endemic corruption which created limited access to education, and justice, economic and social opportunities," and "historical disputes over land acquisition, distribution and accessibility."[20] It is against this backdrop of poverty, corruption and the persistent failure to resolve violent conflict in so many parts of the world that the role of economic violence in transitional justice should be considered today.

---

[16] Indeed, the sheer number of indictments emanating from the International Criminal Court involving African countries has generated significant controversy on the continent, leading in part to an African Union vote to halt cooperation with the Court with respect to the indictment of Sudan's Omar al-Bashir. See BBC News, "African Union in Rift with Court," July 3, 2009, http://news.bbc.co.uk/2/hi/africa/8133925.stm.

[17] See Prisilla Hayner, *Unspeakable Truths: Confronting State Terror and Atrocity* (New York: Routledge, 2011), 75–77. There are exceptions to this trend, however, including Chad, Chile, El Salvador, and Guatemala.

[18] See Paul Collier et al., *Breaking the Conflict Trap*, 20–31, 53 (arguing that civil wars are more likely in low-income countries, have disastrous effects on poverty rates, and cause negative effects which persist well after formal cessation of hostilities).

[19] *Witness to Truth, Report of the Sierra Leone Truth and Reconciliation Commission* (2004), Vol. II, 27.

[20] *Truth and Reconciliation Commission, Consolidated Final Report* (2009) (Liberia TRC Report), Vol. II, 16–17.

Violent conflict devastates both lives and livelihoods, yet ways of understanding what constitutes "violence" and who counts as a "victim" vary a great deal. From the trials at Nuremburg to the international tribunals for the former Yugoslavia and Rwanda, to truth commissions in South Africa and elsewhere, the conception of violence implicit in most transitional justice initiatives has been an exceedingly narrow one. The overwhelming focus of most transitional justice interventions across time has been on accountability for physical violence – murder, rape, torture, disappearances – and violations of civil and political rights more generally.[21] A broader conception of violence that would encompass often equally devastating forms of economic violence – including violations of economic and social rights, endemic corruption, and large-scale looting of natural resources such as oil, diamonds, and timber – has been the exception.

To take a famous example, under the South African Truth and Reconciliation Commission Act, a "victim" was limited to individuals who had suffered gross violations of human rights, including killing, abduction, torture, or ill-treatment.[22] The social, economic, and political system of apartheid – in many ways the very embodiment of the concepts of structural and economic violence – was largely treated as context to instances of egregious bodily harm that became the commission's principal focus. When viewed through this lens, the quotidian violence of poverty and racism, and the victims and beneficiaries of the apartheid system itself, receded into the background.[23] After more than two decades since the end of white rule in South Africa, apartheid has ended, but the de facto economic and social status quo has not changed to the degree many would have hoped. Poverty, inequality, and crime remain high.[24] Although transitional justice has addressed horrific forms of violence in South Africa that took place under the apartheid system, it may have also had the perverse effect of obfuscating and legitimating other abuses of power, leaving many of those who benefited most from the apartheid economic system comfortable in the status quo.

The "constructed invisibility" of economic concerns can have serious long-term effects, both in terms of our understanding of conflict itself and in terms of the remedies thought necessary to prevent recurrence.[25] As Zinaida Miller argues, pushing economic issues to the periphery of transitional justice concerns helps to shape a distorted and one-dimensional narrative of conflict in which economics and conflict can be neatly separated.[26] At best, economic issues become part of the

---

[21] See Nagy, "Transitional Justice as a Global Project," 284.
[22] See Pablo de Greiff, "Repairing the Past: Compensation for Victims of Human Rights Violations," in *The Handbook of Reparations*, ed. Pablo de Greiff (Oxford: Oxford University Press, 2006), 8.
[23] See Nagy, "Transitional Justice as a Global Project," 284 (discussing the standardization of transitional justice).
[24] See Patrick Bond, "Reconciliation and Economic Reaction: Flaws in South Africa's Elite Transition," *International Affairs* 60, no. 1 (2006): 141.
[25] See Miller, "Effects of Invisibility," 280–87. [26] Ibid., 268.

context, helping to explain why the physical violence that is the focus of a truth commission's work may have occurred, but are of little further policy relevance. At worst, a truth commission's work may be almost completely decontextualized, presenting a diagnosis of human rights violations that is abstracted from reality and the dynamics of social power and conflict.[27]

If the dynamics that produced massive human rights violations are poorly understood, creating a distorted narrative of conflict that relegates economic issues to the background, this may in turn limit and bias the range of policies imagined to be necessary in the wake of conflict. When conflicts are viewed through a one-dimensional lens, prevention of human rights abuses becomes a simplistic function of punishment and impunity. At the same time, the emphasis on physical violence and violations of civil and political rights likely means that the issues of economic violence and inequality that may have in part helped to generate the conflict will go unaddressed by the various mechanisms of transitional justice. Thus, we are more likely to see a focus on prosecution of a handful of members of abusive security services, vetting and dismissals and perhaps more general judicial and security-sector reform rather than remedies involving prosecutions for embezzlement that may have impoverished millions, much less some measure of social restructuring, such as affirmative action, redistributive taxation, or land-tenure reform.

UNDERSTANDING THE MARGINALIZATION OF ECONOMIC VIOLENCE IN TRANSITION

From the potential for deterrence inherent in criminal prosecutions to the cries of "never again," transitional justice has long been rooted in the rhetoric of the prevention of future abuses. Given the potential to misdiagnose the causes of conflict and bias the necessary remedies, understanding why an entire subset of issues so central to conflict dynamics has historically been so far from the core of transitional justice work and preoccupation is no easy task. While the factors underpinning such a gaping blind spot are many, there are at least two overlapping factors that are central to understanding the marginalization of economic violence in transitional justice work: (1) an importation of implicit distinctions and hierarchies from mainstream human rights discourse and practice, and (2) the consequences of viewing transitional justice as short-term affair involving a transition to a Western-style (neo)liberal democracy rather than some kind of social democracy or some other form of governance involving a more robust "positive peace."[28]

---

[27] Lisa J. Laplante, "Transitional Justice and Peacebuilding: Diagnosing and Addressing the Socioeconomic Roots of Violence through a Human Rights Framework," *International Journal of Transitional Justice* 2, no. 3 (2008): 337.

[28] The term "negative peace" refers to the absence of direct violence. It stands in contrast with the broader concept of "positive peace," which includes the absence of both direct and indirect violence,

International human rights discourse and practice self-consciously wraps itself in an aura of impartiality and universality. It is ostensibly apolitical, and the rights contained in the core international covenants relating to both civil and political as well as economic and social rights are repeatedly said to be "indivisible," as per the UN mantra.[29] In practice, the seeming consensus regarding universality and indivisibility masks a series of deep and abiding controversies and debates relating to the proper place of economic and social rights under international law. The Cold War roots of this debate, which split the atom of the Universal Declaration of Human Rights into two separate covenants to be championed by competing world powers are well known and will not be rehearsed here in detail.[30] Key for current purposes is the fact that the ripple effects of the implied hierarchical distinction between so-called first-generation and second-generation rights continue to be felt many years after the Cold War's end.

During much of the 1990s, the "formative years" for the field of transitional justice, even the world's largest human rights organizations, Amnesty International and Human Rights Watch, were slow to include documentation of violations of economic and social rights in their work and did so only gradually. Although some of this reluctance has been attributed to "methodological difficulties," it is also true that a number of activist luminaries of the time, including Aryeh Neier, were publicly skeptical as to whether economic and social rights were "real," and staunchly believed that civil and political rights should be the exclusive focus of human rights organizations such as Human Rights Watch.[31] The cross-pollination between human rights and transitional justice communities has been well documented, and many transitional justice scholars and advocates were drawn from the human rights community of this period.[32] One might add that the historic ambivalence toward economic and social rights within the human rights community mirrors a similar ambivalence within mainstream justice and criminal law about social justice more

---

including various forms of "structural violence" such as poverty, hunger, and other forms of social injustice. See generally Galtung, "Violence, Peace, and Peace Research," 167.

[29] See World Conference on Human Rights, June 14–25, 1993, "Vienna Declaration and Programme of Action," UN Doc. A/CONF.157/23, July 12, 1993; see also United Nations General Assembly, Resolution 55/2, "Millennium Declaration," UN Doc. A/RES/55/ 2, September 18, 2000.

[30] See Arbour, "Economic and Social Justice," 6 (discussing the Cold War roots of the current status of economic and social rights).

[31] See Kenneth Roth, "Defending Economic, Social and Cultural Rights: Practical Issues Faced by an International Human Rights Organization," *Human Rights Quarterly* 26, no. 1 (2004): 64 (explaining the particular methodological challenges associated with trying to apply a "naming and shaming" documentation strategy to violations of economic and social rights); see generally Curt Goering, "Amnesty International and Economic, Social, and Cultural Rights," in *Ethics in Action: The Ethical Challenges of International Human Rights Nongovernmental Organizations*, ed. Daniel Bell and Jean-Marc Coicaud (Cambridge: Cambridge University Press, 2006) (tracing the history of Amnesty International's ambivalence toward economic and social rights).

[32] See Paige Arthur, "How 'Transitions' Reshaped Human Rights: A Conceptual History of Transitional Justice," *Human Rights Quarterly* 31, no. 2 (2009): 333.

generally.[33] It is perhaps not surprising, therefore, that many of the lawyers drawn into the early human rights movement may have brought this ambivalence with them, assuming, perhaps, that postconflict justice ought to look an awful lot like a scaled up version of ordinary criminal justice.

Beyond importation of implicit hierarchies from human rights discourse and practice, the second factor key to understanding the peripheral status of economic violence in the transitional justice agenda is found in the historic conceptualization of the idea of transition itself, both as a duration and a destination. In terms of duration, the idea of transition suggests a period of exception, of time-bounded rupture. While the exact duration of the transition in question is never made explicit, the very notion of transition might have the tendency to, first, narrow one's temporal focus to a relatively brief period of the most egregious abuses, excluding the potentially deep and complex socioeconomic roots of conflict, and, second, to suggest corrective measures that are themselves narrowly time limited. Thus, transitional justice institutions are more likely to view human rights abuses – torture, for example – as functions of the excesses of certain segments of the security sector or possibly something done on the orders of higher-level government officials in an attempt to cling to power, and not as deeper expressions of racism, rampant inequality, historic deprivations, or other issues of structural and economic violence. Seen through this lens, the measures implemented to address such excesses within the security sector should be relatively swift – prosecuting and handful of army officers, for example – before the imagined window of transition closes.

Reflecting this view, Lars Waldorf has argued that transitional justice is "inherently short-term, legalistic and corrective."[34] Economic questions, it might be supposed then, will require a far longer time horizon to "fix" than is available for transitional justice, lest the notion of "transition" be strained beyond comprehensibility, and are best left to other institutions. Of course, it might also be said that building institutions that support the rule of law, good governance, and accountability – so critical for respect for civil and political rights – is also a complex, messy, and long-term project. And it is certainly not obvious that the limited prosecutions for torture, rape, and murder typical of transitional justice initiatives are more than symbolic shots fired into space in this regard. One might then ask why short-term remedies to violations of civil and political rights advance peacebuilding and rule-of-law aims more easily or cleanly than efforts to address economic and social rights violations. It would seem that the roots and drivers of both sets of harms are equally complex, and will require both short- and long-term efforts to address.

In terms of the destination of transition, the idea of a particular endpoint may help dictate the exceptional measures thought necessary to reach the intended goal.

---

[33] See Arbour, "Economic and Social Justice," 5.
[34] Lars Waldorf, "Anticipating the Past: Transitional Justice and Socio-Economic Wrongs," *Social & Legal Studies* 2, no. 2 (2012): 179.

Thus, one should ask how different the transitional justice "toolbox" might look if the paradigmatic transitions in the 1980s and 1990s were considered to be transitions to socialism or Scandinavian-style social democracy rather than transitions to neoliberal democracy.[35] Might there have been a greater emphasis on issues of distributive justice, including the need for progressive taxation in countries experiencing radical inequality, land-tenure reform in countries where land-based conflict has been a driver of violence, and affirmative action in countries with historically marginalized classes? While one can only speculate, what can be said is that the notion of transition as transition to (neo)liberal Western democracy surely had a limiting and narrowing effect on the "toolbox" and conceptualization of justice that predominate today, and likely played a key role in sidelining notions of economic justice.

ADDRESSING POTENTIAL OBJECTIONS

Putting these historical roots and limitations aside, even while greater emphasis on issues of economic violence within the transitional justice agenda seems necessary, striking a better balance between physical and economic violence raises difficult questions that have yet to be worked out at the levels of theory, policy, and practice. For example, some would find less objectionable the idea that transitional justice mechanisms should include within their ambit relatively simple and discrete acts of economic violence that took place during the conflict itself. Examples might include prosecutions for a warlord who sold off diamonds and timber to buy weapons to kill civilians, a group of rebels who stole food from a village and burned crops, or perhaps a former official for emptying the national treasury to the detriment of millions. Such crimes could easily be addressed using the traditional toolset of transitional justice and might be aptly characterized as "short-term, legalistic and corrective."[36]

However, the question also arises as to whether we should include deeper issues of distributive justice and structural violence that predate the conflict and which may have in part helped to precipitate it – an unjust tax code or skewed land ownership laws, for example. If we find ourselves focusing on issues of deep-rooted structural violence and fundamentally unjust economic systems, is this the proper work of the field of transitional justice, or should it be left to the work of "development," "peacebuilding," and longer-term political and social processes? In sum, the question of expanding the ambit of transitional justice concern forces us to ask at what point we might be saddling the field with a set of impossible expectations to fix everything that is broken.

We might characterize these as two sets of examples as reflecting "narrow" and "broad" approaches to addressing economic violence in the transitional justice

---

[35] See Arthur, "How 'Transitions' Reshaped Human Rights," 359.
[36] Waldorf, "Anticipating the Past," 179.

context. The majority of skeptics when it comes to the inclusion of economic violence within the transitional justice agenda appear to base their objections largely on the assumption that any embrace of the economic must invariably be a very broad one that would somehow conflate the work of transitional justice with that of social justice writ large or otherwise entail massive redistribution of resources. This, however, is a flawed assumption, since approaches to economic violence can be both broad and narrow, just as approaches to physical violence can be both broad and narrow. At the same time, it is worth considering the potential negative implications of taking a broad approach.

One area to consider in this regard is the question of political backlash that might endanger the larger transitional justice agenda in a given context. Taking a relatively narrow approach and looking only at the economic violence perpetrated during the conflict itself might prove to be relatively uncontroversial (save to those few individuals prosecuted for plunder, that is). Suppose, however, that in a given country there is an attempt during a transitional period to address some of the deeper legacies of abusive systems of governance, such as income inequality, the need for deeply redistributive taxation and wide-scale land-tenure reform. Such was arguably the case in South Africa at the end of apartheid, yet it is also recognized that leaving the economic status quo largely intact was one of the bargains struck and the price paid for a relatively bloodless transition.[37] A group of elites might be willing to see a handful of army officers or warlords prosecuted as sacrificial lambs to the status quo, but attempting radical revision of the political and economic situation that has existed for decades might be another story. In the end, many transitions depend in some measure on the "buy-in," or at least on the lack of resistance on the part of key elite constituencies. Thus, relatively robust or broad approaches to addressing historical economic violence might create the possibility of backlash, reanimating the "peace versus justice" debate along economic lines.

More thinking and research would be needed to predict the potential for backlash based on configurations of elites and their role in the transition itself. Such research would need to consider that, at times, addressing economic legacies of conflict in transition might in fact enlist more support from the general population and therefore be even more feasible than seeking accountability for violations of civil and political rights.[38] Indeed, in Kenya it appears to have been indignation over corruption, land grabbing, and other forms of economic violence that paved the way for broader transitional justice process, with civil and political rights violations riding the proverbial coattails.[39] It should also be borne in mind that the risk

---

[37] See Christine Bell, "Transitional Justice, Interdisciplinarity and the State of the 'Field' or 'Non-Field,'" *International Journal of Transitional Justice* 3, no. 1 (2009): 14.

[38] See Roger Duthie, "Toward a Development-Sensitive Approach to Transitional Justice," *International Journal of Transitional Justice* 2, no. 3 (2008): 307.

[39] Godfrey Musila, "Options for Transitional Justice in Kenya: Autonomy and the Challenge of External Prescriptions," *International Journal of Transitional Justice* 3 (2009): 460.

of a hostile and possibly even violent response on the part of certain elites is not a dilemma unique to addressing economic violence in transition. Indeed, much has already been said about how the parameters of transition justice may be shaped by the extent to which elites and perpetrator groups dictate the terms of the transition.[40] One might note, however, that in those few instances where truth commissions have made penetrating recommendations related to addressing socioeconomic inequalities – in Guatemala and Sierra Leone, for example – those recommendations tend to be ignored by policy makers.[41] The same can often be said of the more far-reaching recommendations relating to civil and political rights. Though hardly a trend worth celebrating, this may be a more likely outcome than backlash. Thus, a truth commission that reaches too far is more likely to be ignored than to upset the entire applecart.

Beyond the potential for backlash, one of the most frequently noted objections to the inclusion of economic violence relates to the additional cost and complexity this would entail.[42] It is a fact widely noted that the costs of even a narrow approach to transitional justice, particularly prosecutions, can be enormous, especially at a time when most governments, reeling from the effects of conflict, have little money to spare.[43] Truth commissions, for their part, are typically understaffed and underbudgeted as it is. Compounding the cost issue is the risk of expanding the mandate of truth commissions and other transitional justice mechanisms so broadly that it will be nearly impossible to fulfill in the limited time typically allotted.[44] In short, it seems clear that the resources devoted to transitional justice – be they financial or temporal – are finite and are unlikely to increase dramatically in the near term. Given these facts, it would seem sensible to question whether this is really the context for trying to grapple with "broad-based development or distributive justice policies that aim to redress widespread violations of the economic and social rights of poor citizens."[45]

While the cost and time issues are far from specious, as already noted, these concerns are most acute if we assume a very broad approach to questions of economic violence. And yet it is entirely possible to address questions of economic violence within the transitional justice process without going so far as to engage "broad-based

---

[40] See, e.g., Samuel P. Huntington, "The Third Wave: Democratization in the Late Twentieth Century," in *Transitional Justice: How Emerging Democracies Reckon with Former Regimes, Volume I. General Considerations*, ed. Neil Kritz (Washington, DC: United States Institute of Peace, 1995), 65–81; Guillermo O'Donnell and Philippe Schmitter, "Transitions from Authoritarian Rule: Tentative Conclusions about Uncertain Democracies," in Kritz, *Transitional Justice*, 57–64.

[41] See, e.g., Laplante, "Transitional Justice and Peacebuilding," 350 (discussing how the Guatemalan government largely ignored key recommendations of the Guatemalan Commission on Historical Clarification, including a progressive tax system and increased state spending on human necessities).

[42] See Rama Mani, "Dilemmas of Expanding Transitional Justice, or Forging the Nexus between Transitional Justice and Development," *International Journal of Transitional Justice* 2, no. 3 (2008): 256 (discussing the problems with the high cost of transitional justice measures in development).

[43] Ibid.   [44] See Duthie, "Toward a Development-Sensitive Approach," 306–7.   [45] Ibid., 299.

development or distributive justice policies." Furthermore, many transitional justice mechanisms are already funded in part by outside actors.[46] It is quite possible that measures to address economic violence in the transitional justice context would find support from complementary constituencies, particularly insofar as they touch upon questions of national economic development. Ruben Carranza has also argued that attempting to recoup money lost to economic violence in the form of embezzlement and corruption could be one way to help fund transitional justice initiatives focusing on economic issues.[47]

Beyond additional cost and complexity, there are also concerns associated with the dilution of the transitional justice enterprise itself. As Naomi Roht-Arriaza has argued, "broadening the scope of what we mean by transitional justice to encompass the building of a just as well as peaceful society may make the effort so broad as to become meaningless."[48] Indeed, if one were to take a robust approach to economic issues during periods of political transition, shifting the paradigm from transition to what some have called "transformation," at what point does the field lose coherence, risking the normative gains that have been made in recent decades? Seeking accountability for physical violence alone has been a monumental task, but over several decades, this work has made an impact on the normative and institutional global landscape.[49] That is no small achievement, and perhaps there is something to be said for doing justice narrowly, but doing it well. On the other hand, while concerns that transitional justice efforts may become too diffuse need to be taken seriously, and while transitional justice must necessarily remain a narrower project than the broader task of true social justice in its fullest sense, the global project of transitional justice cannot be made more meaningful, and the world made more just, if a significant portion of the drivers of conflict and resulting violations of international law are pushed to the side as "someone else's problem." There is no particular reason to think that, absent being taken up by the institutions of transitional justice, questions of economic violence will fare any better in the political marketplace than questions of past physical violence.[50] Such questions are always bothersome for transitional governments, and it is a key task of transitional justice to help shape the postconflict justice agenda by reminding stakeholders of inconvenient truths.

Whatever the harms addressed, there will always be a risk of trying to do too much, risking the legitimacy and capital of the transitional justice enterprise by reaching

---

[46] Ibid., 302–3.   [47] See Carranza, "Plunder and Pain," 324–25.   [48] Ibid., 2.
[49] See Naomi Roht-Arriaza, "The New Landscape of Transitional Justice," in *Transitional Justice in the Twenty-First Century: Beyond Truth versus Justice*, ed. Naomi Roht-Arriaza and Javier Mariezcurrena (Cambridge: Cambridge University Press, 2006), 1–8. See generally Kathryn Sikkink, *The Justice Cascade: How Human Rights Prosecutions Are Changing World Politics* (New York: W. W. Norton, 2011) (discussing accountability in the context of prosecutions for human rights abuses).
[50] See Arbour, "Economic and Social Justice."

beyond the possibilities for social and political change at any given time. And in general, it is very hard to answer the question of "too much" or "too little" in the abstract or in absolute terms. The general argument here is for an approach less based on categorical divisions – between, say, civil and political rights and economic and social rights or physical violence and economic violence – and more based on the dynamics and needs of a specific situation. Thus, the dividing line between "too much" and "too little" transitional justice should not be an arbitrary one based on conceptual categories but on a careful analysis of the drivers of conflict and the social, political and financial capital that can be marshaled to effect change via the various mechanisms of transitional justice in the wake of conflict. Put bluntly, the question of "justice for what" should be driven by context and not preconceived notions and rigid definitions of transitional justice. It may be, for example, that for transitional justice in Argentina, which arose out of a one-sided conflict largely involving disappearances of the outspoken, a narrower focus on civil and political rights made sense. In Sierra Leone and Liberia, on the other hand, which experienced devastating civil wars deeply rooted in poverty and natural resources, a narrow focus on civil and political rights would been inadequate to address the roots and drivers of the conflict.

One key to the challenges of overbreadth and dilution will be to find a legal or conceptual filtering device that opens up the possibility of addressing dimensions of economic violence while maintaining a manageable inquiry. For example, a truth commission might choose to examine plunder, corruption, and other economic crimes, but to impose a tight temporal window upon the inquiry, limiting the investigation to the period of conflict, the last ten years, or some other interval. If such a tightly bounded inquiry might avoid the sprawling and unfocused inquiry in places like Kenya and Liberia where commissions have gone back decades in looking at economic issues, it would of course also be subject to the dilemmas and politics of line drawing and a possible failure to address the deeper roots and drivers of the harms at issue. A second possibility would be for a truth commission or tribunal to look only to those aspects of economic violence that rise to the level of a war crime or violation of international human rights law. By focusing on such a "human rights-economic violence nexus," the inquiry would become much tighter and more manageable. After all, only the more egregious acts of corruption, for example, tend to rise to the level of an economic and social rights violation under international law.[51] The downside of this approach, of course, is that dimensions of economic violence that have caused real harm and served to fuel the conflict itself might slip through the cracks of such a legalistic filter. What is clear is that no

---

[51] See generally Chris Albin-Lackey, "Corruption, Human Rights, and Activism: Useful Connections and Their Limits," in *Justice and Economic Violence in Transition*, ed. Dustin Sharp (New York: Springer, 2014), 139–64.

filtering device will please everyone and each has a significant downside that should be acknowledged. However, such filtering devices could likely be more finely tuned to the context than the crude distinction between civil and political rights, one the one hand, and economic and social rights, on the other, that seems to have been the de facto if implicit filtering device through much of the history of the field of transitional justice.

It should be noted that most transitional justice processes have an explicit or implicit filtering device for physical violence as well. Most truth commissions focus on what they understand to be the most egregious harms. And typically, prosecutions are limited and selective by necessity. In the case of the Special Court for Sierra Leone, for example, only those seen to "bear the greatest responsibility" were supposed to be prosecuted.[52] In short, transitional justice will always be a time and resource bound-inquiry and the need to find ways to make that inquiry manageable is not limited to questions of economic violence.

In the end, working through these and other questions related to the wider acknowledgment of economic and social rights at the level of theory, policy, and practice will require years of effort and study. In this sense, they are little different than the dilemmas and trade-offs associated with civil and political rights in the transitional justice context, most of which have yet to be fully worked out even decades after the birth of the field. As I will argue at greater length in Part II of this book, one key to facilitating such work will be a shift in our mental map of the field in terms of the destination of the transition we have in mind. Reconceptualizing the "transition" of transitional justice as part of a broader transition to "positive peace," as opposed to a narrower transition to Western liberal democracy, could be one useful way to reorient our mental map.[53]

With positive peace as the end goal, the potential need for justice for both physical violence and economic violence would be considered based on an evaluation of the roots and drivers of the particular conflict in question, together with the peacebuilding needs of the present. Such a reorientation would not guarantee or mandate greater emphasis on economic concerns in all cases. However, insofar as the very idea of "positive peace" has at its core more extended concepts of violence and justice, it would provide a conceptual foundation that would more easily lend itself to a broader set of concerns than has historically been considered in transitional justice practice. Reorientation around the concept could therefore be an important step in the direction of bringing economic violence into the foreground of transitional justice policy and practice.

---

[52] Statute of the Special Court for Sierra Leone, Art. 1.
[53] For Galtung, "positive peace" is something that goes beyond "negative peace," or the mere absence of physical violence, and includes the absence of structural and economic violence as well. See generally Galtung, "Violence, Peace, and Peace Research," 167.

LESSONS FROM EVOLVING POLICY AND PRACTICE

Though the marginalization of the economic has been both frequent and persistent, there are increasing signs of a willingness to explore and push the traditional boundaries of the field. At the academic level, a small but growing literature has emerged questioning the marginalization of economic violence in the transitional justice context.[54] At the level of policy, the UN Secretary-General has developed guidelines establishing that transitional justice must seek to address violations of all rights, including economic and social rights.[55] These same guidelines note that approaches to transitional justice should take into account "the root causes of conflict or repressive rule,"[56] an important addition to the individual accountability model that characterized many earlier transitional justice initiatives. Again at the level of policy, the Office of the Prosecutor at the International Criminal Court announced in 2016 that in evaluating the gravity of offenses for purposes of case selection, crimes may be assessed in light of "social, economic and environmental damage inflicted on affected communities."[57] The Office further noted that it will "give particular consideration to prosecuting Rome Statute crimes that are committed by means of, or that result in, inter alia, the destruction of the environment, the illegal exploitation of natural resources or the illegal dispossession of land."[58] Finally, at the level of practice, an increasing number of truth commissions, including Chad, East Timor, Ghana, Kenya, Liberia, and Tunisia have examined questions of economic violence more squarely, even if their recommendations with regard to questions of economic violence have not always been implemented.[59] The trend is therefore a modest one, but it may at least help to shift the terrain of the debate from whether questions of economic violence should be addressed at all, to whether it makes sense to do so in view of the particular roots and drivers of the conflict in question, and how it might be done within the transitional justice context in ways cognizant of prevailing financial and temporal resource limitations.

It is worth briefly mentioning a few of these pioneering efforts by truth commissions as they speak well to both the promises and pitfalls of expanding the mandate of transitional justice institutions. In terms of positive aspects, truth commissions

---

[54] See, e.g., Louise Arbour, "Economic and Social Justice"; the entire volume of *International Journal of Transitional Justice* 2 (2008); Pablo de Greiff and Roger Duthie, eds., *Transitional Justice and Development: Making Connections* (New York: Social Science Resource Council, 2009).

[55] United Nations, *Guidance Note of the Secretary-General: United Nations Approach to Transitional Justice*, March 2010, 7.

[56] Ibid.

[57] International Criminal Court, Office of the Prosecutor, *Policy Paper on Case Selection and Prioritisation*, September 15, 2016, ¶ 41.

[58] Ibid.

[59] Dustin Sharp, "Economic Violence in the Practice of African Truth Commissions and Beyond," in *Justice and Economic Violence in Transition*.

that have looked at dimensions of economic violence have provided a fascinating glimpse at the ways in which physical violence and economic violence are intimately connected, part and parcel of the same sense of impunity on the part of perpetrators. In Chad for example, the truth commission revealed the ways in which the apparatus of state terror was literally funded, at least in part, by stealing the goods of the regime's political opponents.[60] In other words, economic violence was necessary to fuel physical violence. Similarly, truth commissions in Liberia and Sierra Leone powerfully documented the linkages between pillage of natural resources and the perpetuation of horrendous violations of physical integrity.

In some instances, these linkages and the analytical work invested in looking at economic violence is reflected in a truth commission's recommendations. For example, in Sierra Leone, the commission underscored the need to repeal laws preventing women from owning land, strengthen anticorruption initiatives, and develop more transparent systems for the management of diamond revenues, recommendations that were taken up, at least in part, by the government. In general, however, the secondary status of economic and social rights is still reflected in many of these commissions' work. For example, the Commission for Reception, Truth, and Reconciliation in East Timor actually documented violations of economic and social rights in some depth and rigor, yet when it came time to decide who was a "victim" for purposes of receiving reparations, the definition was limited to victims of violations of civil and political rights.[61] Whether justified under the banner of resource constraints or not, such practices have the effect of promoting hierarchies of rights and granting de facto impunity to the architects of economic violence.

Where transitional justice mechanisms have grappled with the economic impacts of conflict and abusive governments, they rarely do so using a human rights paradigm, even though many of the abuses in question may constitute violations of international law. In Chad, Liberia, and Ghana, for example, truth commissions explored various dimensions of what they called "economic crime," but did not frame their analysis or recommendations in terms of violations of international human rights.[62] While the work of such pioneering commissions was helpful in exposing the linkages between physical and economic violence, as Lisa Laplante argues, the failure to help different constituencies understand that in many instances economic violence also constitutes a violation of economic and social rights may have the effect of depriving "national groups a powerful lobbying tool

---

[60] *Les Crimes et Détournements de l'ex-Président Habré et de ses Complices* (Chadian TRC Report) (Paris: L'Harmattan, 1993), 27–28.
[61] See Commission for Reception, Truth and Reconciliation in Timor Leste (CAVR), *Chega!, The Report of the Commission for Reception, Truth and Reconciliation in Timor Leste, Final Report* (2005), 40–41, 140–45.
[62] See generally Dustin Sharp, "Economic Violence in the Practice of African Truth Commissions and Beyond," in *Justice and Economic Violence in Transition*.

to challenge the government's inaction or resistance."[63] Without rights-based scaffolding, subsequent development programs and other initiatives targeting inequality then become mere charity or government largesse rather than responses to concrete violations of international human rights law to which individuals are entitled. And by framing instances of physical violence in terms of violations of rights, yet failing to do the same with respect to violations of economic and social rights, this approach further contributes to the conception that economic and social rights are not "real rights," but mere aspirations.

Finally, the work relating to economic violence of several of these pioneering commissions had a rather loose, sprawling and freewheeling feel, unaccompanied by rigorous documentation that would lend it credibility. This illustrates the potential dangers of overbreadth, together with the need for new kinds of analysis and expertise. In Liberia, for example, the truth commission addressed questions such as land tenure in rather broad-brush fashion, and its recommendations relating to economic violence appear to be unmoored from the same type of rigorous documentation as some of its recommendations relating to civil and political rights. In Chad, the financial crimes division of the truth commission appeared unable to unravel a veritable maze of presidential finances and embezzlement that took place, suggesting the need for greater expertise in forensic accounting. These examples underscore the need for not only for sufficient time, finances, and expertise, but a tighter filter on those forms of economic violence that a commission can reasonably address while keeping the inquiry manageable given various limitations and constraints.

BRINGING THE DEEPER POLITICS OF TRANSITIONAL JUSTICE TO THE SURFACE

In the last two decades, the field of transitional justice has distinguished itself from its parent field of international human rights, in part due to its more overt grappling with the hard policy choices that lie at the intersection of law and politics and of justice and peace. At the same time, there has been an implicit politics at work in the backgrounding and foregrounding of various aspects of transitional justice concern. If mass atrocities and physical violence have been placed in the spotlight, issues of equally devastating economic and social justice have received little attention. The choice of which justice issues to focus on in a given context, be it physical violence, economic violence, or some combination of the two, is itself a political choice with distributional consequences. The goal of reorienting transitional justice as a more open-ended, context-specific project is not to remove politics or pretend that transitional justice is or ever could be an apolitical project. Rather, the hope is to be more attentive to the implications of choosing one form of justice or another.

[63] See Laplante, "Transitional Justice and Peacebuilding," 350.

Thus, the goal is not to do away with politics, but to bring them back to the surface and free them from the confines of a technocratic and legalistic discourse that too often serves to obscure and legitimize the implicit politics at work.

While addressing a wider range of justice concerns than has previously been the case will create serious challenges, failure to address these concerns may ultimately undermine the goals of transitional justice itself, including the prevention of a relapse into conflict. The hope therefore is to replace the historic emphasis and exclusion of economic violence with a more nuanced, contextualized, and balanced approach to the full range of justice issues faced by societies in transition. In this, we would take one step forward in moving beyond the constructed and self-imposed blind spots and biases of the field of transitional justice.

3

Justice for Whom?

If the dominant liberal-legalist script has played a heavy role in shaping our conception of what kind of justice transitional justice is supposed to be, primarily emphasizing physical violence and atrocity justice, decades of transitional justice practice have also raised some very important questions regarding *whose justice* we are really talking about. Transitional justice solutions have at times been imposed from the outside, sparking backlash and resentment. Yet even short of quasi-colonial imposition, interventions across the globe have often generated significant frictions within some of the local communities most affected by the atrocities that transitional justice is supposed to address.[1] While some level of friction between what I will simplistically call "the local" and "the global" dimensions of transitional justice may be inevitable (and even desirable as a source of creative tension), when poorly managed such dynamics can undermine both legitimacy and effectiveness. If the last chapter called for a reexamination of the "what" of transitional justice, this chapter then argues for careful reflection about both the "who" and the "how" of transitional justice.

The need for a better global-local balance is now well recognized, at least rhetorically. Indeed, the importance of "the local" is an increasingly emphasized theme in both postconflict peacebuilding and transitional justice discourse.[2] It is now freely

---

[1] See Alexander Hinton, "Introduction," in *Transitional Justice: Global Mechanisms and Local Realities*, 9 (observing that "transitional justice mechanisms almost always have unexpected outcomes that emerge out of 'frictions' between...global mechanisms and local realities"). As Miller et al. have noted, the "frictions" concept helps to stress the unexpected, unintended, and extremely complex nature of what happens when global meets local. See Gearoid Millar, Jair Van Der Lijn, and Willemijn Verkoren, "Peacebuilding Plans and Local Reconfigurations: Frictions between Imported Processes and Indigenous Practices," *International Peacekeeping* 20, no. 2 (2013): 139.

[2] See, e.g., UN Secretary-General, *Report of the Secretary General on Peacebuilding in the Immediate Aftermath of Conflict*, UN Doc. A/63/881-S/2009/304 (June 11, 2009), ¶ 7 (observing that "[t]he imperative of national ownership is a central theme of the present report"); UN Secretary-General, *The Rule of Law and Transitional Justice in Conflict and Post-Conflict Societies*, UN Doc. S/2004/616

acknowledged that the United Nations (UN) must give "due regard" to local justice and reconciliation traditions.[3] And policy documents across the fields of transitional justice, peacebuilding and development all stress the importance of "local ownership."[4] This emphasis on the importance of the local in policy circles is paralleled by a growing body of scholarship on the topic that has sought to explore the complexities of bringing dimensions of the local from the periphery to the foreground of transitional justice work.[5] All in all, as Shaw and Waldorf have noted, the current moment in transitional justice is marked by a veritable "fascination with locality."[6]

In many ways, this enthusiasm is an important historical corrective, and might be seen to reflect the commonsense (if long overdue) understanding that peace processes and justice mechanisms not embraced by a significant number of those who have to live with them are unlikely to be successful in the long term.[7] As then UN Secretary-General Kofi Annan starkly put it, "no rule of law reform, justice reconstruction, or transitional justice initiative imposed from the outside can hope to be successful or sustainable."[8] In that sense, finding ways to give real meaning to local ownership, agency, values, and priorities, is not an option, but a profoundly pragmatic imperative arising out of a crisis of legitimacy in the field.

The thing is, no one really knows quite how to do this in the real world.[9] Despite the increasingly acknowledged centrality of the local, concepts like "local ownership" remain vague and poorly understood, being marshaled in different ways by

---

(August 23, 2004), ¶¶ 16–17, 36 (arguing that the UN must "learn better how to respect and support local ownership, local leadership and a local constituency for reform").

[3] UN Secretary-General, *The Rule of Law and Transitional Justice in Conflict and Post-Conflict Societies* (2004), ¶¶ 16–17, 36.

[4] Simon Chesterman, "Walking Softly in Afghanistan: The Future of UN Statebuilding," *Survival* 44 (2002): 41 (noting that "[e]very UN mission and development program now stresses the importance of local 'ownership'").

[5] See, e.g., Deborah Isser, ed., *Customary Justice and the Rule of Law in War-Torn Societies* (Washington, DC: USIP, 2011); Rosalind Shaw and Lars Waldorf, eds., *Localizing Transitional Justice: Interventions and Priorities after Mass Violence* (Stanford: Stanford University Press, 2010); Alexander Hinton, ed., *Transitional Justice: Global Mechanisms and Local Realities after Genocide and Mass Violence* (Newark: Rutgers University Press, 2010); Erin Baines, "Spirits and Social Reconstruction after Mass Violence: Rethinking Transitional Justice," *African Affairs* 109, no. 436 (2010): 409; Elizabeth Stanley, "Transitional Justice: From the Local to the International," in *The Ashgate Research Companion to Ethics and International Relations*, ed. Patrick Hayden (Farnham: Ashgate, 2009).

[6] Rosalind Shaw and Lars Waldorf, "Introduction," in *Localizing Transitional Justice*.

[7] See Timothy Donais, "Haiti and the Dilemmas of Local Ownership," *International Journal* 64 (2008–9): 759.

[8] UN Secretary-General, *The Rule of Law and Transitional Justice*, ¶ 17.

[9] Leopold von Carlowitz has observed that while policy makers, academics, and practitioners generally agree on the importance of the local, local ownership has nevertheless proven difficult to operationalize in practice. *Local Ownership in Practice: Justice System Reform in Kosovo and Liberia*, Occasional Paper 23 (Geneva: DCAF, 2011), 1.

different actors for different ends,[10] often reflecting more aspirational rhetoric than concrete policy reality.[11] Moreover, in the transitional justice context – a context permeated with liberal (and primarily Western) international normative frameworks, institutions, donors, and technocratic expertise – the odds are often stacked against giving greater primacy to the local in a meaningful sense.[12]

THE DILEMMAS OF THE LOCAL

Contributing to these long odds is that underneath the platitudes lies a profound ambivalence arising out of what we might call "the dilemmas of the local." Building upon local ownership, priorities, practices, and values is recognized as among the keys to success for transitional justice interventions. And yet local practices and traditions can also lead to stark clashes with international law – anathema to the very human rights community who helped give birth to the field of transitional justice. The appeal to the local can also be used by Machiavellian elites for their own political agendas, including to reinforce the very oppressive power structures that may have led to the conflict in the first place.[13] For these and others reasons, there is a deep distrust of local agency in the postconflict context that abides beneath the rhetorical embrace.[14]

Such dilemmas arise in part due to a clash between universalism and particularism, between Global North and Global South, reflecting dynamics at the heart of the cultural relativism debate in human rights. As Peter Uvin has noted, "when internal or local solutions emerge, they often take forms that do not conform to

---

[10] See Daniel Bendix and Ruth Stanley, "Deconstructing Local Ownership of Security Sector Reform: A Review of the Literature," *African Security Review* 17, no. 2 (2010): 101.

[11] Timothy Donais, "Empowerment or Imposition? Dilemmas of Local Ownership in Post-Conflict Peacebuilding Processes," *Peace and Change* 34, no. 1 (2009): 5 (observing that in the broader field of peacebuilding, "local ownership has rarely moved beyond the level of rhetoric"); Simon Chesterman, "Ownership in Theory and in Practice: Transfer of Authority in UN Statebuilding Operations," *Journal of Intervention and Statebuilding* 1, no. 1 (2007): 9 (noting that in the fields of postconflict reconstruction and development, ownership "has frequently been of more rhetorical significance than anything else").

[12] See Jaya Ramji-Nogales, "Designing Bespoke Transitional Justice: A Pluralist Process Approach," *Michigan Journal of International Law* 21 (2010–11): 21 (noting that "[i]n transitional justice mechanisms to date, the international justice proponents' concerns have generally been paramount, perhaps because they often provide much of the funding and technical support for transitional justice mechanisms in the developing world").

[13] See Patricia Lundy, "Paradoxes and Challenges of Transitional Justice at the 'Local' Level: Historical Enquiries in Northern Ireland," *Contemporary Social Science* 6, no. 1 (2011): 93 (reviewing arguments in the literature that "transitional justice can be used by elites for a variety of purposes and to serve or conceal other very different political agendas").

[14] Florian Kuhn, "The Peace Prefix: Ambiguities of the Word 'Peace,'" *International Peacekeeping* 19, no. 4 (2012): 402.

western ethical ideals of international legal principles."[15] Yet often overlooked is that fact that that concepts like participation, inclusion, and tolerance – liberal ideas often invoked in debates about local justice – are themselves seemingly put forth as quasi-universal values intended to trump others. At times, such values are invoked as a shield to protect local autonomy and decision making and at others as a sword against local or traditional practices that might discriminate or otherwise fail to be fully inclusive. Thus, the dilemmas of the local are generated in no small part due to conflicting commitments within liberalism itself: between, for example, a liberal interventionist internationalism that seeks to wage peace and prevent atrocities and principles of local sovereignty and autonomy; and between competing internationally recognized human rights such the right of access to justice, on the one hand, and fair-trial rights on the other.

The result of this ambivalence, as played out through global-local power disparities, has typically been accommodation of the local to the extent of conformity with the global, co-option and not co-existence.[16] Conflicting rights and values call for a complicated balancing act, and in some contexts, too much local may be as problematic as too much global.[17] While it may be an all-but-impossible needle to thread,[18] finding a better balance between global and local agency, priorities, practices, and values stands out as one of the key policy challenges of twenty-first-century transitional justice – central to the future legitimacy of the field.[19]

To this end, this chapter will begin by canvassing several decades of transitional justice practice, a history punctuated by imposition and the marginalization of the local, which has in turn given rise to calls for greater "local ownership." As a potentially radical concept now on its way to becoming an empty signifier, I will argue for the need to dissect and disaggregate local ownership into its constituent parts: distinguishing concerns about actual *control* (agency, decision making, funding), *process* (bottom-up, participatory, homegrown), and *substance* (values, practices, priorities). The greater clarity afforded by addressing local ownership along these multiple axes may facilitate better diagnosis of global-local transitional justice frictions, and help to generate new and innovative approaches, including hybrid global-local initiatives,

---

[15] See Peter Uvin, "Difficult Choices in the New Post-Conflict Agenda: The International Community in Rwanda after the Genocide," *Third World Quarterly* 22, no. 2 (2001): 185–86.

[16] See Stephanie Vielle, "Transitional Justice: A Colonizing Field?," *Amsterdam Law Forum* 4, no. 3 (2012): 66.

[17] See Donais, "Empowerment or Imposition?," 21.

[18] See Roland Paris and Timothy Sisk, *Managing Contradictions: The Inherent Dilemmas of Postwar Statebuilding* (International Peace Academy/Research Partnership on Postwar Statebuilding, 2007), 5 (suggesting that insofar as the dilemmas of postwar statebuilding stem from "compelling but mutually conflicting imperatives," they may prove unresolvable).

[19] I have elsewhere outlined this and other key dilemmas that characterize what I call "fourth generation transitional justice." Dustin Sharp, "Interrogating the Peripheries; The Preoccupations of Fourth Generation Transitional Justice," *Harvard Human Rights Journal* 26 (2013): 149.

that take us beyond the transitional justice "toolbox" going forward.[20] Finally, I will argue that managing the tensions between the global and the local might be facilitated somewhat though the recovery and emphasis of several principles worked out in historically liberal societies, including pluralism, subsidiarity, and the margin of appreciation. In other words, if liberalism has been part of the problem, it might also be part of the solution to more innovative and contextually adapted transitional justice practice.

A HISTORY OF FRICTIONS AND IMPOSITION

While the ideological and professional origins of transitional justice theory and practice discussed in Chapter 1 helped to shape the conceptual boundaries of the field and to set in motion some of the global-local frictions experienced today, it would be too simple to attribute everything to those origins. We must also look to several decades of transitional justice practice to better understand the dilemmas of the local. Transitional justice practice is, of course, not a monolith, and where trenchant critiques have been raised, there are always notable exceptions to the more general trend.[21] And to be clear, much of the work of transitional justice – be it national-level human rights prosecutions or locally initiated and driven restorative justice practices – is carried out without significant tension with the global.[22] Yet a persistent critique of many transitional justice initiatives is that they pay insufficient attention to questions of locality and have been distant from the victims and larger communities they were at some level intended to serve. Examples here will be largely drawn from transitional justice initiatives with a significant international component or where global-local frictions have otherwise risen to the surface most palpably. International prosecutions, in particular, have tended to set global-local frictions in sharpest relief, and will be examined in some detail before turning more briefly to the work of truth commissions.[23]

---

[20] The phrase "transitional justice toolbox" refers to the mechanisms and interventions most associated with the field: prosecutions, truth-telling, reparations, vetting and dismissals, institutional reform, etc. The toolbox metaphor is increasingly critiqued as suggesting a set, one-size-fits-all template ignorant of context, and because the tool idea implies that transitional justice interventions are somehow neutral, acultural, and apolitical.

[21] See Jenny Peterson, "A Conceptual Unpacking of Hybridity: Accounting for Notions of Power, Politics and Progress in Analyses of Aid-Drive Interfaces," *Journal of Peacebuilding and Development* 7, no. 2 (2012): 12 (noting the tendency of assessments of liberal interventions to homogenize).

[22] At the same time, as I explore later on in this chapter, great caution with categories of "global" and "local" is warranted. What may look like a purely "local" effort or initiative may turn out to have been in part initiated by internationals, and receive international funding, framing, and technical assistance. Thus, in practice, there is often a blurring of categories.

[23] By "international prosecutions," I include purely international tribunals such as the international criminal tribunals for the Former Yugoslavia (ICTY) and Rwanda (ICTR) and the International Criminal Court (ICC) and the so-called hybrid tribunals, such as the Special Court for Sierra Leone (SCSL). Though one could argue for a distinction between "international criminal justice," limited

In many ways, the paradigm for modern-day international tribunals can be found in the Nuremburg International Military Tribunal (IMT) established by the victorious Allied powers shortly after the Second World War in order to try senior Nazi leaders for aggression, war crimes, and crimes against humanity.[24] From the outset, the tribunal was dogged with criticism that it exemplified a form of victor's justice and made little attempt to secure what we might today call local ownership, drawing both judges and prosecutors from the ranks of the victors.[25] Indeed, quite apart from a preoccupation with such niceties, one of the chief policy debates in the lead up to the creation of the tribunal was whether to summarily execute senior Nazi leaders, with options ranging from 50 to 50,000 executions.[26] The trial option prevailed, however, and unlike some modern international tribunals the IMT was located in country, and in Nuremburg no less, the ceremonial birthplace of the National Socialist (Nazi) party and site of annual propaganda rallies. The choice of a trial (rather than executions) and a symbolic location in Germany were intended to help to generate a sense of defeat among the vanquished (i.e., the locals), but also to serve an educational function for ordinary Germans in conveying some sense of the scope of the atrocities committed by the Nazis in their name.[27] Ultimately, though better than the alternatives debated at the time, there can be little doubt that the Nuremburg (and lesser known Tokyo) tribunals were an imposed justice and that the ability of local constituencies to have meaningful input into the process was limited to nonexistent.[28]

---

primarily to international and hybrid criminal tribunals, and the broader work of "transitional justice," the fact remains that since Nuremburg international tribunals have often been associated with transitional and postconflict contexts, and tend to generate similar legal, political, and moral dilemmas. Because it has the potential to hear cases from a great variety of countries, the International Criminal Court is not of course limited to addressing crimes in postconflict or transitional contexts, yet its work in places like Uganda and Côte d'Ivoire has become central to postconflict dynamics in both countries. Even when operating where there is no political transition to speak of, the ICC has demonstrated a capacity to generate very sharp global-local frictions. Thus, for purposes of analyzing global-local frictions at least, a sharp line between international criminal justice, on the one hand, and transitional justice on the other need not be drawn.

[24] For a fascinating account of the establishment of the Nuremburg tribunal and recap of the debates that it engendered, see Gary Bass, *Stay the Hand of Vengeance: The Politics of War Crimes Tribunals* (Princeton: Princeton University Press, 2002), 147–205.

[25] With respect to the victor's justice charge, Chief Justice Stone of the US Supreme Court famously called the trials a "high-grade lynching party" and a "sanctimonious fraud." Louise Arbour, "The Rule of Law and the Reach of Accountability," in *The Rule of Law*, ed. Cheryl Saunders and Katherine Le Roy (Annandale: Federation Press, 2003), 104.

[26] Gary Bass, *Stay the Hand of Vengeance*, 158–95.

[27] See ibid., 154 (noting President Roosevelt's desire that "every person in Germany should realize that this time Germany is a defeated nation" and speculating that the aspect of the Nuremburg trials that may have most appealed to President Roosevelt was their educational value for the local population in terms of conveying some of the truth of what was done during the war). Beyond its symbolic value, Nuremburg was also chosen out of convenience since its Palace of Justice was large and relatively undamaged by the war.

[28] The majority of defense counsel were German lawyers.

Despite some of the controversy generated by the Nuremburg and Tokyo tribunals, they helped to spark an interest in the creation of a permanent international criminal court.[29] However, Cold War frictions soon made consensus on the parameters of such an institution impossible.[30] Nevertheless, the Nuremberg model remains important because it was in some respects resurrected in the mid-1990s with the creation of the ad hoc tribunals for the former Yugoslavia (ICTY) and Rwanda (ICTR). The first major post–Cold War experiments in international justice, both tribunals served as a lightning rod for critiques and concerns relating to their engagement with the local. Neither tribunal was fully supported by the national governments most concerned, and the tribunals themselves were set up far from the victim communities and publics on whose behalf, at least in part, they ostensibly worked.[31] Focusing on this sense of almost imperial remoteness, one early critic argued that the tribunals "orbit in space, suspended from political reality and removed from both the individual and national psyches of the victims as well as the victors in those conflicts."[32]

Perhaps predictably, the distanced and isolated nature of the tribunals led to a lack of understanding of their work in both regions.[33] Nationals of the affected states were excluded from holding high-level positions within the tribunals, further eroding a sense of ownership, and leading to a situation where those doing the prosecuting and judging not only did not share the traditions of the alleged perpetrators, but in many cases were almost totally ignorant about local history and culture.[34] Despite expectations that the tribunals would contribute to peace in the respective regions, it has been argued that, in the case of the ICTY, the tribunal's architects "gave little

---

[29] See John Dugard, "Obstacles in the Way of an International Criminal Court," *Cambridge Law Journal* 56, no. 2 (1997): 329 (noting that "[t]he enthusiasm generated by Nuremberg and Tokyo for a permanent court").

[30] See ibid. Between 1949 and 1954, the International Law Commission prepared several draft statutes that would have led to the creation of a permanent international criminal court, but they were eventually shelved.

[31] The ICTY is located in the Hague, the Netherlands, far from the killing fields of Bosnia. The ICTR is located in Arusha, Tanzania. Unlike the ICTY, the Rwandan government actually asked the Security Council to create a tribunal, though it eventually cast the sole dissenting vote against the tribunal due to its location outside of Rwanda, its primacy over Rwandan courts, and its lack of ability to impose the death penalty. Its relations with the tribunal have ranged from coolness to hostility. See Alison Des Forges and Timothy Longman, "Legal Responses to Genocide in Rwanda," in *My Neighbor, My Enemy*, 54.

[32] Makau Mutua, "Never Again: Questioning the Yugoslav and Rwanda Tribunals," *Temple International and Comparative Law Journal* 11 (1997): 168.

[33] See Laurel Fletcher and Harvey Weinstein, "A World unto Itself? The Application of International Justice in the Former Yugoslavia," in *My Neighbor, My Enemy*, 29; Timothy Longman et al., "Connecting Justice to Human Experience: Attitudes toward Accountability and Reconciliation in Rwanda," in *My Neighbor, My Enemy*, 206.

[34] See Fletcher and Weinstein, "A World unto Itself?," 32; Des Forges and Longman, "Legal Responses to Genocide in Rwanda," 53 (noting that in the early years of the ICTR, "[v]irtually none of the tribunals staff... knew anything about the history and culture of Rwanda").

thought to how it would relate to those most affected by the carnage" ultimately threatening "the legitimacy of the court in the eyes of the society it was trying to help."[35] Given the misunderstandings and lack of local legitimacy, it is perhaps not surprising that some local constituencies have come to see the work of the ICTY as a form of victor's justice.[36] While the ICTR has provoked less overt hostility among ordinary Rwandans, many see it as largely useless, an affair conducted by the international community for the international community.[37]

Mounting criticism of the ad hoc tribunals eventually led to the creation of "community outreach" units, though turning around perceptions of the tribunals' work has proved to be a tall order, and such outreach and other community-centered objectives have always been ancillary to the primary task of securing convictions.[38] Writing in 2003, some five years after the creation of the ICTR's outreach program, Uvin and Mironko note that "[t]he main sentiment in Rwanda regarding the ICTR may well be massive ignorance: ordinary people know or understand next to nothing about the tribunal's work, proceedings, or results."[39] These are disappointing results, and it is hard to see how a tribunal could contribute to broader efforts at reconciliation and postconflict peacebuilding when so many are not familiar with its work in the first place.[40] Lack of information likely also contributes to distortions

---

[35] See Fletcher and Weinstein, "A World unto Itself?," 32–33.
[36] Ibid., 40. With regard to the ICTR, the tribunal's failure to prosecute crimes committed by the Rwandan Patriotic Front has been seen by some as a form of victor's justice. International Crisis Group, *International Criminal Tribunal for Rwanda: Justice Delayed*, Africa Report 30 (Brussels: ICG, 2001), iii.
[37] Ibid. See also Bert Ingelare, "The Gacaca Courts in Rwanda," in *Traditional Justice and Reconciliation after Violent Conflict: Learning from African Experiences*, ed. Luc Huyse and Mark Salter (Stockholm: IDEA, 2008), 31–45 (arguing that "[o]n Rwandan soil, the International Criminal Tribunals for Rwanda is portrayed and perceived as an instance of the western way of doing justice – highly inefficient, time-consuming, expensive and not adapted to Rwandan custom").
[38] See David Cohen, "'Hybrid' Justice in East Timor, Sierra Leone, and Cambodia: 'Lessons Learned' and Prospects for the Future," *Stanford Journal of International Law* 43 (2007): 5–6; Varda Hussain, "Sustaining Judicial Rescues: The Role of Judicial Outreach and Capacity-Building Efforts in War Crimes Tribunals," *Virginia Journal of International Law* 45 (2005): 551; see also Victor Peskin, "Courting Rwanda: The Promises and Pitfalls of the ICTR Outreach Programme," *Journal of International Criminal Justice* 3 (2005): 950–61.
[39] Peter Uvin and Charles Mironko, "Western and Local Approaches to Justice in Rwanda," *Global Governance* 9 (2003): 221. This ICTR is not alone in this regard. Though hailed as modestly innovative, it has been argued that the Outreach Section of the Special Court for Sierra Leone "largely failed in its primary goal of educating Sierra Leoneans about the Special Court." Stuart Ford, "How Special Is the Special Court's Outreach Section?," in *The Sierra Leone Special Court and Its Legacy: The Impact for Africa and International Law*, ed. Charles Jalloh (Cambridge: Cambridge University Press, 2013), 505.
[40] The preamble to the United Nations Security Council resolution establishing the ICTR provides that "the prosecution of persons responsible for serious violations of international humanitarian law, would enable this aim [bringing effective justice] to be achieved and would contribute to the process of national reconciliation and to the restoration and maintenance of peace." UNSCR 955, S/RES/955, November 8, 1994.

promoted by those opposed to the work of the tribunals, including elites and former perpetrators attempting to sway public opinion against them.[41]

Much has therefore been said about the potential for more and better outreach.[42] However, even a well staffed, well funded and brilliantly executed outreach program can only do so much to bridge the substantial gap that can exist between local populations and international justice efforts. In and of itself, outreach does little to address the marginalization of local agency, priorities, values, and practice in the setup and operation of the tribunals, and carries with it a subtext of locals as passive recipients of international justice discourse and practice. Outreach does not, for example, change the fact that Rwandans are being judged outside of Rwanda by non-Rwandans using Western-style judicial practices not all Rwandans agree with or understand in an international tribunal that has primacy over national proceedings within Rwanda, the very creation of which was opposed by the Rwandan government in the first place. It also does not change the fact that defendants found guilty by the ICTR will serve their sentences outside of Rwanda in conditions far superior to that of anyone found guilty on similar charges by Rwanda's national courts.[43] Outreach does not change the fact that, at the end of the day, neither the Rwandan government nor the so-called international community solicited the views of the Rwandan people regarding how justice should best be achieved in postgenocide Rwanda.[44] Thus, while being better informed about a distant process is better than being wholly ignorant, it is still very different than having a meaningful say about the setup and implementation of justice processes that might deeply affect a community.

Of course, one could debate to what extent international tribunals *should* spend valuable time and resources trying to be more communicative, be more connected to local communities, and pursue wider social aims beyond delivering judgments.[45] There may indeed be cause to be modest in our expectations for what a tribunal can meaningfully accomplish given historic resource limitations and established bureaucratic incentives and priorities.[46] Yet one danger in not doing a better job

---

[41] See Fletcher and Weinstein, "A World unto Itself?," 32.

[42] See, e.g., Ramji-Nogales, "Designing Bespoke Transitional Justice," 29–38; Etelle Higonnet, "Restructuring Hybrid Courts: Local Empowerment and National Criminal Justice Reform," *Arizona Journal of International and Comparative Law* 23 (2005–6): 363–76, 387–88, 410–13, 425.

[43] The disparate treatment of defendants and those convicted has been a source of some resentment in Rwanda as it gives the impression that the "big fish" who orchestrated the genocide are being given better treatment than "rank-and-file" offenders. See Jennie Burnet, "The Injustice of Local Justice: Truth, Reconciliation, and Revenge in Rwanda," *Genocide Studies and Prevention* 3, no. 2 (2008): 175.

[44] Longman et al., "Connecting Justice," 206.

[45] See, e.g., Marlies Glasius, "Do International Criminal Courts Require Democratic Legitimacy?," *European Journal of International Law* 23, no. 1 (2012) (reviewing critiques of international courts).

[46] See Padraig McAuliffe, "Hybrid Tribunals at Ten: How International Criminal Justice's Golden Child Became an Orphan," *Journal of International Law and International Relations* 7 (2011): 64 (arguing that without a significant reorientation of the priorities of international criminal justice policy makers, expectations for tribunals should be dampened).

engaging in questions of locality than the ICTY and ICTR is a potential loss of legitimacy and a sense that the tribunals are little more than a "theoretical exercise in developing international humanitarian law."[47] While scrupulously run proceedings and eventual convictions are unquestionably important, a process viewed by locals with indifference (at best) to hostility (at worst) would seem to represent a lost opportunity when it comes to deeper projects of accountability and the rule of law associated with long-term peacebuilding.

Amid the many challenges, successes, and failures of the ad hoc tribunals, a new international tribunal model emerged, that of the so-called hybrid or mixed tribunals of Sierra Leone (Special Court for Sierra Leone), Kosovo ("Regulation 64" Panels in the Courts of Kosovo), East Timor (the Serious Crimes Panels of the District Court of Dili), and Cambodia (the Extraordinary Chambers in the Courts of Cambodia).[48] Unlike the ICTY and ICTR, hybrid tribunals are generally located in the country most affected by the conflict, and comprise national and international judges and staff.[49] This model was initially greeted with some enthusiasm, being thought to hold the promise of greater local legitimacy, greater norm penetration at the local level and the ability to do more local capacity building, including strengthening domestic judicial systems.[50] In the literature, they are often presented as a sort of evolution from and response to the failures and critiques of the ad hoc tribunals,[51] representing a sort of middle ground that harnesses the power and legitimacy of international law, remains connected to local expertise and populations, while avoiding the staggering costs of purely international prosecutions.[52] Yet closer study of the creation of the various hybrid tribunals reveals a process of quick decisions and tough compromises more than a conscious process of experimentation as part of an effort to improve upon past failures.[53] It should also be noted that the exceptional cost of the ad hoc tribunals (which represented a full 15 percent

---

[47] See Fletcher and Weinstein, "A World unto Itself?," 30.
[48] A great deal has been written about the establishment, functioning, and failures of hybrid tribunals. See, e.g., McAuliffe, "Hybrid Tribunals at Ten"; Cohen, "'Hybrid' Justice in East Timor"; Higonnet, "Restructuring Hybrid Courts."
[49] There have been slight deviations from this norm. The trial of Charles Taylor before the Special Court for Sierra Leone was held in the Hague, due primarily to fears about security. See generally Giulia Bigi, "The Decision of the Special Court for Sierra Leone to Conduct the Charles Taylor Trial in The Hague," *Law and Practice of International Courts and Tribunals* 3 (2007): 303.
[50] McAuliffe, "Hybrid Tribunals at Ten," 10–22.
[51] See Cohen, "'Hybrid' Justice in East Timor," 1; Olga Martin-Ortega and Johanna Herman, "Hybrid Tribunals: Interaction and Resistance in Bosnia and Herzegovina and Cambodia," in *Hybrid Forms of Peace: From Everyday Agency to Post-Liberalism*, ed. Oliver Richmond and Audra Mitchell (New York: Palgrave Macmillan, 2012), 73.
[52] Higonnet, "Restructuring Hybrid Courts," 349 (outlining the potential power of hybrid tribunals in theory if not reality); Ellen Stensrud, "New Dilemmas in Transitional Justice: Lessons from the Mixed Courts in Sierra Leone and Cambodia," *Journal of Peace Research* 46, no. 1 (2009): 7 (arguing that "[t]he combination of international standards through UN involvement and local ownership through physical proximity and national participation may increase the legitimacy of these mechanisms").
[53] McAuliffe, "Hybrid Tribunals at Ten," 23.

of the UN budget at the time of their full operation) made the possibility of creating additional courts modeled on the ICTY and ICTR impossible as a practical matter.[54] Thus, the narrative of progress and institutional learning regarding the best relationship between tribunals and the local may not be as straightforward as once imagined.

Over a decade after the enthusiasm that greeted the first hybrid tribunals, evaluations of their success have become more circumspect. McAuliffe argues that some of the hybrid tribunals were often more hybrid in principle than in practice.[55] That is, far from being paragons of shared or local ownership, in the case of a number of the tribunals, "domestic authorities were largely marginalized or disengaged" while internationals dominated the process.[56] This may have resulted in part from ambiguity over allocation of responsibility and in part out of a seeming reluctance by some national governments to share blame and responsibility.[57] Compounding matters, tribunals in Sierra Leone, East Timor, and Cambodia have also been severely underfunded, particularly when it comes to activities such as outreach.[58]

If the ad hoc tribunals orbited in space,[59] the hybrid tribunals have been also described as a "spaceship phenomenon," with the tribunals' physical headquarters a strange and alien hive of activity largely seen as an irrelevant curiosity by the local population.[60] In practice, some critics argue, far from being the goldilocks solution some had hoped for that brings together the best of the global and the local, hybrid tribunals may sometimes turn out to be the worst of both worlds, bringing together the remoteness of purely international tribunals like the ICTR and ICTY with the shoestring budgets and occasional lack of rigor that can at times undermine purely local efforts.[61] Thus, while hybrid tribunals *as a theoretical model* continue to hold much promise,[62] some have argued that without a radical shift in priorities and funding, we may need to be modest in our expectations as to what they can accomplish beyond the fairly straightforward work of trying defendants and rendering judgments.[63]

---

[54] George Yacoubian, "Evaluating the Efficacy of the International Tribunals for Rwanda and the Former Yugoslavia: Implications for Criminology and International Criminal Law," *World Affairs* 165 (2003): 136.

[55] See McAuliffe, "Hybrid Tribunals at Ten," 36 (noting that the hybrid tribunals were "hybrid in form but never in ethos"); Higonnet, "Restructuring Hybrid Courts," 349.

[56] McAuliffe, "Hybrid Tribunals at Ten," 36.

[57] Ibid., 35; see also Cohen, "'Hybrid' Justice in East Timor," 36 (discussing challenges arising from unclear or contested ownership).

[58] Cohen, "'Hybrid' Justice in East Timor," 36.   [59] Makau Mutua, "Never Again," 168.

[60] Tom Perriello and Marieke Wierda, *The Special Court for Sierra Leone Under Scrutiny* (New York: ICTJ, March 2006), 2 (defining the spaceship phenomenon as "a Court that is perceived as a curiosity and an anomaly with little impact on citizens' everyday lives").

[61] See, e.g., Caitlin Reiger, "Hybrid Attempts at Accountability for Serious Crimes in Timor Leste," in *Transitional Justice in the Twenty-First Century: Beyond Truth versus Justice*, ed. Naomi Roht-Arriaza and Javier Mariezcurrena (Cambridge: Cambridge University Press, 2006), 143–70.

[62] Higonnet, "Restructuring Hybrid Courts," 349.

[63] McAuliffe, "Hybrid Tribunals at Ten," 53–65.

Given that enthusiasm for hybrid tribunals has waned and additional ad hoc tribunals modeled on the ICTR and ICTY seem unlikely for the foreseeable future, the ability of the International Criminal Court (ICC) to better engage with questions of locality and to avoid some of the failures of the past becomes especially important.[64] Yet as an overall model, the institution created by the Rome Statute seems to harken back to Nuremburg and the ad hoc tribunals, suggesting, even in the absence of any practice, that the potential to generate significant global-local frictions would be high. Of course, there are some notable structural differences. One obvious distinction between the ad hoc tribunals and the ICC is that while the former were created by fiat of the United Nations Security Council (UNSC), accession to the Rome Statute is voluntary, even if the UNSC retains the power to refer cases involving non states parties to the Court under Article 13(b).[65] In addition, provisions in the Rome Statute relating to victim access, participation, and compensation, as well as some flexibility as to where the court may sit represent a distinct improvement compared to the ad hoc tribunals, at least in principle.

However, despite these theoretical improvements, with a headquarters far removed both physically and culturally from the conflicts and perpetrators it has thus far addressed, the ICC's practice has been regularly punctuated by what one could characterize as a clash between global and local.[66] In Uganda, for example, some members of Acholi constituencies in the North have expressed a strong preference for using local reconciliation and reintegration practices to address crimes committed by former members of the Lord's Resistance Army rather than the ICC's retributive justice.[67] With respect to Kenya, a variety of African states and the African Union (AU) once attempted to pressure the Court to drop charges against Kenyan President Uhuru Kenyatta, with the AU chairman going so far as to accuse the ICC of being racist for only prosecuting cases in Africa.[68] With respect to

---

[64] This is not to deemphasize the importance of national-level or "domestic" human rights prosecutions. Indeed, Kathryn Sikkink has shown that the worldwide crescendo of human rights prosecutions in recent decades rests upon a bedrock of national trials. See Sikkink, *The Justice Cascade*, 21.

[65] See generally Rome Statute of the International Criminal Court, July 17, 1998, 2187 UNTS 90 (July 2002). For review of the Court's outreach work in practice, see Marlies Glasius, "What Is Global Justice and Who Decides? Civil Society and Victim Responses to the International Criminal Court's First Investigations," *Human Rights Quarterly* 31, no. 2 (2009): 509–20.

[66] Thus far, all of the Court's official investigations, save Georgia, have been in Africa: Central African Republic, Côte d'Ivoire, Democratic Republic of Congo, Kenya, Libya, Mali, Sudan (Darfur), and Uganda. Though it has yet to take advantage of it, it should be noted that a degree of flexibility has been built into the Rome Statute, allowing the Court to sit in locations outside of the Hague. See Rome Statute of the International Criminal Court, Art. 3 (While "[t]he seat of the Court shall be established at The Hague in the Netherlands," "[t]he Court may sit elsewhere, whenever it considers it desirable").

[67] See Tim Murithi, "African Approaches to Building Peace and Social Solidarity," *African Journal on Conflict Resolution* 6 (2006): 23–27.

[68] BBC News, "ICC Delays Cases"; Jenny Vaughan and Aude Genet, "Africa Closes Ranks to Condemn 'Racist' ICC on Kenya Cases," AFP, May 27, 2013. Perspectives among ordinary Kenyans are highly

Sudan, members of the African Union voted to refuse cooperation with the indictment of Omar Al-Bashir.[69] In 2016, these mounting tensions came to a head when Burundi, the Gambia, and South Africa signaled their intention to withdraw from the Rome Statute.[70] Taken together, declining enthusiasm for the Court, particularly in Africa, constitutes a serious challenge to the future health and legitimacy of the fledgling institution, highlighting the importance of taking questions of locality seriously.[71]

It would be easy to write off some criticism of the ICC as a sort of rearguard effort by autocratic leaders and regimes to preserve some of the privileges and impunity associated with power. Indeed, as demonstrated in Kenya, support for the work of the Court was at times higher among ordinary citizens than in segments of a self-interested political class, even if the views of the former were eventually susceptible to elite manipulation.[72] At the same time, one should note that the possibility of having a former president or senior official tried for human rights abuses in a foreign country or before an international tribunal has almost always generated significant tensions and feelings of ambivalence, from Augusto Pinochet, to Charles Taylor, to Laurent Gbagbo today.[73] Thus, one should expect that prosecutions of the type carried out by the ICC will generate controversy even in the best of circumstances.

However, though important, overemphasis of these factors would serve to ignore some of the deeper issues driving the global-local frictions that seem to plague the Court's work, issues stemming from the way global and local responsibilities and powers are structured under the Rome Statute. Put simply, the very architecture the Rome Statute hinges on a delicate and unstable compromise between global and

---

varied, ranging from support for the ICC's work in Kenya, to ambivalence, to opposition. See generally Thomas Obel Hansen, "Kenya's Power-Sharing Arrangement and Its Implications for Transitional Justice," *International Journal of Human Rights* 17 (2013): 307.

[69] See "African Union in Rift with Court," BBC News, July 3, 2009, http://news.bbc.co.uk/2/hi/africa/8133925.stm.

[70] Somini Sengupta, "As 3 African Nations Vow to Exit, International Court Faces Its Own Trial," *New York Times*, October 26, 2016. As of this writing, the Gambia indicated that it would not in fact withdraw from the Rome Statute, and South African courts ruled that the executive branch of government did not have the ability to withdraw unilaterally.

[71] See William Schabas, "The Banality of International Justice," *Journal of International Criminal Justice* 11, no. 3 (2013): 545.

[72] See generally Obel Hansen, "Kenya's Power-Sharing Arrangement."

[73] Consider in this regard the potential controversy if George W. Bush or Donald Rumsfeld were arrested and put on trial outside of the United States. The possibility of similar scenarios helped spawn the American Service-Members Protection Act of 2002, 22 USC § 7427, a federal law adopted with a stated purpose "to protect United States military personnel and other elected and appointed officials of the United States government against criminal prosecution by an international criminal court to which the United States is not party." It authorizes the president to use "all means necessary and appropriate to bring about the release of any US or Allied personnel being detained or imprisoned by, on behalf of, or at the request of the International Criminal Court." Because "all means necessary" would not seem to preclude the use of force, the law has been nicknamed the "Hague Invasion Act." See Human Rights Watch, "US: 'Hague Invasion Act' Becomes Law," Press Release, August 4, 2002, www.hrw.org/en/news/2002/08/03/us-hague-invasion-act-becomes-law.

local sovereignty in matters of justice.[74] Under the principle of complementarity, which has been described as the "cornerstone" of the Rome Statute, member states exercise primary but only conditional sovereignty in matters of justice, with power effectively ceded to the ICC where a member is "unwilling or unable" to prosecute a case itself.[75] The "unwilling or unable" standard echoes other emerging international norms and practices associated with the "responsibility to protect" and the US war on terror that are serving to reconfigure the relationship between global and local by replacing traditional notions of sovereignty with a sense of conditionality.[76] As Pierre Hazan has noted, by using the law to transform adversaries into criminals, intervention beyond state boundaries is increasingly permitted in the name of protecting humanity.[77]

While the principle of complementarity is in many ways a form of deference to the local, and stands in contrast to the primacy of jurisdiction exercised by the ad hoc tribunals, it also establishes a potential tension between the global and the local insofar as it invites the Court to stand as ultimate arbiter as to the adequacy of local effort and capacity.[78] The principle of complementarity would also seem to

---

[74] See Shaw and Waldorf, "Introduction," in *Localizing Transitional Justice*, 19 (describing the ICC as "an uneasy and unstable compromise between international justice and state sovereignty").

[75] Rome Statute of the International Criminal Court, Art. 17. Thomas Obel Hansen, "A Critical Review of the ICC's Recent Practice Concerning Admissibility Challenges and Complementarity," *Melbourne Journal of International Law* 13 (2012): 217 (noting that "the principle of complementarity has often been pointed to as the cornerstone of the Rome Statute"). The phrase "unwilling or unable" is defined in only the broadest terms in the Statute, but under the Court's emerging jurisprudence, it has largely come to pivot on a determination of inactivity. See ibid., 218.

[76] Consider, for example, the various formulations of the emerging principle of the responsibility to protect, or "R2P," where a nation-state's sovereignty effectively becomes conditional on its ability or willingness to protect its people from mass atrocities. See The International Commission on Intervention and State Sovereignty, *The Responsibility to Protect* (2001), xi (providing that while "primary responsibility" for protection lies with each individual state, "the principle of non-intervention yields to the international responsibility to protect" where the state is "unwilling or unable" to protect its people from serious harm); UN Secretary-General, Report of the High-Level Panel on Threats, Challenges and Change, UN Doc. A/59/565 (December 2, 2004), ¶ 201 (noting that there "is a growing acceptance that while sovereign Governments have the primary responsibility to protect their own citizens... when they are unable or unwilling to do so that responsibility should be taken up by the wider international community"). The threshold for intervention was arguably raised in 2005 with the language adopted in the World Summit Outcome Document, where it was agreed that national authorities must "manifestly fail" to protect before intervention is warranted. UN General Assembly, A/60/L.1 (September 15, 2005), ¶ 139. Beyond R2P, a similar construction of a conditional sovereignty can be seen in the Obama administration's controversial claim to the right to unilaterally pursue and kill targets in states without consent if that country is deemed "unable or unwilling to suppress" what the United States believes to be a threat. See Department of Justice White Paper, *Lawfulness of a Lethal Operation Directed against a U.S. Citizen Who Is a Senior Operational Leader of Al-Qaida or an Associated Force*, copy leaked to NBC News, 2013, http://msnbcmedia.msn.com/i/msnbc/sections/news/020413_DOJ_White_Paper.pdf.

[77] Pierre Hazan, "Transitional Justice after September 11," in *Localizing Transitional Justice*, 52.

[78] See William Schabas, *An Introduction to the International Criminal Court* (Cambridge: Cambridge University Press, 2007), 175 (observing that the relationship between international justice and national justice established under the principle of complementarity is "far from 'complementary,'" with the

preclude local approaches to atrocity that differ from a retributivist approach in some instances.[79] Consider in this regard the possible response of the ICC not just to a local pardon or grant of amnesty, but an effort to address offenses using restorative, "traditional," or otherwise alternative local practices of justice and reconciliation.[80] In instances without concurrent prosecutions, would such alternative approaches to justice be tantamount to "unwilling or unable" under the terms of the Rome Statute? While former Chief Prosecutor Louis Moreno-Ocampo has suggested that there should be great flexibility when it comes to lower-level offenders and the modalities of justice applied, the possibility for deviating from international retributivism when it comes to high-level offenders is more doubtful.[81]

Building upon the principle of complementarity and the notion of the primary responsibility of national governments, the ICC has no enforcement mechanisms of its own, but is completely dependent on state cooperation to carry out investigations and enforce its judgments.[82] Particularly in cases of self-referral under Article 14 of the Rome Statute, this can create special challenges to the Court's legitimacy as ICC intervention is played through the prism of local politics.[83] In Uganda, for example, a 2003 referral by the Ugandan government has resulted in the indictment of senior-level commanders in the Lord's Resistance Army.[84] This has been divisive for several reasons. First, because it is arguably subverting local judicial and reconciliation practices in Northern Uganda where segments of the population would prefer the use of customary justice practices to the Western retributive justice of the ICC.[85] Second, because it would seem to turn a blind eye to violations committed by the Ugandan army at the height of the civil war in Northern Uganda,

---

two systems functioning "in opposition and to some extent with hostility *vis-à-vis* each other"). Aside from deference, it should be noted that the principle of complementarity also acknowledges the reality that the ICC is a court of limited jurisdiction without the resources to address the great bulk of the world's human rights atrocities.

[79] See Alexander Greenawalt, "Complementarity in Crisis: Uganda, Alternative Justice, and the International Criminal Court," *Virginia Journal of International Law* 50 (2009): 141–44.

[80] Some scholars take exception to the word "traditional" as a description of such practices because it can imply that local are static and because it can also have pejorative implications. As noted later in this chapter, "traditional" practices used in the modern-day transitional justice context tend to be adaptations of much older forms of local justice and reconciliation practices.

[81] See Greenawalt, "Complementarity in Crisis," 141–44.

[82] See Charles Jalloh, "What Makes a Crime against Humanity a Crime against Humanity," *American University Law Review* 28, no. 2 (2013): 419.

[83] Under Art. 14(1), a "State Party may refer to the Prosecutor a situation in which one or more crimes within the jurisdiction of the Court appear to have been committed requesting the Prosecutor to investigate the situation for the purpose of determining whether one or more specific persons should be charged with the commission of such crimes."

[84] See generally Tim Allen, *Trial Justice: The International Criminal Court and the Lord's Resistance Army* (London: Zed Books, 2006).

[85] See Adam Branch, "Uganda's Civil War and the Politics of ICC Intervention," *Ethics and International Affairs* 21, no. 2 (2007): 195. It should be noted, however, that the Acholi population is not a monolith, and there are also segments of the population that support ICC intervention. See ibid., 192.

potentially giving the impression that the ICC is taking sides in a conflict rather than meting out impartial justice.[86] Similarly, in Côte d'Ivoire, former President Laurent Gbagbo stands indicted as an indirect co-perpetrator of crimes against humanity while crimes committed by forces loyal to his erstwhile political opponent, current president Alassane Ouattara, are largely overlooked.[87] In this and other cases, it may prove difficult for the ICC to serve as a credible check on state power while needing to tread lightly enough to ensure local cooperation.[88]

Both the Ugandan and Ivorian cases illustrate one of the key challenges for the ICC and international tribunals more generally vis-à-vis the local. To stand wholly aloof and independent from the local invites mistrust and misunderstanding, ultimately undercutting the potential to do more than develop abstract international legal precedents. Yet the ICC is also dependent on the local for its day-to-day work, and this carries with it the possibility of playing into local political agendas that may further notions of victor's justice, besmirch the impartiality and credibility of the ICC and play into narratives that would see in the ICC a Western project that picks winners and plays favorites.[89] What seems clear is that an international tribunal that ignores the complexity of local context (history, politics, culture, etc.) does so at its own peril.[90] Building the legitimacy of transitional and postconflict justice

---

[86] See ibid., 187–90 (2007). The suggestion of partiality was not helped when then Chief Prosecutor Louis Moreno-Ocampo appeared at a joint press conference in London with President Museveni in January 2004. See Michael Otim and Marieke Wierda, "Justice at Juba: International Obligations and Local Demands in Northern Uganda," in *Courting Conflict? Justice, Peace and the ICC in Africa*, ed. Nicholas Waddell and Phil Clark (London: Royal African Society, 2008), 22. There are also suggestions that it was actually Moreno-Ocampo who first persuaded Museveni to file the "self-referral" in the first place, further giving the impression of some kind of unseemly partnership. See Phil Clark, "Law, Politics and Pragmatism: The ICC and Case Selection in the Democratic Republic of Congo and Uganda," in *Courting Conflict?*, 43.

[87] See Human Rights Watch, *Turning Rhetoric into Reality: Accountability for Serious International Crimes in Côte d'Ivoire* (New York: HRW, 2013), 10; see also Pascal Airault, "Côte d'Ivoire – CPI: Gbagbo ou le Bénéfice du Doute," *Jeune Afrique*, June 14, 2013.

[88] See Janine Clark, "Peace, Justice and the International Criminal Court: Limitations and Possibilities," *Journal of International Criminal Justice* 9 (2011): 527–29.

[89] See Glasius, "What Is Global Justice," 519 (arguing that "[o]n the basis of current indictments he [the ICC prosecutor] could even be accused of exercising victor's justice... He has helped governments, including some that are none too friendly to human rights, to constrain rebels and rogue states under the banner of international law").

[90] For this reason, it has been argued that a "stakeholder assessment" employing qualitative interviews, ethnographies, focus groups, or population-based surveys should be carried out prior to a transitional justice intervention in order to discern local preferences, values, and cultural knowledge. See Ramji-Nogales, "Designing Bespoke Transitional Justice," 63–67. Nogales argues that under this model, the ICC prosecutor "would issue an indictment only if the population expresses a preference for international prosecutions in a distance location." Ibid., 70. While efforts along these lines to gain a greater appreciation of context would be a welcome step forward in many instances, at the same time, in the case of a potential ICC intervention based on a self-referral by a national government, this would raise some serious questions about sovereignty in the context of international justice. Even where a government might not be fully representative or a population divided, one could ask whether

interventions over time will likely require an exquisite sensitivity to context, and this may, as Greenawalt has argued, "call for as much, if not more, open-ended political assessment and balancing than for legal expertise."[91]

While the dilemmas of the global and the local are perhaps most acute in the realm of international and mixed tribunals, truth commissions often raise similar issues, though perhaps in subtler ways. Over the last thirty years, the truth commission has become a truly global phenomenon, with some forty commissions having been created, and new ones emerging on a fairly regular basis.[92] Though their mandates, composition, and powers vary greatly, most truth commissions attempt to accomplish three essential tasks: (1) diagnosing "what went wrong" in the lead up to the conflict or period of abuses; (2) documenting and analyzing the human rights abuses that were perpetrated; and (3) offering prescriptions for the future with a view to preventing recurrence of conflict.[93]

These tasks would seem to require an approach that is much more open-ended, context sensitive, and participatory than most tribunals. And indeed, truth commissions tend to be located in the affected region, largely staffed by locals, and typically involve the direct participation of a greater number of members of the affected public than a tribunal.[94] At the same time, as Rama Mani has noted, owing to restricted mandates and budgets, participation of the local population can still be quite limited, and the dissemination of reports can be erratic, incomplete, or even nonexistent.[95] Nevertheless, truth commissions have, by and large, been spared the trenchant critiques directed toward tribunals vis-à-vis their rather clumsy engagement with the local.

Even so, there is also a sense in which truth commissions have become part of a global project rather than a local initiative, a box to tick on postconflict checklist funded by international donors and assisted by a shadow staff of international

---

it is appropriate for an international treaty-based institution to do an end run around a state party in this way.

[91] See Greenawalt, "Complementarity in Crisis," 159.

[92] In her authoritative book on the topic, Priscilla Hayner documents the existence of forty modern-day truth commissions. Hayner, *Unspeakable Truths*, 256–62. Since that volume's publication, new commissions have emerged in Brazil, Côte d'Ivoire, and Tunisia.

[93] Sharp, "Economic Violence in the Practice of African Truth Commissions," in *Justice and Economic Violence in Transition*.

[94] There has been at least one call for a permanent international truth commission. See generally Michael Scharf, "The Case for a Permanent International Truth Commission," *Duke Comparative and International Law Journal* 7 (1997): 375. That said, as Hayner has noted, "[m]ost truth commissions are predominantly national, in both commission members and staff." Hayner, *Unspeakable Truths*, 214–15. A notable exception is El Salvador, where the truth commission was under the administration and oversight of the United Nations, with an entirely foreign staff and set of commissioners. Ibid., 214.

[95] Rama Mani, "Rebuilding an Inclusive Political Community after War," *Security Dialogue* 36, no. 4 (2005): 519.

consultants, rather than the result of a homegrown push for the particular type of truth and accountability that a truth commission can deliver.[96] One might consider in this regard the truth commission in East Timor, established not by domestic actors, but by a legal act of the UN's Human Rights Unit,[97] or the extremely close association between the International Center for Transitional Justice and the work of the Moroccan Equity and Reconciliation Commission (Instance Équité et Réconciliation, IER).[98] The result may often be a truth-seeking process that is not as attuned to local needs and realities as one might expect. Thus, Cavallaro and Albuja observe that in some respects truth commissions tend to hew to a "dominant script" that has been established over time not because it was necessarily perfectly attuned to each new context, but as a result of "repeated information exchange and consultations" between experts.[99] Funding from international donors, training workshops by international NGOs, and the occasional "technical assistance" provided by international consultants likely contribute to this phenomenon.

More fundamentally, anthropologist Rosalind Shaw has argued that the truth commission as a global phenomenon is rooted in Western modes of truth-telling and traditions of public confession and may not be appropriate in cultures with a different historical grounding.[100] In Sierra Leone, for example, many people preferred a "forgive and forget" approach rooted in local practices of memory, healing, and social forgetting.[101] Similarly, in Mozambique, Mani argues, the desire to remember the truth did not even exist.[102] The prevailing sentiment seemed to be that "the less we dwell on the past, the more likely reconciliation will be," and traditional cleansing rituals were used to help reintegrate combatants into their communities and at the sites of massacres.[103] Assumptions about the purportedly universal benefits of verbally remembering violence that appear to undergird the work of most truth commissions, Shaw argues, may undermine and serve to displace these alternative approaches to dealing with the past.[104] This may explain why many Sierra Leoneans attending truth commission hearings appeared to be less than enthusiastic about the process, though Kelsall notes that some hearings may have had unintended

---

[96] See David Mendeloff, "Truth-Seeking, Truth-Telling, and Postconflict Peacebuilding: Curb the Enthusiasm?," *International Studies Review* 6 (2004): 355–56 (noting that truth-telling is increasingly considered a necessary component of the postconflict peacebuilding process, together with demobilization, disarmament, and the holding of postwar elections).

[97] See Carsten Stahn, "Justice under Transitional Administration: Contours and Critique of a Paradigm," *Houston Journal of International Law* 27 (2004–5): 335–36.

[98] See Mark Freeman and Veerle Opgenhaffen, *Transitional Justice in Morocco: A Progress Report* (New York: ICTJ, 2005); see also International Center for Transitional Justice, *Morocco, ICTY's Role,* http://ictj.org/our-work/regions-and-countries/morocco.

[99] Cavallaro and Albuja, "The Lost Agenda," 125.

[100] See generally Rosalind Shaw, *Rethinking Truth and Reconciliation Commissions; Lessons from Sierra Leone*, United States Institute for Peace Special Report 130 (Washington, DC: USIP, 2005).

[101] See ibid., 9.   [102] Mani, "Rebuilding an Inclusive Political Community," 519.

[103] Hayner, *Unspeakable Truths*, 197–203.

[104] See Shaw, *Rethinking Truth and Reconciliation Commissions*, 1.

benefits once locals started to transform them though the incorporation of a process of community ritual.[105]

From this, it can be said that many of the assumptions of truth commissions – including the notion that personal healing promotes national healing, that truth-telling promotes reconciliation, and that forgetting the past necessarily leads to war – even if valid in some contexts and cultures, may not hold in others. For these and other reasons, Mendeloff argues that one should not be so quick to proclaim the necessity of truth commission in the aftermath of violent conflict.[106] As with tribunals, the need for context-specific approaches that take into account questions of local ownership, agency, priorities, values and practices must be given greater weight if truth-seeking practices and institutions are to live up to their many promises.[107]

THE PROMISES AND PITFALLS OF LOCAL OWNERSHIP

> Ultimately, no rule of law reform, justice reconstruction, or transitional justice initiative imposed from the outside can hope to be successful or sustainable... [w]e must learn better how to respect and support local ownership, local leadership and a local constituency for reform, while at the same time remaining faithful to United Nations norms and standards.
>
> – UN Secretary-General, *The Rule of Law and Transitional Justice in Conflict and Post-Conflict Societies*

If an imperious global justice has in some contexts been undermined by a ham-fisted engagement with the local that has served to blunt both legitimacy and effectiveness, making the global in some ways part of the problem, can it be that giving greater weight to principles like "local ownership" will lead to better solutions in the transitional justice context? The concept of local ownership is often traced to the field of economic development, and represents the evolution of concepts like "participatory development,"[108] but can now be found across a range of fields including peacebuilding and transitional justice. In the UN policy literature in particular, the concept of local ownership has become a sort of mantra. A 2011 UN report on the rule of law, for example, invokes the word "ownership" no less than seventeen times.[109] While this may be an extreme example, Simon Chesterman, who has

---

[105] See generally Kelsall, "Truth, Lies, Ritual," 361. [106] See Mendeloff, "Truth-Seeking," 355.
[107] See ibid., 358–361 (2004) (outlining claims made with respect to the beneficial effects of truth commissions on social healing and reconciliation, justice, the official historical record, public education, institutional reform, democracy, and deterrence).
[108] See Simon Chesterman, "Ownership in Theory and in Practice: Transfer of Authority in UN State-building Operations," *Journal of Intervention and Statebuilding* 1, no. 1 (2007): 7; see also Benjamin de Carvalho and Niels Nagelhus Schia, *Local and National Ownership in Post-Conflict Liberia: Foreign and Domestic Inside Out?*, NUPI Working Paper 787 (Oslo: NUPI, 2011), 6.
[109] See UN Secretary-General, *Strengthening and Coordinating United Nations Rule of Law Activities*, UN Doc. A/66/133 (August 8, 2011).

written widely about the concept of ownership in postconflict peacebuilding, has noted that "[e]very UN mission and development program now stresses the importance of local 'ownership.'"[110]

Some see in the prominence of the concept an attempt to paper over the legitimacy crisis in UN peacekeeping and peacebuilding, sparked in part by criticism emphasizing their neocolonial and overly Western character.[111] But whatever the exact impetus, it is painfully clear that rhetorical tribute to local ownership has often failed to translate into meaningful changes "on the ground," making the concept superficial and slippery in practice.[112] Indeed, far short of giving meaningful content to "ownership," Longman has argued that "[g]overnments and international institutions, such as the United Nations, rarely, if ever, consult affected populations when formulating policies aimed at rebuilding post-war societies."[113] Thus, to paraphrase the character Inigo Montoya from the film The Princess Bride, "ownership" does not appear to mean what we think it means. At the same time, because of the intellectual currency that the concept has achieved in donor and policy circles, it continues to be invoked by different actors in different ways to assert influence over postconflict policy processes.[114] Bendix and Stanley, for example, observe that in the context of security-sector reform donors demand local ownership to legitimize donor-driven policy prescriptions, local governments demand local ownership to secure their own power and influence, and nonstate actors want local ownership as a means to give themselves access to the policy process.[115]

Taken together, local ownership has become something of an empty signifier, employed by nearly everyone while at the same time remaining vague and poorly understood.[116] Yet the opacity of the concept does not diminish its importance. As Donais has argued, "there are real limits on the ability of outsiders to shape, direct, and influence events within states emerging from conflict," meaning that there is no real alternative to substantive local ownership over the longer term.[117] International experts can run an international or hybrid tribunal in the short term and donors can fund a truth commission, but ultimately only "deep and locally owned

---

[110] See Chesterman, "Walking Softly," 41.
[111] See Carvalho and Schia, *Local and National Ownership*, 1–6.
[112] See Donais, "Empowerment or Imposition?," 5; see also Chesterman, "Ownership in Theory and in Practice," 9.
[113] Longman et al., "Connecting Justice to Human Experience," 206. But see Anna Triponel and Stephen Pearson, "What Do You Think Should Happen? Public Participation in Transitional Justice," *Pace International Law Review* 22 (2010): 103 (examining a trend toward increasing public consultation in the setup phase of transitional justice mechanisms).
[114] See Patricia Lundy, "Exploring Home-Grown Transitional Justice and Its Dilemmas: A Case Study of the Historical Enquiries Team, Northern Ireland," *International Journal of Transitional Justice* 3, no. 3 (2009): 329 (arguing that "the concept of local/home-grown transitional justice is capable of being expropriated and manipulated to mask or serve other interests and 'unjust' practices").
[115] Bendix and Stanley, "Deconstructing Local Ownership," 101.
[116] Chesterman, "Ownership in Theory and in Practice," 7–10.
[117] See Donais, "Haiti and the Dilemmas of Local Ownership," 772.

social and political dynamics" can guarantee "well functioning institutions that produce substantive results."[118] Compounding matters, successful initiatives require the kind of profound local knowledge of context and culture that international actors almost never possess.[119] Yet even with ample awareness of context, interventions felt to be imposed "from the outside" are more likely to be seen as illegitimate, raising the possibility of backlash and ill will toward reforms.[120] In this sense, the struggle to give greater significance to local ownership can be seen as profoundly pragmatic.

More fundamentally, however, the concept of local ownership raises important normative questions, asking us to consider whether people have the right to determine their own destiny and make their own mistakes.[121] As Stahn observes, to even ask the question suggests a certain paternalism,[122] and could risk pathologizing and infantilizing entire postwar populations.[123] The normative pull of principles of self-determination and democratic control emanating from the concept of local ownership is especially strong when you consider that even with the best of intentions, errors of intervention are likely, yet it is locals who must live with and bear the costs of these errors over the long term.[124] International actors, in contrast, will pack their bags and move on to the next crisis. In this sense, the concept of local ownership asks us to recognize that if the goals of postconflict peacebuilding include classic liberal goods of democracy, good governance, and the rule of law, divorcing control and agency over a set of postconflict initiatives from accountability and cost bearing is ultimately a self-defeating exercise in contradiction.[125]

Despite its obvious importance, the turn to the local in matters of postconflict justice and peacebuilding is no panacea. In calling for better engagement with questions of locality, there is danger of propagating the myth of a virtuous local that may

---

[118] See Uvin, "Difficult Choices in the New Post-Conflict Agenda," 186.
[119] von Carlowitz, *Local Ownership in Practice*, 54 (observing that while they often possess technical knowledge and professional skills, international actors mostly lack sufficient knowledge of local structures and traditions).
[120] Talentino, "Perceptions of Peacebuilding," 153.
[121] See Stahn, "Justice under Transitional Administration," 326; von Carlowitz, *Local Ownership in Practice*, 54 (observing that "local ownership might remain rhetoric because international actors are unwilling to allow their local counterparts to make their own mistakes"); An-Na'im, "Editorial Note," 199 (arguing that "the practice of justice for every society can only emerge through an indigenous process of trial and error").
[122] Stahn, "Justice under Transitional Administration," 326.
[123] See Vanessa Pupavac, "Pathologizing Populations and Colonizing Minds: International Psychosocial Programs in Kosovo," *Alternatives: Global, Local, Political* 27 (2002): 490.
[124] See Uvin, "Difficult Choices in the New Post-Conflict Agenda," 185; Stahn, "Justice under Transitional Administration," 330.
[125] See Gerald Knaus and Felix Martin, "Travails of the European Raj," *Journal of Democracy* 14, no. 3 (2003): 64 (exploring tensions between unaccountable international intervention and the need to plant the seeds of democratic politics in Bosnia); see also Stahn, "Justice under Transitional Administration," 330 (exploring how the United Nations Mission in Kosovo absolved itself of legal checks on its power, making accountability a one-way street where locals are expected to bear the costs).

lead to a tendency to overlook its complexities.[126] Even without such romanticization, making local ownership meaningful in the postconflict context is extraordinarily challenging. The more intrusive international peace and justice interventions often occur in regions where there has been a profound breakdown in local political and normative structures and ordering.[127] In some cases, the formal institutions of governance have been hollowed out or collapsed entirely, and much of the expertise that may have helped to rebuild the country has fled, resulting serious deficits in terms of capacity and technical expertise. As an example, the brutal Liberian civil war spanned more than a decade, resulting in the loss of as many as 250,000 lives and the displacement of one million individuals. These are staggering numbers for a country whose prewar population numbered just over two million.[128] In Rwanda, 10 percent of the population of eight million had been killed and over two million had fled to neighboring countries.[129]

Complicating matters further, with the ethnic, political, and economic cleavages that often lead to and continue in the aftermath of conflict, there is often no coherent set of "local owners" in the first place.[130] Indeed, it has been argued that "[p]ostconlict spaces, almost by definition, are characterized far more by diversity and division than by unity."[131] In this context, postconflict justice, like other interventions affecting distributions of power, can be utilized by postwar elites as a means of jockeying for gain, furthering partisan political agendas, and attempting to reimpose preconflict power structures that may be discriminatory or otherwise not in keeping with international human rights standards.[132] Ultimately, therefore, as one set of waggish commentators put it, "the local ownership championed by the international community is not local ownership *tout court* but local ownership of a *specific* kind: the good kind."[133]

If the postconflict waters are sewn with mines that serve to make local ownership difficult in practice, navigation is made all the more complex by the role,

---

[126] See Richmond, "The Romanticisation of the Local," 149; Mazlish, "The Global and the Local," 95.
[127] Examples are not in short supply, but postwar Sierra Leone and Liberia would be among the more challenging of such contexts.
[128] See Sharp, "Economic Violence in the Practice of African Truth Commissions and Beyond," 98.
[129] See Barbara Oomen, "Donor-Driven Justice and Its Discontents: The Case of Rwanda," *Development and Change* 36, no. 5 (2005): 900.
[130] See Donais, "Haiti and the Dilemmas of Local Ownership," 759; see also Edward Joseph, "Ownership Is Over-rated," *SAIS Review* 27 (2007): 119 (contending that in some instances locals "do not take ownership of their problems primarily because they do not agree on who ought to be the owner").
[131] See Donais, "Haiti and the Dilemmas of Local Ownership," 759.
[132] Of course, the dangers of insertion of self-interest by international elites into the peacebuilding process can be equally problematic. See Kristoffer Liden, Roger Mac Ginty, and Oliver Richmond, "Introduction: Beyond Northern Epistemologies of Peace: Peacebuilding Reconstructed?," *International Peacekeeping* 16, no. 5 (2009): 594; see also Knaus and Martin, "Travails of the European Raj," 66 (noting that like all institutions, international peacebuilding missions have a tendency to pursue self-interest).
[133] de Carvalho and Schia, *Local and National Ownership in Post-Conflict Liberia*, 5.

expectations, and financial power of the international actors drawn to the scene. Taking concepts like local ownership seriously necessarily involves significant additional time and expense, yet international actors and donors tend to be impatient and anxious for results.[134] At the same time, international standards for transitional justice interventions are institutionally demanding, tending to privilege technocratic expertise over deep local contextual knowledge.[135] When coupled with global-local imbalances in terms of financial capacity, the end result is that all too often post-conflict justice interventions tend to place less of a premium on local ownership in practice than the global policy rhetoric would suggest.

Taken together, in many instances it might be said that true local ownership in the sense of full local agency and control is simply unrealistic.[136] In the context of international and hybrid tribunals in particular, it may well be impossible.[137] How, for example, could one truly have local ownership – again in the sense of agency and control – of a prosecution by the ICC, ICTY, or SCSL?[138] Even outside the context of such tribunals, global power, and funding structures, together with the momentum and politics of the international justice advocacy movement would seem to suggest that some degree of international involvement is inevitable as a practical matter.

Building on this, it has been argued that in some cases full local ownership may not even be desirable, and that some degree of international involvement is necessary in at least a supporting role if not more.[139] In many instances for example, "local violent conflicts are no longer local or traditional in their causation or dynamics," having been transformed by "interventions of regional and global actors."[140] In such cases, simple concepts of "local solutions to local problems" would seem to fail to capture the complexity of the situation. There are also arguments that some kind of global-local balance is required due to "capacity gaps" and the possibility of

---

[134] See Lucius Botes and Dingie van Rensburg, "Community Participation in Development: Nine Plagues and Twelve Commandments," *Community Development* 35 (2000): 50–51 (discussing the tensions in the context of development projects between pressures for results and the process demands of community participation); Stahn, "Justice under Transitional Administration," 336–37 (noting that greater local ownership with respect to judicial reconstruction in Afghanistan led to a slower process that was less protective of individual rights).

[135] See Bosire, "Overpromised, Underdelivered," 72.

[136] See Simon Chesterman, *You, the People: The United Nations, Transitional Administration, and State-Building* (Oxford: Oxford University Press, 2004), 242.

[137] See Matthew Saul, "Local Ownership of the International Criminal Tribunal for Rwanda: Restorative and Retributive Effects," *International Criminal Law Review* 12 (2012): 434 (arguing that one cannot always assume that "more local ownership will always be desirable"; rather, "it is possible that in some contexts where it is self-evident that there is a need for an international criminal tribunal, it might be in the best interests of the situation overall for there to not be any particular effort to incorporate local ownership into the establishment process").

[138] In the case of the ICC, one might say that the opportunity for full local ownership effectively disappears the moment a state is deemed "unwilling or unable" to prosecute under the terms of Art. 17 of the Rome Statute.

[139] See Joseph, "Ownership Is Over-rated," 115–16.   [140] An-Na'im, "Editorial Note," 202.

excessive parochialism.[141] Might it be, for example, that a better global-local balance in the trial of Saddam Hussein could have resulted in something less like a show-trial?[142] Similar weaknesses in the national judiciaries of Kosovo, East Timor, Sierra Leone, and Cambodia led in part the creation of international hybrid tribunals.[143] Finally, outside of the courtroom, other local experiments in transitional justice such as *Gacaca* in Rwanda, described in greater detail later on in this chapter, can and do conflict with international human rights standards – raising difficult question about whether and how to balance individual freedoms against principles of self-determination.[144]

For these and other reasons, while the local is often seen as one of the keys to the legitimacy of transitional justice initiatives, perceived legitimacy is in practice quite complex and there are no guarantees that a process will be seen as legitimate at any level simply because there is a high degree of local ownership.[145] In some instances, local constituencies might actually express a preference for an international prosecution, for example, due to perceptions that national courts are corrupt, discriminatory, lack independence, and so on.[146] In the end, therefore, too much local may raise as many questions as too much global.[147] As Mazlish argues, the local cannot simply be used as a talisman to ward off all possible intervention.[148] The world over, someone's local has often given way to a larger local – with the dismantling of segregation in the southern United Sates being one example – the results of which are hard to disagree with in the long term.[149]

Simply put, while there is no alternative to local ownership in the long run, in the short-run at least, local ownership may at times be an impossible ideal. If this makes for a very difficult needle to thread in terms of postconflict programming, it may explain why so much of the literature on local ownership does little more than say that it is both important and hard.[150] At the policy level, the tendency in the face of these dilemmas is to elide complexity, with local ownership becoming a sort

---

[141] See Joseph, "Ownership Is Over-rated," 115–16.   [142] Ibid.
[143] See McAuliffe, "Hybrid Tribunals at Ten," 24–28; see also Stahn, "Justice under Transitional Administration," 318–20 (reviewing some of the challenges of national courts that may bolster an argument for some international involvement).
[144] This dilemma is particularly acute in the case of *Gacaca* given the strong argument that it would have been impossible for Rwanda to comply with all international standards relating to accountability norms, victims' rights, and due process.
[145] See Saul, "Local Ownership of the International Criminal Tribunal for Rwanda," 434 (noting that an increase in local ownership could come with complications that can actually reduce legitimacy). Consider in this regard the example of *Gacaca* in Rwanda, which, though locally owned in the sense of literal control by the Rwandan government, has minimal legitimacy in the eyes of many local constituencies. See Burnet, "The Injustice of Local Justice," 188.
[146] Observation based on the author's experience documenting human rights violations in Guinea and Côte d'Ivoire for Human Rights Watch.
[147] Such preferences were often expressed to the author during his time documenting human rights violations in Guinea and Côte d'Ivoire for Human Rights Watch.
[148] Mazlish, "The Global and the Local," 98–99.   [149] Ibid.
[150] de Carvalho and Schia, *Local and National Ownership in Post-Conflict Liberia*, 5.

of cheap bureaucratic trope to signal the need for local "buy-in" and support rather than meaningful input or control.[151] Moving past this state of affairs in order to strike a better balance between global and local requires that we look more deeply into constructions of "global" and "local."

GLOBAL AND LOCAL: BREAKING DOWN THE BINARIES

For all of their importance, there is a sense in which the dilemmas of the global and the local are false dilemmas created by rigid intellectual categories.[152] As Goodale has observed, outside of the academic and policy literature, there is no place called "local" or "global."[153] Similarly, there is no "international plane," "international community" or places called "on the ground" and "in the field," yet these concepts are often spoken of as if they actually existed. The global-local binary is also problematic insofar as it implies that there are only two levels at which social processes emerge or unfold and implicitly invokes a normative hierarchy and teleology.[154] Thus, both categories tend to essentialize and depoliticize sets of actors that are neither ideologically monolithic nor politically homogenous. For these and other reasons, some scholars have questioned the value of the concept of the local, arguing instead for more complicated notions of "glocality" and "translocality."[155]

Despite these problems, the global-local distinction remains a central theme in human rights discourse, and is useful for its ability to underscore power asymmetries in the transitional justice context.[156] Similarly, as a policy trope and as an ideal, the concept of the local can provide an important counterweight to the centralizing and universalizing tendencies of transitional justice and liberal international peacebuilding more generally.[157] There may therefore be times when it is useful to categorize and essentialize to avoid pushing power differentials to the background, somewhat in keeping with Spivak's concept of "strategic essentialisms."[158] Thus, concepts of the local and the global retain utility for purposes of both analysis and policy making, even if they do not accurately describe the full complexity of all

---

[151] See Chesterman, *You, the People*, 242 (arguing that in practice "ownership... is usually not intended to mean control and often does not even imply a direct input into political questions").

[152] See Lundy, "Exploring Home-Grown Transitional Justice," 329 (cautioning against using the local in simply binary terms).

[153] See Mark Goodale, "Locating Rights, Envisioning Law between the Global and the Local," in *The Practice of Human Rights: Tracking Law between the Global and the Local*, ed. Mark Goodale and Sally Engle Merry (Cambridge: Cambridge University Press, 2007), 15–16.

[154] See Goodale, "Locating Rights," 14–15.

[155] See Lundy, "Paradoxes and Challenges," 93; Mazlish, "The Global and the Local," 99.

[156] See Goodale, "Locating Rights," 23.

[157] See Susan Thomson and Rosemary Nagy, "Law, Power and Justice: What Legalism Fails to Address in the Functioning of Rwanda's Gacaca Courts," *International Journal of Transitional Justice* 5, no. 1 (2010): 11 (positioning the turn to the local in transitional justice as a "corrective to the shortcomings of internationalized, 'one-size-fits-all' approaches").

[158] See Peterson, "A Conceptual Unpackaging of Hybridity," 14.

transitional justice processes as they emerge and unfold. Working through the dilemmas of the local therefore requires a complicated analytical tightrope act. On the one hand, the global-local binary remains a useful construct for the reasons articulated. At the same time, understanding the complexity of global-local dynamics requires some deconstruction and destabilization, breaking down simple binary notions.

The analytical and practical utility of breaking down simple binary notions of local and global can be illustrated by examining the *Gacaca* process in Rwanda. In using *Gacaca* as the central case study, I do not mean to conflate the local with customary law and tradition or to suggest that the dilemmas of the local can be solved by mere incorporation of local ritual. Ultimately, giving greater weight to the local in matters of postconflict justice must address the deeper and fundamental privileging of Western liberal-legalist responses to atrocity that may crowd out other ways of understanding and doing justice. Nevertheless, examination of the tensions associated with the embrace of local ritual and tradition as seen in the *Gacaca* process is useful to help complicate simplistic binary notions of global and local and to help tease out what local ownership might actually mean beyond the platitudes.

Historically, *Gacaca* served as a form of community-based informal arbitration employed to resolve minor disputes at the village level.[159] Following the arrests of suspected *génocidaires* in the years that followed the 1994 genocide, Rwanda's prisons population swelled to well over 130,000.[160] These figures grossly overwhelmed the capacity of Rwanda's legal system, creating the very realistic possibility that thousands of individuals would either die in Rwanda's severely overcrowded prisons before they would be granted a trial, or need to be released without trial.[161] This led to pressure from a variety of actors to solve a very palpable human rights problem, and the idea adapting *Gacaca* to address genocide-related crimes emerged.[162]

While its exact provenance is somewhat murky, the idea of using *Gacaca* may have arisen out of a conversation between a researcher for Human Rights Watch and some professors from the National University.[163] Alternatively, Oomen points to "evidence that it was representatives of the donor community who first raised the idea."[164] Others point to a 1996 report by the United Nations High Commission for Human Rights, which concluded that *Gacaca* might play a role in dealing with genocide-related crimes, but only as a sort of truth-seeking adjunct to the work of

---

[159] There is an ample literature on *Gacaca*, including its historical origins and evolution. See, e.g., Phil Clark, *The Gacaca Courts, Post-Genocide Justice and Reconciliation in Rwanda; Justice without Lawyers* (Cambridge: Cambridge University Press, 2010); Burnet, "The Injustice of Local Justice," 177; Lars Waldorf, "Mass Justice for Mass Atrocity: Rethinking Local Justice as Transitional Justice," *Temple Law Review* 79 (2006): 1; Longman, "Justice at the Grassroots? Gacaca Trials in Rwanda," in *Transitional Justice in the Twenty-First Century*, 206–28.
[160] See Burnet, "The Injustice of Local Justice," 177.
[161] See Des Forges and Longman, "Legal Responses to Genocide in Rwanda," 58.
[162] See Burnet, "The Injustice of Local Justice," 175.   [163] Ibid., 176.
[164] See Oomen, "Donor-Driven Justice and Its Discontents," 902.

Breaking Down the Binaries 65

tribunals or a community reconciliation mechanism that should be buffered from too much government interference.[165] Whatever the precise origins, the idea of drafting *Gacaca* into national service to address Rwanda's postgenocide justice challenges was eagerly seized upon by the Rwandan government and members of the international donor community.[166]

As adopted and adapted, the *Gacaca* of "tradition" was effectively transformed by the Rwandan government from a relatively informal community-driven conflict resolution mechanism to a modernized and formalized public punitive justice institution backed by the power of the state.[167] Whereas pregenocide *Gacaca* was not applied in cases of murder or other serious crimes, it was adapted to complex circumstances involving mass atrocities and genocide.[168] This proved especially troubling to international human rights groups who questioned the lack of protections for the accused, minimal training for *Gacaca* judges, and issues of corruption, among other things.[169]

Despite some of the controversy, *Gacaca* was initially welcomed by many outside Rwanda as a creative and pragmatic means to address a troubling backlog of cases relating to the 1994 genocide.[170] It also appeared to enjoy widespread support by ordinary Rwandans.[171] From a distance, it seemed to be the embodiment of a homegrown, locally owned, culturally embedded process – a Rwandan solution to Rwandan problems – yet this brushes over some of the complex reality.[172]

---

[165] See Ingelare, "The Gacaca Courts in Rwanda," 31–36.
[166] See Oomen, "Donor-Driven Justice," 897 (noting the "massive support" on the part of donors for *Gacaca*).
[167] In describing the ways in which *Gacaca* was adapted, I do not mean to suggest that its pregenocide or "traditional" form was static. As noted by Luc Huyse, "traditional techniques, in Rwanda and in other African post-conflict countries, have been greatly altered in form and substances by the impact of colonization, modernization, and civil war"). Luc Huyse, "Introduction: Tradition-Based Approaches in Peacemaking, Transitional Justice, and Reconciliation Policies," in *Traditional Justice and Reconciliation after Violent Conflict*, ed. Huyse and Salter, 6–7. In this sense, the label "traditional" is potentially problematic insofar as it suggests a practice not subject to constant change. See ibid., 7. Bert Ingelare argues that the "new" *Gacaca* is such a radical departure from the "old" that it represents an "invented tradition." Ingelare, "The Gacaca Courts in Rwanda," 32. Others have suggested terms such as *reinvented tradition* and *neotraditional*.
[168] See Waldorf, "Mass Justice for Mass Atrocity," 48 (noting that "traditional *gacaca* generally did not treat cattle theft, murder, or other serious crimes, which were handled by chiefs or the king's representatives").
[169] See Human Rights Watch, *Justice Compromised: The Legacy of Rwanda's Community Based Gacaca Courts* (New York: HRW, 2011), 4.
[170] For a more upbeat, though cautious assessment at the outset of the implementation of *Gacaca*, see generally Longman, "Justice at the Grassroots?"; see also Oomen, "Donor-Driven Justice," 902 (noting that *Gacaca* was once heralded as "ground-breaking" and "revolutionary").
[171] Paul Gready, "Reconceptualizing Transitional Justice: Embedded and Distanced Justice," *Conflict, Security, and Development* 5, no. 1 (2005): 13.
[172] See Christine Venter, "Eliminating Fear through Recreating Community in Rwanda: The Role of the Gacaca Courts," *Texas Wesleyan Law Review* 13 (2007): 580 (describing Gacaca as a "uniquely Rwandan...grassroots [effort] to deal with the genocide...from the bottom up"). Of course, the

As noted, while loosely based on a traditional dispute resolution process and championed by the Rwandan government as the only possible solution, the impetus for *Gacaca* also owes much to discussion generated by Rwandan scholars, international human rights activists, UN reports, and donors to say nothing of sustained pressure from international NGOs and other entities to address Rwanda's serious prison overcrowding problem. It was carried out in large part as a result of support from international donors.[173] What was presented as "traditional" and "community based" was really a hybrid that moved back and forth between historical origins and capture by the nation-state.[174] Thus, to adopt the neologism of some scholars, it might indeed be correct to say that the origins and unfolding of the *Gacaca* process were very much "glocal" or "translocal."[175] In this way, the emergence and shaping of transitional justice processes might be seen as part of a continued dialectical process between multiple "levels" – global, regional, national, and community. Simple categories of global and local fail to capture this complexity.

Just as *Gacaca* shows that the global-local binary must be questioned and blurred, making better sense of global-local dilemmas and interactions also requires us to break down and unpack concepts like "local ownership" into constituent parts. In practice, I argue, the term has become a catchall of sorts for concerns relating to actual *control* (agency, decision making, funding), *process* (whether a transitional justice initiative is "bottom-up," participatory or homegrown, being shaped by input from "the grassroots," or "top-down" and imposed; whether it is driven by the state or "the community"), and *substance* (whether a transitional justice initiative honors and resonates with local values and practices). While the control, process, and substance dimensions of local ownership are in practice often going to be highly related, it may not be necessary to satisfy concerns relating to all three for a transitional justice program to be perceived as legitimate. For example, hypothetically, a UN or otherwise "externally" controlled and funded program might be seen as legitimate by many local constituencies if it were heavily shaped by a bottom-up participatory process that put local priorities and practices at the heart of the program. In contrast, a transitional justice program might be fully controlled by a national government or other locals, and yet still be part of a state-centric solution imposed from the top-down upon local peasant communities without significant input, and ultimately be seen by many locals as lacking legitimacy.

Both hypotheticals presented here would seem to suggest that the process dimension of local ownership is especially key to the design of transitional justice interventions, not simply because process can help to generate feelings of (il)legitimacy, but also because, in practice, satisfying process concerns may tend to lead to

---

Rwandan government itself was also at some pains to present *Gacaca* as homegrown and locally devised. See Oomen, "Donor-Driven Justice," 902.
[173] See generally Oomen, "Donor-Driven Justice."
[174] Huyse, "Introduction: Tradition-Based Approaches in Peacemaking, Transitional Justice," 8.
[175] See Lundy, "Paradoxes and Challenges," 93.

transitional justice modalities that hit positive notes on the substance axis.[176] At the same time, undue focus on the process dimension alone is potentially problematic as it has been observed in other contexts that ideas like "participatory development" can easily be co-opted by states and international institutions to their own ends.[177] In the transitional justice context, it has similarly been noted that where efforts at "consultation" do take place, local communities are often asked for input into project implementation long after more fundamental questions of design and setup have already been established, suggesting that process concerns are often treated as a shallow, technical exercise.[178] There is therefore a danger that as notions of process, including participation, are mainstreamed, they become yet another bureaucratic planning tool, muddying useful distinctions between genuinely people-centered, bottom-up processes and top-down, technocratic ones.[179] Finally, beyond process, one should not dismiss the importance of the control dimension, which – being intimately linked to the power and politics of transitional justice interventions – still plays an important role in global-local frictions and feelings of legitimacy.

By offering this schema, the intent is not to suggest that categories of control, process, and substances are in any way definitive, or that local ownership could not be broken down into alternative or additional categories. The key point is that thinking of local ownership *multidimensionally* based on the unique history of each particular context is a much more useful exercise than the loose sloganeering that often takes place around the concept today. Thus, the question should not be whether there is "local ownership" writ large, but *what kind of ownership*, and across which dimensions. Again, the *Gacaca* process serves as a useful real-world illustration of some of these complex dynamics.

At the most superficial level, the *Gacaca* process was very much "locally owned" as compared to the ICTR, for example, in the sense that formal control was retained by Rwandans. Yet to end there would be to confuse local ownership with ownership by the national government, a distinction that is potentially problematic in a context where the government cannot be assumed to represent many local constituencies or to be subject to checks and balances if it fails to consider their input.[180] The results of the *Gacaca* process illustrate that this kind of national ownership alone will often

---

[176] See generally Triponel and Pearson, "What Do You Think Should Happen" (examining trend toward increasing public consultation in the setup phase of transitional justice mechanisms).

[177] See Lundy, "Exploring Home-Grown Transitional Justice," 329. The concept of participation has a long history in the field of development and is both revered and reviled in the literature for its power to both empower and co-opt. For a review of the history and trajectory of the concept, see generally Sam Hickey and Giles Mohan, "Towards Participation as Transformation: Critical Themes and Challenges," in *Participation: From Tyranny to Transformation?*, ed. Samuel Hickey and Giles Mohan (New York: Zed Books, 2004).

[178] See Rubli, *Transitional Justice: Justice by Bureaucratic Means*, 12.

[179] See Hickey and Mohan, "Towards Participation as Transformation," 4.

[180] Oomen, "Donor-Driven Justice," 899–902 (discussing the "increasingly oppressive" and authoritarianism climate in Rwanda).

not be sufficient to create legitimacy in the eyes of many local constituencies.[181] Thus, the process dimension of local ownership, including whether a transitional justice initiative is carried out in a manner that is "bottom-up," drawing upon meaningful input and participation by affected communities, remains critical.[182] While the *Gacaca* process certainly involved a lot of participation by ordinary Rwandans in the hearings themselves, attendance at *Gacaca* hearings eventually dwindled and had to be coerced, and Rwandans had little space to contest dimensions of the larger *Gacaca* process itself.[183] Thus, there was a very real sense in which the process was imposed from the top-down (with the top being Kigali rather than New York or Geneva).[184]

Beyond control and process, there is also a substantive dimension to questions of local ownership, including the extent to which a transitional justice initiative honors and resonates with local values and practices. Even on this score, the *Gacaca* process receives mixed results. While initially greeted with enthusiasm by the Rwandan population as a distinctively Rwandan approach to postconflict justice in contrast with the remote and Western ICTR, many Rwandans were ultimately alienated by the process and felt that it lacked legitimacy.[185] In many respects, the process appeared to be more in tune with national (or government) values and priorities than community-based ones in the sense that it was engineered to reinforce longstanding partisan narratives favored by the Rwandan Patriotic Front (RPF) political party by excluding crimes committed by the RPF from the *Gacaca* process.[186] Thus, *Gacaca* illustrates that adapting the trappings of local practices, traditions and rituals alone is not sufficient to generate a sense of legitimacy and good will toward a transitional justice program.

With the process concluded as of 2012, *Gacaca* leaves an ambiguous legacy.[187] While it constitutes an important experiment in postconflict justice programming, its glaring gaps and deficiencies also serve as something of a cautionary tale.[188]

---

[181] Many ordinary Rwandans prefer the *Gacaca* courts over Rwanda's national courts and the ICTR. See Ingelare, "The Gacaca Courts in Rwanda," 51. At the same time, other Rwandans see it as an imposition from Kigali. See Burnet, "The Injustice of Local Justice," 188; see also Oomen, "Donor-Driven Justice," 904 (noting that "the public at large seemed to increasingly consider the [*Gacaca*] meetings as mandatory events to sit through, just like community service").

[182] See generally Triponel and Pearson, "What Do You Think Should Happen?"

[183] See Ingelare, "The Gacaca Courts in Rwanda," 31, 46–47.

[184] See Burnet, "The Injustice of Local Justice," 188.   [185] See ibid.

[186] See Christopher Le Mon, "Rwanda's Troubled Gacaca Courts," *Human Rights Brief* 14 (Winter 2007): 16. The RPF was the military victor in the Rwandan conflict and has effectively set the agenda for post-genocide Rwanda without much restraint. See Ingelare, "The Gacaca Courts in Rwanda," 31–32.

[187] Phil Clark has written a comprehensive review of *Gacaca*, delving into strengths and weaknesses in great detail. See generally Phil Clark, *The Gacaca Courts, Post-Genocide Justice and Reconciliation in Rwanda*; see also Ingelare, "The Gacaca Courts in Rwanda," 51–57 (evaluating the strengths and weaknesses of *Gacaca*).

[188] These include the fact that the *Gacaca* process actually led to *increases* in the numbers of the accused and detained. See Burnet, "The Injustice of Local Justice," 178. It may have also increased conflict in some communities. See ibid., 74.

Initially projected as an exemplar of local ownership in transitional justice, *Gacaca* was in practice another top-down, state-based solution imposed on affected communities, and ultimately suffered a loss of legitimacy as a result.[189] Given the authoritarian political climate in Rwanda, this should not be surprising.[190] Rather than transcending Rwanda's postgenocide political culture, *Gacaca* was simply played out through its prism.[191]

Of course, it is important to note that not all attempts to integrate local or "traditional" approaches to postconflict justice and reconciliation have been as controversial as *Gacaca*. These efforts have not typically substituted for trials and truth commissions, but have served as an important complement to them. For example, in East Timor's Community Reconciliation Process, reconciliation between perpetrators and former combatants with members of their estranged communities was facilitated by drawing upon elements of local ritual, arbitration, and mediation practice.[192] This served to complement the work of a hybrid tribunal for criminal prosecutions and a national truth commission. In Sierra Leone, the formal, state-sanctioned truth commission incorporated aspects of local ritual into its work.[193] And the nongovernmental organization Fambul Tok ("Family Talk" in the Krio language) has also worked to facilitate a context-specific response to reconciliation.[194] While far from perfect, all of these initiatives show some of the promise of the local, and the reasons for which it is worth attempting future experiments along these lines.

GLOBAL AND LOCAL: STRIKING A BETTER BALANCE GOING FORWARD

At a deeper level, *Gacaca* illustrates the almost inescapable pull of both universalism and particularism in transitional justice processes, with notions of what it means to do justice in the aftermath of conflict invariably shaped by contested global and local norms.[195] More than that, however, it represents a clash of purportedly universal commitments, between liberal internationalism and international human rights,

---

[189] See Oomen, "Donor-Driven Justice and Its Discontents," 906–07; see also Thomson and Nagy, "Law, Power and Justice," 13 (describing *Gacaca* as a "state-imposed" project).

[190] See Thomson and Nagy, "Law, Power and Justice," 13 (noting that legal systems, traditional or otherwise, "inescapably embody prevailing constellations of power").

[191] See Andrew Iliff, "Root and Branch: Discourses of 'Tradition' in Grassroots Transitional Justice," *International Journal of Transitional Justice* 6, no. 2 (2012): 8 (arguing that *Gacaca* was used to "bolster[] the current Rwandan government's framing of the genocide as a singular event legitimating its authoritarian rule").

[192] See generally Patrick Burgess, "A New Approach to Restorative Justice – East Timor's Community Reconciliation Process," in *Transitional Justice in the Twenty-First Century*, ed. Roht-Arriaza and Mariezcurrena, 176–205.

[193] See generally Kelsall, "Truth, Lies, Ritual."

[194] See generally Park, "Community-Based Restorative Transitional Justice."

[195] For a review of the ways in which the universality debate in human rights can inform dilemmas of the global and the local that arise in the transitional justice context, see generally Lieselotte

on the one hand, and conceptions of self-determination, sovereignty, and pluralism on the other. As noted at the outset of this chapter, these are as much about competing *liberal* commitments as they are a clash between the liberal and illiberal. Given the seeming inevitability of these competing forces in many transitional justice interventions, the disappointments and politics of *Gacaca* point not to the need to abandon alternative approaches to postconflict justice, but to consider possibilities that offer a better balance, including global-local balance, along the multiple axes of local ownership.

In thinking of future experiments, the concept of "hybridity" might prove more useful than the simple binary lens of global-local. The notion of hybridity evokes two related ideas, and both are worth exploring in future transitional justice experiments:

In the first instance, the concept of hybridity is used descriptively, attempting to capture the complex and messy "glocal" reality of processes like *Gacaca* in Rwanda and *Lisan* in East Timor, processes that upon deeper analysis are neither purely local nor global. This dimension of the concept of hybridity has been offered in the broader context of peacebuilding as one way to begin to move beyond simple global-local debates and to better capture the complexity of the relationships between the many actors involved.[196] In other words, the first step to striking a better global-local balance is to better *understand* the ways in which both dimensions are often inextricably intertwined and transformed through their encounter with one another. In this way, hybridity goes hand in hand with disaggregating local ownership and thinking of it multidimensionally.

In the second instance, the concept of hybridity is used more prescriptively, as a "desirable political project[] that could stimulate alternatives and counter what is perceived to be hegemonic, externally driven liberal programming."[197] Hybridized forms of transitional justice that involve a mixture of conventional (Western) and local practices and models would be an example of this latter use of the term, and might be thought of as one way to begin to move beyond, or at least to accompany, liberal-legalist transitional justice. As previously noted in the area of hybrid courts, practices of genuine global-local hybridity hold promise, yet have not been adequately tested in practice, suggesting the need for further innovation. As a

---

Viaene and Eva Brems, "Transitional Justice and Cultural Contexts: Learning from the Universality Debate," *Netherlands Quarterly of Human Rights* 28 (2010): 199; see also Alexander Betts, "Should Approaches to Post-conflict Justice and Reconciliation Be Determined Globally, Nationally, or Locally?," *European Journal of Development Research* 17 (2005): 740–44 (discussing the ways in which the universalism-versus-relativism debate played out in post-genocide Rwanda).

[196] See Edward Newman et al., "Introduction," in *New Perspectives on Liberal Peacebuilding*, ed. Edward Newman et al. (New York: United Nations University, 2009), 16.

[197] Peterson, "A Conceptual Unpackaging of Hybridity," 7. For the application of a hybridity lens to postconflict justice more specifically, see generally, Chandra Lekha Sriram, "Post-Conflict Justice and Hybridity in Peacebuilding: Resistance or Cooptation," in *Hybrid Forms of Peace*, ed. Richmond and Mitchell.

programmatic project, hybridity asks us to see global and local not as competitors, but as complementary dimensions of postconflict justice, with each seeking to fill in gaps and weaknesses in the other.

Of course, for all of their promise, future experiments in alternative or hybridized justice and reconciliation are unlikely to involve easy compromise or simple solutions. Better global-local balance requires some give and take on *both* "sides," and yet existing UN doctrine does not really allow for this. In a landmark 2004 report on transitional justice, for example, former Secretary-General Kofi Annan notes that "due regard must be given to indigenous and informal traditions" yet suggests in the same breath that "due regard" will only be extended insofar as there is "conformity" with international standards.[198] This echoes what in colonial times was known as the "repugnancy clause" where local laws and traditions were tolerated insofar as they did not violate things like "conscience," "natural justice," the "principles of civilization," and so on. If we are honest, however, it will become clear that moving beyond superficial concepts of local ownership will necessarily require a deeper reconsideration of what it means to do "justice," and *whose justice* should be done, in times of transition. After all, it would be all too easy for transitional justice programs and professionals to embrace the local to the extent that it resonates with and resembles Western norms and institutions, using the trappings of the local in an attempt to boost legitimacy and buy-in to a larger set of projects.[199] Yet this would represent at best a form of co-option, a leveraging of the local only insofar as it stands in conformity with the global. Reflecting this impasse, An-Na'im has lamented that "even the possibility of an indigenous alternative conception of justice is not taken seriously at a theoretical or empirical level."[200]

If striking a better global-local balance will entail a more fundamental reconsideration of the primacy of Western approaches to mass atrocity than has typically been the case, this does not of itself require the abandonment of liberal principles, but a more careful consideration of a larger number of them. Indeed, concepts worked out in historically liberal societies, including pluralism, subsidiarity, and the margin of appreciation, might all prove to be constructive conceptual tools in attempting to strike a better global-local balance in transitional justice going forward.

To begin with the concept of pluralism, we should acknowledge that as a matter of pure description, transitional justice contexts (and many others) are almost inevitably legally plural in the sense that multiple legal systems coexist in the same social field.[201] If not the product of colonialism and transplanted laws, then

---

[198] UN Secretary-General, *The Rule of Law and Transitional Justice in Conflict and Post-Conflict Societies* (2004), ¶¶ 16–17, 36.
[199] See Baines, "Spirits and Social Reconstruction," 411–12, 414–15.
[200] See An-Na'im, "Editorial Note," 197 (observing that the dominant transitional justice paradigms are so strong that "even the possibility of an indigenous alternative conception of justice is not taken seriously at a theoretical or empirical level").
[201] Sally Engle Merry, "Legal Pluralism," *Law and Society Review* 22, no. 5 (1988): 870.

modern-day projects conducted under the aegis of human rights, good governance, and the rule of law have certainly created highly legally plural environments. In such contexts, hybridity and pluralism are then simply a fact of life. At a more normative level, a pluralistic approach to human rights and transitional justice is one that acknowledges the importance of values of diversity, autonomy, difference, and self-governance.[202] In this sense, even robust normative pluralism should not be equated with "anything goes" relativism, but rather as an attempt to balance competing liberal human rights commitments. In effect, accepting such normative pluralism by acknowledging and attempting to balance multiple completing values forces us to stand on that tenuous yet inevitable middle ground between universalism and relativism – a precarious perch that will prove uncomfortable to many human rights lawyers.[203] Contributing to the complexity is the fact that legal pluralism is an arena in which conflicting agendas and claims to authority are played out, making it a ripe terrain for moral, political, and ideological contestation.[204]

At the same time, striking a global-local balance also means that one particular local will at times have to give way to a larger local.[205] This reflects the simple recognition that neither global nor local dimensions of justice holds a monopoly on emancipatory projects, possibilities, and wisdom. For these and other reasons, what has been described in this chapter as global-local tensions can never be fully eliminated. In some instances, eliminating tensions may not even be desirable insofar as a certain degree of friction between global and local may generate a sort of creative tension, pushing practitioners to look beyond the increasingly rote transitional justice toolbox. As Paul Berman has noted in describing federal systems, the "preservation of diverse legal spaces makes innovation possible."[206] If this does not make things easy, one might at least note that persistent frictions and debates

---

[202] Douglas Lee Donoho, "Autonomy, Self-Governance, and the Margin of Appreciation: Developing a Jurisprudence of Diversity within Universal Human Rights," *Emory International Law Review* 15 (2001): 397.

[203] Using different terminology, scholars from a range of disciplines have made attempts to carve out a position between strong universalism and strong relativism. See, e.g., Paul Healy, "Human Rights and Intercultural Relations," *Philosophical and Social Criticism* 32 (2006): 513 (arguing for a middle ground between ethnocentric universalism and radical cultural relativism); Gérard Cohen-Jonathan, "Universalité et Singularité des Droits de l'Homme," *Revue Trimestrielle des Droits de l'Homme* 53 (2003): 11 (discussing a "pluralist" conception of human rights); Anne Hellum, "Women's Human Rights and African Customary Laws: Between Universalism and Relativism – Individualism and Communitarianism," in *Development and Rights; Negotiating Justice in Changing Societies*, ed. Christian Lund (New York: Frank Cass, 1999), 96 (using the idea of "cultural pluralism" to create a space between universalism and relativism); Ronald Cohen, "Human Rights and Cultural Relativism: The Need for a New Approach," *American Anthropologist* 91, no. 4 (1989): 1015–16 (calling for a middle ground between "simplistic polarities of relativism versus universalism").

[204] Deborah Isser, "The Problem with Problematizing Legal Pluralism," in *Legal Pluralism and Development; Scholars and Practitioners in Dialogue*, ed. Brian Tamanaha, Caroline Sage, and Michael Woolcock (Cambridge: Cambridge University Press, 2013), 240.

[205] See Mazlish, "The Global and the Local," 99 (discussing the idea of local giving way to larger local).

[206] Paul Schiff Berman, "Global Legal Pluralism," *Southern California Law Review* 80 (2005): 1190.

might not so much undermine human rights as emphasize its nature as "a privileged site for the engagement with diversity."[207] That said, tensions are not always productive and may, if unmitigated, undermine the legitimacy and effectiveness of transitional justice interventions to an unacceptable degree. In a world of multiple competing norms, perhaps the best that can then be hoped is that we learn to better manage the tensions, which will likely often involve rather uninspiring "provisional compromises."[208]

To these ends, giving greater weight to principles of "subsidiarity" and the "margin of appreciation" in the transitional justice context could prove useful. As Yuval Shany has argued, policy arguments surrounding the practice of international institutions – including legitimacy and capacity concerns – favor pushing agency and decision making wherever possible to national and local levels pursuant to principles of subsidiarity.[209] Such a presumption would likely be less intrusive and more politically acceptable in the long term, promoting a flexible and decentralized vision of international law that strengthens compliance pull over time. In this sense, subsidiarity is both normative and pragmatic. In the European Court of Human Rights, these principles have been largely managed via the "margin of appreciation" doctrine, which accepts pluralism over strict uniformity so long as fundamental guarantees are observed, effectively granting local authorities a degree of latitude in the interpretation and application of the European Convention on Human Rights.[210] In this, the level of Europe-wide consensus or dissensus on the right in question is key to the level of deference afforded to national-level courts.[211] However, though easily confused, the margin of appreciation is not driven by a loose cultural relativism but by restraint and flexibility as a means to securing effectiveness and legitimacy over time.[212]

It is likely that transitional justice could learn a great deal from such a pragmatic, incremental approaches. However, finding ways to operationalize such principles would no doubt often prove highly contentious. After all, one might expect the level of dissensus involved in many transitional justice contexts to be much higher than among European states with comparatively homogenous traditions, making the question of tension management much more fraught and tenuous. And of course, there is no global arbiter of transitional justice norms and practices akin

---

[207] René Provost and Coleen Sheppard, "Introduction, Human Rights through Legal Pluralism," in *Dialogues on Human Rights and Legal Pluralism* (New York: Springer, 2013), 4.
[208] Berman, "Global Legal Pluralism," 1165.
[209] Yuval Shany, "Toward a General Margin of Appreciation Doctrine in International Law," *The European Journal of International Law* 16, no. 5 (2006): 908.
[210] See Viaene and Brems, "Transitional Justice and Cultural Contexts," 210 (reviewing the margin of appreciation doctrine that has developed under the European Convention on Human Rights).
[211] Dean Speilmann, "Whither the Margin of Appreciation?," *Current Legal Problems* 67 (2014): 53.
[212] James Sweeney, "Margins of Appreciation: Cultural Relativity and the European Court of Human Rights in the Post–Cold War Era," *International and Comparative Law Quarterly* 54, no. 2 (2005): 459.

to the European Court of Human Rights. That said, as a set of guiding principles and presumptions, these concepts would provide a useful starting point for thinking about the design of transitional justice programs that do not always hew to the liberal-legalist dominant script to the detriment of the local. In this way, these principles could provide a useful counterweight to the seemingly inevitable slide toward the global in disputed questions of postconflict justice.

4

Justice to What Ends?

The felt need to grapple with the moral, legal and political dilemmas that arise in the aftermath of periods of intense repression and large-scale human rights abuses, has, for the past several decades, been conceptualized and institutionalized through the lens of "transitions." While sometimes taken for granted, such a choice was hardly inevitable. Over the years, there have been proponents of a number of other ways of framing the goals, challenges and problems at stake, including "overcoming the past,"[1] Rama Mani's concept of "reparative justice"[2] and the idea of "transformative justice."[3] While each of these proposals has had its strengths, attempting to address some of the shortcomings and blind spots of the field, it is the name and conceptual lens of *transitional* justice that has stuck, now adorning NGO letterhead, job titles, official governmental policy documents, and an array of programmatic initiatives across the globe. What we call the field might seem like an obscure academic debate about terminology and definitions. And yet, the conceptual lens we use has heavy implications for the shared mental maps that transitional justice experts use to structure their thinking, debates, and practice, ultimately touching the lives of people all over the world.

In the abstract at least, the "transition" of transitional justice connotes unspecified change, suggesting a number of open-ended possibilities. We might be discussing, for example, a transition from war to peace, a transition from less to more just or peaceful relations in society,[4] or perhaps even normative, ideological, or

---

[1] Timothy Garton Ash, "The Truth about Dictatorship," *New York Review of Books*, February 19, 1998, 35–40.
[2] Rama Mani, "Rebuilding an Inclusive Political Community after War," *Security Dialogue* 36, no. 4 (2005): 521.
[3] See Lambourne, "Transitional Justice and Peacebuilding after Mass Violence," 46; Paul Gready and Simon Robins, "From Transitional to Transformative Justice: A New Agenda for Practice," *International Journal of Transitional Justice* 8, no. 3 (2014): 339–61.
[4] Jennifer Balint, Julie Evans, and Nesam McMillan, "Rethinking Transitional Justice, Redressing Indigenous Harm: A New Conceptual Approach," *International Journal of Transitional Justice* 8, no. 2 (2014): 214.

conceptual transitions. For legal theorist Ruti Teitel, however, who arguably coined the term "transitional justice" in 1991,[5] the transition at issue is defined as a political one involving "the move from less to more democratic regimes."[6] This conceptualization of transition is hardly unique to Teitel, and indeed it can be said that liberal democratic transitions constitute the "paradigmatic transition" of transitional justice[7] and form a core component of the field's dominant script. As the introduction to an influential compendium of transitional justice materials from the 1980s and 1990s made clear: "These volumes are limited... to the way that emerging *democratic* societies address the legacy of their repression of their own people."[8] Implicit in this understanding of transition is a sort of teleological or "stage theory" view of history.[9] If barbarism, communism, and authoritarianism lie at one end of the narrative, then Western liberal democracy sits at the other "end of history,"[10] and its proponents stand ready and willing to help any and all along to the promised land.[11] With law as the master discipline and lawyers as the high priests, the mechanisms of transitional justice become a sort of secular right of passage symbolizing a political evolution to be midwifed, where necessary, by a cadre of international experts.[12]

In addition to implying a political destination, this conceptualization of transition has also often been understood to involve a process or window for activity that is more short-term, radical, and disruptive than long-term and incremental.[13]

---

[5] Ruti Teitel, "Transitional Justice Globalized," *International Journal of Transitional Justice* 2, no. 1 (2008): 1.

[6] Ruti Teitel, *Transitional Justice* (New York: Oxford University Press, 2000), 5.

[7] Padraig McAuliffe, "Transitional Justice's Expanding Empire: Reasserting the Value of the Paradigmatic Transition," *Journal of Conflictology* 2, no. 2 (2011): 34–35.

[8] Charles Smith, "Introduction," in *Transitional Justice*, vol. 1, ed. Neil Kritz (Washington, DC: USIP, 1995): xvi, emphasis original.

[9] See Alexander Hinton, "Introduction," in *Transitional Justice: Global Mechanisms and Local Realities after Genocide and Mass Violence*, ed. Alexander Hinton (New Brunswick: Rutgers Press, 2010), 6–7.

[10] See generally Francis Fukuyama, *The End of History and the Last Man* (New York: Avon Books, 1992).

[11] The triumphal and euphoric sentiment of the foundational era of transitional justice is well captured in the opening paragraph to the introduction of Neil Kritz's three-volume work:

> When the communist world began its collapse in the late 1980s and the post–Cold War period opened, newly democratic nations, some with vibrant histories of democracy, others ruled only by tyrants, and a few enjoying the promise of new nationhood, looked to the democracies, especially the United States, for help in creating democratic institutions and the complex foundation of a citizenry of democrats so necessary to traverse the inevitable rough waters ahead. How, they asked, might we best inspire our people with the habits of democracy and establish legal institutions to propel and protect our new freedoms.

Charles Smith, "Introduction," xv.

[12] See Michael Rothberg, "Progress, Progression, Procession: William Kentridge and the Narratology of Transitional Justice," *Narrative* 20, no. 1 (2012): 5.

[13] See, e.g., Samuel P. Huntington, "The Third Wave: Democratization in the Late Twentieth Century," in *Transitional Justice*, vol. 1, ed. Neil Kritz (Washington, DC: USIP, 1995), 79.

In some ways, this is a curious assumption since transitions might just as easily be thought of as long term as short, and there is no particular reason to limit our view of them to a sort of "big bang" event.[14] Nevertheless, taken together, understanding the field as involving both a political destination and a relatively short-term process has come to shape ideas about what is both prudent and possible within the time and space of transitional justice, leading some to view the field as *"inherently short-term, legalistic and corrective."*[15] Taken together, this conceptualization has also furnished answers to deeper purposive questions regarding "why" and "to what ends" the particular types of justice understood as "transitional justice" should be mobilized.

In this chapter, I will put this conceptualization of the field – both in terms of destination and duration – under the microscope, with a particular view to examining the ways in which it has failed to keep up with the empirical developments in transitional justice practice around the world. For example, while the field grew out of the paradigmatic transitions to liberal democracy in places like Argentina and Chile, transitional justice practice has for some time been applied to a range of contexts (both transitional and nontransitional; democratic and nondemocratic), and can be leveraged by elites to serve a number of purposes, both "good" and "bad." In some instances, transitional justice might even be more accurately seen to have produced a sort of "transitional injustice."[16] In terms of time and process, it is now clear that transitional justice efforts can be initiated prior to a political transition and often extend for decades after the process of democratization has begun, calling into question earlier ideas about the field being limited to short-term, corrective measures during a brief window of transitional opportunity.

All of these developments call for careful consideration of the continued relevance of the paradigmatic transition model at the core of the dominant script. In this chapter, I call for a more open-ended transitional justice project, seeking to understand how practice works in a range of contexts, from paradigmatic transitions, to autocratic transitions, to nontransitions in consolidated democracies. I also suggest that while looking at longer-term problems – potentially involving deep-rooted historical injustices – calls for a degree of caution, to avoid doing so out of a conviction that transitional justice must be *inherently* short term is simply unwarranted. I will conclude the chapter with a brief look at the possibility of reconceptualizing the field as a transition not to Western liberal democracy but to "positive peace," an idea that I will explore in much greater detail in Part II of this book.

---

[14] Harry Hobbs, "Locating the Logic of Transitional Justice in Liberal Democracies: Native Title in Australia," *UNSW Law Journal* 39, no. 2 (2016): 521.

[15] Lars Waldorf, "Anticipating the Past: Transitional Justice and Socio-Economic Wrongs," *Social & Legal Studies* 2, no. 2 (2012): 179, emphasis added.

[16] See generally Cyanne Loyle and Christian Davenport, "Transitional Injustice: Subverting Justice in Transition and Postconflict Societies," *Journal of Human Rights* 15 (2016): 126–49.

TRANSITION AS NARROW LIBERAL TELEOLOGY?

When it first burst upon the world stage in the 1980s and 1990s, transitional justice was understood as an important vehicle for securing liberal goods in postconflict and postauthoritarian societies. With some sixty countries converging toward democracy after extended periods of severe repression, the dominant understanding of the "transition" of transitional justice as involving "the move from less to more democratic regimes"[17] certainly resonated with the global political climate of the times. Given that a number of those same countries chose to experiment with trials, truth commissions, and other iconic transitional justice practices, the idea of transitional justice as a partial vector for consolidating important political changes and therefore as part of a rather narrow liberal teleology likely seemed quite plausible, especially given some of the prevailing assumptions about democratic transitions at the time. In particular, Thomas Carothers has skewered the then fashionable notion that democratization is a natural and inevitable process, less dependent on underlying conditions and history than decisions and bargains by enlightened elites.[18]

Of course, in 2017 the global outlook appears rather different than it did at the end of the Cold War. For one thing, given the rise of religious extremism and the resurgence of geopolitics, spheres of influence, and muscular authoritarianism,[19] it is harder to be optimistic that the playing field of history tilts toward liberal democratic ends than it used to be. Not only are a number of great and regional powers not trending democratic, but human rights monitoring organizations like Freedom House have lamented democratic backsliding across the globe in a range of countries.[20] Externally sponsored democracy and human rights programs, which enjoyed a wave of popularity through the 1990s and beyond, are now being restricted and undermined by both authoritarian and democratic governments as never before.[21] The most recent "wave" of (attempted) democratization resulted not in a Chile or an Argentina, but Libya, Syria, and Egypt. If history ended in the early 1990s, it appears to have come back with a vengeance in the new century.

Beyond these worrisome geopolitical trends, one fundamental problem with the historic and narrow conception of transitions in transitional justice is that it is simply empirically inaccurate when we look at transitional justice practice from its very beginnings. The label "transitional justice" has for some time been applied to

---

[17] Teitel, *Transitional Justice*, 5.
[18] See generally Thomas Carothers, "The End of the Transition Paradigm," *Journal of Democracy* 13 (2002): 5–21.
[19] Walter Russell Mead, "The Return of Geopolitics; the Revenge of Revisionist Powers," *Foreign Affairs*, May/June 2014.
[20] See, e.g., Freedom House, "Freedom in the World 2016: Anxious Dictators, Wavering Democracies: Global Freedom under Pressure," https://freedomhouse.org/report/freedom-world/freedom-world-2016.
[21] Thomas Carothers, "Closing Space for International Democracy and Human Rights Support," *Journal of Human Rights Practice* 8, no. 3 (2016): 358–77.

contexts that do not involve a liberal political transition at all. For example, in Chad, Idriss Déby came to power in 1990 in a bloody coup, ousting the paranoid and repressive dictator Hissène Habré. Déby clearly understood that the end of the Cold War necessitated new gestures and rhetoric, initially making noises about greater respect for human rights, and even authorizing the creation of a truth commission that implicated Habré in the deaths of more than 40,000 people.[22] In practice, however, the commission was seen by many as a sort of hatchet job intended primarily to make Habré look worse than Déby.[23] Few of its recommendations were heeded, and torturers identified in its final report continued to serve openly in government positions decades later. Some twenty-five years after his successful putsch, Déby continues to rule Chad – a country formally ranked by Freedom House as "not free" – and the principal justice done for Habré's victims has been carried out not in Chad but in Senegal where a coalition of NGOs and torture victims have successfully driven the prosecution and eventual conviction of Habré in 2016.[24]

In Rwanda, the site of some of the most intensive transitional justice activity anywhere on the planet, President Paul Kagamé and his Rwandan Patriotic Front (RPF) political party continue to rule over twenty years after the end of the genocide in a political climate that is increasingly authoritarian and repressive, with worsening harassment of journalists, NGOs, and the political opposition.[25] Opponents of the regime are repeatedly accused of "divisionism" or having a "genocidal ideology" – serious crimes in Rwanda – when they oppose an array of government programs.[26] Every transitional justice initiative, from the *Gacaca* process of community-level hearings discussed in the last chapter, to national prosecutions in Rwandan courts, to the International Criminal Tribunal for Rwanda has been aggressively manipulated by the government in order to almost entirely exclude RPF crimes from prosecution and discussion and cement a political narrative of the RPF as a national savior without which the country would implode. Where Rwandans have sought to resist through refusal to attend or participate in such one-sided processes, attendance has been coerced.[27] Thus, not only is Rwanda not getting any more democratic – Kagamé is set to run for a third term in office in 2017 following constitutional changes to allow it – but the tools of transitional justice have been used to enforce a

---

[22] The Commission's final report was published as *Les Crimes et Détournements de l'ex-Président Habré et de ses Complices* (Chadian TRC Report) (Paris: L'Harmattan, 1993).

[23] Priscilla Hayner, "Fifteen Truth Commissions – 1974 to 1994: A Comparative Study," *Human Rights Quarterly* 16 (1994): 625.

[24] See Human Rights Watch, "Chad's Ex-Dictator Convicted of Atrocities," Press Release, May 30, 2016, www.hrw.org/news/2016/05/30/chads-ex-dictator-convicted-atrocities.

[25] Freedom House, "Rwanda," in *Freedom in the World 2016* (Washington, DC: Freedom House, 2016).

[26] See Human Rights Watch, *Law and Reality: Progress in Judicial Reform in Rwanda* (New York: HRW, 2008), 37–41.

[27] Bert Ingelare, "The Gacaca Courts in Rwanda," in *Traditional Justice and Reconciliation after Violent Conflict: Learning from African Experiences*, ed. Luc Huyse and Mark Salter (Stockholm: IDEA, 2008), 46–47.

victor's justice that fosters selective denial and forgetting and legitimates authoritarianism and state repression, all under the most superficial veneer of reconciliation.[28]

Similarly, in Uganda, there is a long history of using the mechanisms of transitional justice for illiberal ends. In 1971, Idi Amin Dada established the Commission of Inquiry into the Disappearance of People in Uganda to examine disappearances during the early years of the Amin government. The report was never made public, and did nothing to affect the extreme brutality of Amin's bloody 8-year rule.[29] Years later, one of Amin's successors, Yoweri Museveni, established another commission of inquiry to look at the abuses of his predecessors.[30] The report was never widely disseminated and, like Uganda's earlier commission, had "no significant impact."[31] Museveni has also successfully instrumentalized the International Criminal Court, agreeing to a state party referral to prosecute members of the Lord's Resistance Army in order to advance his own military objectives, while the significant crimes committed by the Ugandan army go largely overlooked both nationally and internationally.[32] Years later, Museveni declared his opposition to the Court when it no longer seemed to suit his agenda.[33] Some thirty years after he came to power, Museveni continues to rule an autocratic Uganda – his fifth consecutive term began in 2016 – where civil society and the political opposition are increasingly repressed.[34] As in Chad and Rwanda, therefore, transitional justice in Uganda has been more a tool for settling political scores than one of democratization, reconciliation, and accountability.

In other instances, the tools of transitional justice have been mobilized in transitions involving a move from one nominally liberal ethno-regime to another. In Côte d'Ivoire, for example, President Laurent Gbagbo was ousted from power by a combination of Ivorian rebel forces and UN and French firepower after he refused to concede defeat in 2010 elections. The successor government, led by Alassane Ouattara, though more democratic than its predecessors, has carefully manipulated the transitional justice process to protect its allies and preserve its own version of history. A truth commission report was shelved for years after its completion and scarcely outlines some of the crimes committed by the rebel forces that helped bring Ouattara to power. And prosecutions, both at the national level and at the ICC, continue to focus almost exclusively on crimes committed by Ggabgo-era officials even though erstwhile pro-Ouattara rebel forces also committed war crimes and crimes

---

[28] See generally Loyle and Davenport, "Transitional Injustice."
[29] See International Center for Transitional Justice, "Confronting the Past: Truth Telling and Reconciliation in Uganda," ICTJ Briefing, September 2012, www.ictj.org/sites/default/files/ICTJ-Briefing-Uganda-Confronting-Past-2012-English.pdf.
[30] Ibid.   [31] Ibid.
[32] See generally Adam Branch, "Uganda's Civil War and the Politics of ICC Intervention," *Ethics and International Affairs* 21, no. 2 (2007): 195.
[33] See "Walkout at Ugandan President's Inauguration over ICC Remarks," *The Guardian*, May 12, 2016.
[34] Freedom House, "Uganda," in *Freedom in the World 2016* (Washington, DC: Freedom House, 2016).

against humanity.[35] Ironically, though he now stands trial before the ICC, it was former president Gbagbo's government that initially granted the ICC jurisdiction in Côte d'Ivoire pursuant to a 2003 ad hoc declaration under Article 12(3) of the Rome Statute,[36] based on what appears to have been the assumption that the Court would play a useful role in bringing the then rebels to justice while ignoring crimes by pro-Gbabgo forces.[37] (Of course, given the way the ICC would later behave in Uganda, targeting only the Lord's Resistance Army, perhaps this assumption was not unjustified.) In these ways, transitional justice in Côte d'Ivoire has been less about reconciliation and the rule of law than selective victor's justice and the construction of particular narratives friendly to the party in power. While this is perhaps not surprising at the national level, it is troubling that leaders in Rwanda, Uganda, and Côte d'Ivoire have also managed to manipulate the mechanisms of international justice to suit their own domestic agendas, making institutions like the International Criminal Tribunal for Rwanda and the International Criminal Court, at least in the eyes of some critics, their "useful idiots."

Beyond these less-than-liberal transitions, the concept of transitional justice has in limited instances been invoked to describe the use of truth commissions and other commissions of inquiry in consolidated liberal Western democracies in regard to abuses against Indigenous peoples in the absence of any paradigmatic political transition. In Australia, a 1997 Commission of Inquiry examined the forced removal of Aboriginal children from their families, culminating in the "Bringing them Home Report," which concluded that Indigenous families had endured gross violations of their human rights.[38] In Canada, a truth and reconciliation commission was established in 2008 to examine abuses against First Nations peoples within residential schools, documenting a pattern of sexual and psychological abuse, neglect, and a larger aim of eradicating First Nation cultures.[39] In 2008, prime ministers in both countries formally apologized for the respective harms.[40]

Both the Australian and Canadian examples stand as exceptions to the more general trend of seeing the West as the agent who intervenes and supports transitional

---

[35] See Human Rights Watch, *"Justice Reestablishes Balance": Delivering Credible Accountability for Serious Abuses in Côte d'Ivoire* (New York: HRW, 2016).

[36] Republic of Côte d'Ivoire, Declaration Accepting Jurisdiction of the International Criminal Court, April 18, 2003, www.icc-cpi.int/NR/rdonlyres/74EEE201-0FED-4481-95D4-C8071087102C/279844/ ICDEENG.pdf.

[37] See Human Rights Watch, *Country on Precipice: The Precarious State of Human Rights and Civilian Protection in Côte d'Ivoire* (New York: HRW, 2005).

[38] See generally Balint et al., "Rethinking Transitional Justice."

[39] See generally Rosemary Nagy, "The Scope and Bounds of Transitional Justice and the Canadian Truth and Reconciliation Commission," *International Journal of Transitional Justice* 7, no. 1 (2013): 52–73.

[40] Indigenous and Northern Affairs Office Canada, statement of apology to former students of Indian Residential Schools, June 11, 2008, www.aadnc-aandc.gc.ca/eng/1100100015644/1100100015649; Australian Government, "Apology to Australia's Indigenous Peoples," February 13, 2008, www.australia .gov.au/about-australia/our-country/our-people/apology-to-australias-indigenous-peoples.

justice in the non-Western world rather than the one who needs transitional justice itself.[41] This appears to reflect an ignorance of the potential need for reconciliation and restorative justice in liberal democracies, together with the acute need to address present-day systemic structural injustices rooted in the violence of the past.[42] While the Australian and Canadian examples are a far cry from a holistic attempt to address the egregious injustices meted out to Indigenous peoples, at their best, such efforts might at least begin to promote a justice-based rather than welfare or charity-based model for dealing with the past in colonial-settler societies.[43]

Taken together, these and other similar cases make clear that the mechanisms of transitional justice have been applied in a range of contexts – both democratic and nondemocratic, both transitional and nontransitional (at least in the democratic sense). They help illustrate that the concept of "transition" has tended to lump together transitions from authoritarianism to democracy and transitions from civil war to (illiberal) peace even though the parameters for justice are often more optimistic in the former than the latter. This variety of contexts and uses suggests that transitional justice is protean and dynamic. The so-called transitional justice toolbox is not a one-way ratchet of liberal betterment, but can in fact be used to reinforce illiberal ideologies and to consolidate the power of illiberal regimes. According to Hansen, scholarship has largely ignored the complexity and diversity of such patterns because of a deep-rooted assumption that transitional justice is inherently "good."[44] Loyle and Davenport have similarly argued that these patterns have been overlooked because of "normative assumption that relevant processes are put in place with the intention of advancing liberal democratic goals, disregarding research critical of this claim."[45] It may also be that the faith in the law associated with transitional justice, especially the tendency to see law as enabler of positive transformation rather than constitutive of violence and the status quo, serves to obfuscate some of the very real power dynamics and contestable political choices at the heart of any set of transitional justice mechanisms.

Yet if transitional justice may be used to promote forms of injustice – selective, partisan, or incomplete – the Australian and Canadian examples show that transitional justice can also be invoked in regimes that are decidedly liberal but which may be undergoing normative transitions with respect to historic injustices, potentially slowly transitioning from less to more just relations.[46] This suggests that despite its roots in moments of democratic political regime change, transitional justice may

---

[41] Balint et al., "Rethinking Transitional Justice," 194–95.   [42] Ibid., 194–95.   [43] Ibid., 213.
[44] Thomas Obel Hansen, "Transitional Justice: Toward a Differentiated Theory," *Oregon Review of International Law* 13, no. 1 (2011): 17; see also Siphiwe Ignatius Dube, "Transitional Justice beyond the Normative: Towards a Literary Theory of Political Transitions," *International Journal of Transitional Justice* 5, no. 2 (2011): 181.
[45] Loyle and Davenport, "Transitional Injustice," 128.
[46] On the concept of transition without actual regime transition, see, e.g., Andrew Vails, "Racial Justice as Transitional Justice," *Polity* 36, no. 1 (2003): 53–71.

offer a flexible and broader justice model that has important relevance and appeal outside of the paradigmatic context.[47] Indeed, insofar as it might plausibly help to facilitate a more just social contract for Indigenous or other historically abused and marginalized populations, its need outside of the paradigmatic context is clear.[48]

Even in the autocratic context, one can still find value in some of the transitional justice work that was carried out. In Chad, for example, the work of the truth commission in the early 1990s would lay part of the predicate for the eventual successful conviction of Hissène Habré in Senegal in 2016 after decades of struggle. This was the first time a former head of state from one country has been successfully tried in the court system of another country under the principle of universal jurisdiction, a "milestone for justice in Africa"[49] and indeed the world. Decisions handed down by the International Criminal Tribunal for Rwanda, even if they did not involve RPF perpetrators, set important legal precedents regarding genocide, war crimes, and crimes against humanity that might assist judges, lawyers, and victims the world over.[50] To find transitional justice efforts severely wanting in such contexts is not, therefore, to find them worthless.

TRANSITION AS A TIME-BOUND WINDOW OF OPPORTUNITY?

As transitional justice practice gained momentum throughout the 1980s and 1990s, scholars and practitioners attempted to distill best practices across countries, many of which have been captured in the time capsule of Neil Kritz's seminal edited volumes published by the United States Institute for Peace in 1995.[51] Consistent with the temporality implied by "transitions," the field of fruitful transitional justice activity was seen as being circumscribed by time. Going beyond this, however, it was also assumed that the window of opportunity presented by political change was going to be relatively short term, requiring one to strike while the proverbial iron was hot. This is an important assumption to examine since it is not self-evident that a transition should be necessarily considered short term. One could, for example, easily speak or conceive of "long-term," "gradual," and "incremental" transitions without doing violence to the concept; and there is a role for justice both in the short and longer term.

Despite this, in an excerpt published in the Kritz volume, political scientist Samuel Huntington invoked political exigencies to underscore the imperative of timely transitional justice action:

---

[47] Balint et al., "Rethinking Transitional Justice," 196.
[48] Hobbs, "Locating the Logic of Transitional Justice in Liberal Democracies," 525.
[49] New York Times Editorial Board, "A Milestone for Justice in Africa," July 22, 2015.
[50] See generally Human Rights Watch, *Genocide, War Crimes and Crimes against Humanity: A Digest of the Case Law of the International Criminal Tribunal for Rwanda* (New York: HRW, 2010).
[51] See generally Neil Kritz, ed., *Transitional Justice: How Emerging Democracies Reckon with Former Regimes* (Washington, DC: USIP, 1995).

> Democratic justice cannot ... be slow justice. The popular support and indignation necessary to make justice a political reality fade; the discredited groups associated with the authoritarian regime reestablish their legitimacy and influence. In new democratic regimes, justice comes quickly or it does not come at all.[52]

In fact, while perhaps plausible at the time he wrote it, Huntington's prognostication proved inaccurate, and subsequent decades have made clear that transitional justice processes are not confined to a narrow window of opportunity immediately after the transition. Rather, the political opportunity structures that make a degree of transitional justice possible appear to vary over time, potentially increasing, decreasing, or proceeding in fits and starts after the immediate transition. Sometimes, "discredited groups associated with the authoritarian regime" eventually become politically weaker with the passage of enough time, just as those harmed by the former regime might eventually rise to the levels of power and prominence that allow them to kick-start or reenergize the transitional justice agenda.

In the case of Argentina, for example, transitional justice initially appeared to follow Huntington's short-term, window-of-opportunity model. In 1984, a groundbreaking truth commission (Comisión Nacional sobre la Desaparición de Personas, CONADEP) charged with investigating disappearances in the course of Argentina's dirty war published its final report, *Nunca Más* (Never Again), which became a best seller.[53] This was followed by nine successful prosecutions against senior members of the military for their role in the dirty war, including former presidents Jorge Rafael Videla and Roberto Eduardo Viola.[54] However, the Argentine "justice cascade" appeared to come to a crashing halt in 1986 when President Raúl Alfonsín ceded to pressure from the military to halt the prosecutions with passage of the "Full Stop" law, to be followed by the "Due Obedience" law in 1987, effectively granting a blanket amnesty to the military.[55] Adding insult to injury, between 1989 and 1990, Alfonsín's successor, Carlos Menem, granted presidential pardons to those few who were convicted.

This was the end of the story from the perspective of Samuel Huntington quoted above in 1991; however, it was far from the end of the story of justice in Argentina. In the years that followed, a vigorous civil-society-led effort at home and abroad for accountability, involving efforts before the Inter-American Commission on Human Rights, Spanish courts, and so-called truth trials in national federal courts that could obtain official information without imposing criminal penalties would ensure that

---

[52] Huntington, "The Third Wave," 79.
[53] *Nunca Más, Report of the Argentine National Commission on the Disappeared* (New York: Farar, Strauss, and Giroux, 1986).
[54] See generally Carlos Nino, *Radical Evil on Trial* (New Haven: Yale University Press, 1998).
[55] See José Zalaquett, "Confronting Human Rights Violations Committed by Former Governments: Principles Applicable and Political Constraints," in *Transitional Justice*, vol. 1, ed. Neil Kritz (Washington, DC: USIP, 1995), 20–27.

the question of accountability was not forgotten.[56] Meanwhile, the internationally famous Mothers of the Plaza de Mayo continued to march to keep the memory of their disappeared children alive.[57] In 2003, both the Full Stop and Due Obedience laws were repealed by the National Congress, and ultimately ruled unconstitutional by the Supreme Court in 2005 in the *Simón* case, leading to the reopening of a flood of cases.[58] The first of as many as 600 potential convictions involved Miguel Etchecolatz, a high-ranking police officer who was found guilty in 2006 of kidnapping, torture, and murder. In 2007, the Supreme Court deemed unconstitutional the earlier pardons by President Menem. In 2010, former junta leader and president Jorge Rafael Videla was sentenced to life in prison, where he died in 2013. Thus, in 2017, it is clear that the story of what has been called "posttransitional justice"[59] is still unfolding in Argentina and that just because justice does not come quickly, does not mean that it will not come at all. This may be particularly true as perpetrators age and retire, becoming less of a threat to the new government and their former victims.

With all of the twists and turns in the plot, the Argentinian story is a compelling one, but it is not unique. Efforts to secure justice in Chile, for example, also spanned several decades after the removal of a brutal dictator from power. Formal initiatives began shortly after dictator General Augusto Pinochet's 1989 electoral loss with a truth commission (known as the Rettig Commission) that investigated deaths and disappearances, followed by a reparations program for select victims. In 1998, Pinochet was famously arrested in Great Britain – ultimately leading not to a conviction, but nevertheless establishing an important legal precedent that was later built upon in the trial of Hissène Habré.[60] That same year, Pinochet's stature was further diminished when a state holiday celebrating his 1973 coup was abolished. But perhaps more significantly, the Chilean Supreme Court also held that a 1978 amnesty law should not apply to human rights violations, opening the door to around a thousand investigations and hundreds of prosecutions.[61] In 2003, a second truth commission was created (known as the Valech Commission), charged with investigating torture, followed by a 2009 reparations program for this additional class of victims.

[56] See generally International Center for Transitional Justice, "Criminal Prosecutions for Human Rights Violations in Argentina," Briefing, November 2009, www.ictj.org/sites/default/files/ICTJ-Argentina-Prosecutions-Briefing-2009-English.pdf.
[57] See generally Marguerite Bouvard, *Revolutionizing Motherhood: The Mothers of the Plaza de Mayo* (New York: SR Books, 2004).
[58] See Christine Bakker, "A Full Stop to Amnesty in Argentina: The Simón Case," *Journal of International Criminal Justice* 3, no. 5 (2005): 1106–20.
[59] Cath Collins, *Post-Transitional Justice: Human Rights Trials in Chile and El Salvador* (University Park: Penn State University Press, 2010).
[60] Krishnadev Calamur, "The Legacy of the Pinochet Trial: Hissène Habré and Chile's Augusto Pinochet Have Seemingly Little in Common – Except a Legal Precedent," *The Atlantic*, October 17, 2015, www.theatlantic.com/international/archive/2015/10/chad-habre-trial-pinochet/411004/.
[61] Amnesty International, "Chile: Amnesty Law Keeps Pinochet's Legacy Alive," September 11, 2015, www.amnesty.org/en/latest/news/2015/09/chile-amnesty-law-keeps-pinochet-s-legacy-alive.

Finally, in 2014, Chile's parliament began debating whether to formally overturn the 1978 amnesty law.[62] Thus, like Argentina, transitional justice in Chile has proceeded in fits and starts, but has had a much longer arc than Huntington's 1991 assertion would have foretold.

Beyond Chile and Argentina, one could also point to the example of Brazil, which in 2011 created a truth commission to investigate a military dictatorship that ended in 1985.[63] The commission was supported by then President Dilma Rousseff, herself a former prisoner and torture victim of the junta.[64] And of course, the cases of investigative commissions in Canada and Australia suggest that at times the political context that determines readiness for transitional justice will come even longer after the abuses in question, reflecting gradual shifts in historical understanding and moral sentiment.

All of these cases raise difficult questions about the coherence of the term "transition" and the continued relevance of the transitions paradigm as a lens for thinking about justice for massive human rights violations. If the decades-long processes in Argentina and Chile are not seen as "transitional justice," are they then "posttransitional justice,"[65] or might they simply, at some undefined stage, be understood as some kind of "ordinary justice"?[66] And if it turns out that transitional justice is not *inherently* short term, might this liberate thinking and practice in ways that allow us to focus both on short-term and longer-term peacebuilding goals?

CONTINUED RELEVANCE OF THE TRANSITIONS PARADIGM?

As the preceding sections have made clear, the concept of transitional justice has for some time been applied well outside of the paradigmatic context both in terms of liberal democratic destination and short-term temporal scope. Observing these patterns, Padraig McAuliffe has argued for the retention of a traditional and somewhat narrow understanding of "transitional justice" on the grounds that transitional justice mechanisms can best and most fairly be evaluated under the conditions of the classic paradigmatic liberal democratic transition.[67] McAuliffe also worries that the

---

[62] See generally Cath Collins, "Human Rights Trials in Chile during and after the 'Pinochet Years,'" *International Journal of Transitional Justice* 4, no. 1 (2010): 67–86.

[63] See generally Nina Schneider, "'Too Little Too Late' or 'Premature'? The Brazilian Truth Commission and the Question of 'Best Timing,'" *Journal of Iberian and Latin American Research* 19, no. 1 (2013): 149–62.

[64] "Leader's Torture in '70s Stirs Ghosts in Brazil," *New York Times*, August 4, 2012, www.nytimes.com/2012/08/05/world/americas/president-rousseffs-decades-old-torture-detailed.html?pagewanted=all&_r=0.

[65] Collins, *Post-Transitional Justice*.

[66] Eric Posner and Adrian Vermeule have argued more broadly that the so-called dilemmas of transitional justice are no different – theoretically or empirically – from the dilemmas of domestic (nontransitional) justice, a claim that has gone largely unanswered in the academic literature. See generally "Transitional Justice as Ordinary Justice," *Harvard Law Review* 117, no. 3 (2003): 761.

[67] McAuliffe, "Transitional Justice's Expanding Empire," 34–35.

range of contexts to which the term "transition" is being applied might be stretching the coherence of the term. Under this line of reasoning, it is hardly fair to criticize the results of transitional justice mechanisms when applied in contexts and by elites where there is really no pretension of promoting genuine truth, accountably, reconciliation, or democratization in the first place, as the cases of Chad, Rwanda, and Uganda might be taken to illustrate. Thus, McAuliffe suggests, we might want to make a distinction between paradigmatic transitional justice as applied in the context of liberal democratic transitions, and the mere use of transitional justice mechanisms "in societies which radically depart from the traditional type of transitions where it is most useful."[68] Following this logic, one might say that both Rwanda and Canada may have used some of the *mechanisms* of transitional justice, but this should not be conflated with true "transitional justice."

McAuliffe's arguments certainly have some cogency and appeal, and are buttressed by empirical data suggesting that transitional justice initiatives may have the largest positive impact in countries already well on the path to democracy.[69] At the same time, it seems clear that accepting these arguments would likely restrict the field of transitional justice to a very small subset of countries around the world. As Carothers noted in 2002 in questioning assumptions about the democratic transitions paradigm, most countries captured under the lens of "transitions" are neither dictatorial nor headed toward democracy, and this "political grey zone" might actually be "the most common political condition today of countries in the developing world and the postcommunist world."[70] Yet is it also important to note that such configurations are hardly permanent, and "[c]ountries can and do move out of them."[71] If justice initiatives should only be understood as "transitional justice" when applied by earnest leaders in the context of "true" democratization, excluding weak and partial democracies, then we will have excluded from the field by definition many of the most challenging, fascinating, and, yes, ambiguous, uses of transitional justice around the world. The losers of such definitional exclusion might be scholars, activists, and policy makers, who stand to learn as much if not more from "bad" transitional justice as "good" transitional justice. It may also be that looking at paradigmatic and nonparadigmatic examples together reveals as much continuity as discontinuity. After all, politicians the world over, both liberal and illiberal, attempt to shape and manage pressure for justice to suit their own political ends, some in ways cruder than others.

In addition, it is important to note that our empirical understanding about the relationship between transitional justice, democracy, and human rights protection is far from complete, suggesting a degree of caution in tethering definitions of the

---

[68] Ibid., 33.
[69] Oskar N. T. Thoms, James Ron, and Roland Paris, "State-Level Effects of Transitional Justice: What Do We Know?," *International Journal of Transitional Justice* 4, no. 3 (2010): 35.
[70] Carothers, "The End of the Transition Paradigm," 9, 18.   [71] Ibid., 14.

field to the context and fruits of democratization. A 2010 meta study looking at the state-level effects of transitional justice – including effects on levels of political violence, adherence to the rule of law, democratization, and a political culture of human rights and pluralism – concludes that there is a "prevailing ambiguity surrounding TJ impacts."[72] While Kathryn Sikkink's 2011 work is more sanguine, concluding that countries with human rights prosecutions are less repressive long term than countries without,[73] empirical work by Olsen, Payne, and Reiter suggests that no transitional justice mechanism standing alone – be it trials, truth commissions, or amnesties – appears to strengthen democracy or reduce human rights violations long term, and in the case of truth commissions, may even be associated with significant negative impacts.[74] Rather, it is the combination of mechanisms that appears to produce positive effects, and those effects take significant time to appear, at least a decade or more.[75] For these reasons, it may be premature in any given instance to assume that transitional justice outside of the paradigmatic context is useless, or should otherwise be excluded from the field's ambit and concern. By the same token, transitional justice mechanisms, even in more liberal contexts, are hardly a guarantee of further liberalization.

Thus, rather than reserving the term "transitional justice" for a narrow subset of paradigmatic transitions where it might work optimally, what is needed is a better understanding of the ways in which transitional justice mechanisms function in a range of contexts, from the paradigmatic political transition, to the normative and ideological transitions seen in consolidated democracies, to war-to-peace transitions whose eventual result is more autocratic than democratic. Such understandings might lead to the development of transitional justice practice better suited to each specific context. As Harry Hobbs has observed, dominant transitional justice practice has been largely drawn from strongly institutionalized states transitioning from dictatorship to democracy, and it is not especially surprising that simply transposing these initiatives to weakly institutionalized states experiencing recurrent conflict has resulted in limited success.[76]

Moreover, to the extent that the intelligibility of the term "transition" is being stretched by application to contexts other than that of the paradigmatic political transition, any incoherence depends in large measure on the extent to which the field remains intellectually wedded to an exclusively liberal and political understanding of that term. There is certainly nothing inherently political about the concept of "transition" itself, and, as developed below, there are other and broader ways to conceptualize "transition" than a liberal political one. Finally, given the field's

---

[72] Thoms et al., "State-Level Effects," 332.
[73] Kathryn Sikkink, *The Justice Cascade* (New York: W. W. Norton, 2011), 183.
[74] Tricia Olsen, Leigh Payne, and Andrew Reiter, *Transitional Justice in Balance* (Washington, DC: USIP, 2010), 153.
[75] Ibid., 146, 153.
[76] Hobbs, "Locating the Logic of Transitional Justice in Liberal Democracies," 524.

unabashedly normative origins rooted in human rights advocacy, the label "transitional" might at times be seen as more of a normative assertion about what should happen rather than an empirical description of what in fact is happening at the time.

One might also note that, for better or worse, the horse of a more expansive notion of transitional justice may be out of the proverbial barn. The current transitional justice moment is characterized precisely by a willingness to question and push back on the historical peripheries and paradigms of the field.[77] Whether this expansion is due to resistance to the limitations of the narrow founding paradigm of transitional justice, or simply the result of an emerging industry that seems eager to make itself increasingly relevant to new contexts, the result is much the same: returning to a more narrow conception of applicable context and aspirations seems improbable. More pragmatically, what is needed is a (re)conceptualization of our understanding of transitions that captures the complex realities of an expanding field, while addressing some of the blind spots and limitations of the founding paradigm.

One possible reason for the expansion and growth of transitional justice in situations far removed from the "third-wave" democratic transitions that helped to establish the original mold is an increasing tendency to see transitional justice as a tool for promoting not just democracy, but peace and human security more broadly in a more diverse range of contexts.[78] This raises the question as to whether the transition of transitional justice might be better seen as a transition to peace, broadly understood, and perhaps specifically as a transition to "positive peace," rather than something like liberal democracy, more narrowly understood, or some otherwise more "negative peace."[79] As defined by Johan Galtung, the term "negative peace" refers primarily to the absence of direct, personal violence. It stands in contrast with the broader concept of "positive peace," which includes the absence of both direct, personal violence and more indirect, "structural" violence (understood to comprise poverty and power and resource inequalities more generally).[80]

In considering such a (re)conceptualization, one must of course acknowledge that many have questioned the utility of the "transitions" lens altogether, irrespective of the imagined destination.[81] And as noted in the introduction to this chapter, multiple alternatives have already been proposed that exclude or de-emphasize the concept of transition, including "overcoming the past"[82] and Rama Mani's concept of "reparative justice," a concept that is at once holistic, placing a greater emphasis on distributive justice and "root causes," while also suggesting something permanent

---

[77] See generally Dustin Sharp, "Interrogating the Peripheries; the Preoccupations of Fourth Generation Transitional Justice," *Harvard Human Rights Journal* 26 (2013): 150.

[78] Teitel, "Transitional Justice Globalized," 2–3.

[79] The idea of a "positive peace" foundation will be introduced briefly here and then explored in much greater depth in Chapter 7.

[80] See Johan Galtung, "Violence, Peace, and Peace Research," *Peace Research* 6, no. 3 (1969): 175, 183.

[81] Thomas Carothers, "The End of the Transition Paradigm," *Journal of Democracy* 13 (2002): 4.

[82] Ash, "The Truth about Dictatorship," 35–40.

and incremental, rather than transitional, temporal, and incomplete.[83] In a similar vein, Wendy Lambourne and, more recently, Paul Gready and Simon Robins have argued for the adoption of a "transformative justice" approach with a view to placing greater emphasis on, among other things, structural violence and local agency as part of the transitional justice process.[84] Each of these proposals has, in its own way, attempted to address some of the assumptions and limitations of the field's foundational paradigm and has been anchored in the broader and more holistic conceptions of peace and peacebuilding associated with "positive peace." In that sense, (re)conceptualizing the transition of transitional justice as a transition to positive peace is meant to build upon and draw together these various proposals rather than oppose or replace them, while expressing a particular and explicit consonance with a conception or transitional justice as a form of peacebuilding.

While a (re)conceptualization of the field to involve a transition to positive peace would of course retain the transitions lens and while peace is itself a teleological concept, it might nevertheless distinguish itself from the paradigmatic transition model insofar as all countries have gone through war and peace throughout history, and all countries could stand to benefit from a move to more just and peaceful relations. In this sense, transitional justice as a transition to positive peace might come to suggest not a specific destination, and not a project for the backward rest rather than the liberal West – a moment that occurs at "the end of history" – but something that all societies will need to revisit at multiple junctures. As (re)conceptualized, transitional justice would be as relevant to addressing historical injustices in consolidated democracies like Australia and the United States as it is to the immediate postconflict context of Liberia or Sierra Leone.

Positive peace is inherently holistic, and a destination never fully arrived at. In this sense, it carries with it the potential to address issues relating to the narrowness of the paradigmatic transitions lens. It suggests a project that is clearly normative, yet more flexible in terms of destination, as well as one that is more incremental and long term than previous conceptualizations of justice in times of democratic transition. And if transitional justice is not *inherently* short term, this should inform debates about inclusion of questions of economic and structural violence within the ambit of activity and concern discussed in Chapter 2. As I discuss in Part II of this book, however, peace, and even "positive peace," may be subject to narrow and limiting constructions. After all, what has become known as "liberal peacebuilding," with its shallow emphasis on free markets and democracy as the pathway to "peace," reflects much more than a simple attempt to guarantee "negative peace," understood as the absence of overt hostility. Liberal peacebuilders might rightly claim that they are working toward a sort of "positive peace." Yet Galtung's concept of positive peace

---

[83] Mani, "Rebuilding an Inclusive Political Community after War," 521.
[84] See Lambourne, "Transitional Justice and Peacebuilding after Mass Violence," 46; Gready and Robins, "From Transitional to Transformative Justice: A New Agenda for Practice," 339.

would not stop there, and is intimately bound up with considerations of social and distributive justice that have been largely absent from mainstream practice in the fields of both peacebuilding and transitional justice.[85] I explore these distinctions in greater detail in the following chapters, including the necessity of conjugating positive peace with other concepts from critical peacebuilding theory.

[85] Galtung, "Violence, Peace, and Peace Research," 183.

PART II

Building a Better Foundation

5

Peacebuilding and Liberal Postconflict Governance

With the passage of time and the expansion of the field to new contexts, the overt preoccupation with democratization that heavily marked transitional justice in the 1980s and 1990s has become less pronounced. Even so, the idea of transitional justice as handmaiden to liberal political transitions – the "paradigmatic transition" of transitional justice – remains a deeply embedded narrative that continues to shape dominant practices and conceptual boundaries,[1] including answers to the questions that were the focus of Part I of this book: *justice for what, justice for whom, and justice to what ends?*

In more recent years, this traditional transitional justice narrative has become increasingly intertwined with a view of transitional justice (along with human rights and rule-of-law assistance programs) as a component of postconflict peacebuilding more generally, including in societies not undergoing a paradigmatic liberal transition. To the extent that "peace" invokes more holistic and varied sets of objectives than the narrower goals associated with facilitating liberal political transitions, the turn to peacebuilding might be seen to represent a broadening and a loosening of earlier paradigms and moorings, making this a significant moment in the normative evolution of the field. Yet with few exceptions, there has thus far been little scrutiny as to what "transitional justice as peacebuilding" might actually mean or how, if at all, it might be different than "transitional justice as liberal democracy building."[2]

---

[1] See generally Paige Arthur, "How 'Transitions' Reshaped Human Rights: A Conceptual History of Transitional Justice," *Human Rights Quarterly* 31, no. 2 (2009): 321.

[2] For the most part, transitional justice scholars have not framed their work in terms of peace or peacebuilding. Kora Andrieu, "Civilizing Peacebuilding: Transitional Justice, Civil Society and the Liberal Paradigm," *Security Dialogue* 41, no. 5 (2010): 539. There are, of course, notable exceptions to this trend, including Rami Mani, Chandra Lekha Sriram, and Wendy Lambourne. See, e.g., Rama Mani, *Beyond Retribution: Seeking Justice in the Shadows of War* (Malden: Blackwell, 2002); Chandra Lekha Sriram, "Justice as Peace? Liberal Peacebuilding and Strategies of Transitional Justice," *Global Society* 21, no. 4 (2007): 580–81; Wendy Lambourne, "Transitional Justice and Peacebuilding after Mass Violence," *International Journal of Transitional Justice* 3, no. 1 (2009): 28–48.

In many instances, analysis of the linkages between transitional justice and peacebuilding goes little further than the loose sloganeering of "no peace without justice" or simplistic assertions that peace and justice go hand in hand.[3]

Considered more critically, it is entirely possible that "transitional justice as peacebuilding" will prove to be a distinction without a difference from what came before. Historically, the "peace" associated with international postconflict peacebuilding efforts spearheaded by the United Nations and major international donors has typically been conceived of as a narrow liberal peace predicated on free markets and Western-style democracy.[4] Thus, insofar as the goals of liberal international peacebuilding and the historic goals of transitional justice are essentially one and the same, "transitional justice as peacebuilding" may be little more than a dressed up tautology. More darkly, an amorphous transitional-justice-as-peacebuilding narrative may prove useful to autocratic regimes that would seek to use the tools and rhetoric of transitional justice to consolidate abusive regimes in the name of "peace," just as victors have often done in the name of "justice."[5]

Bearing in mind Robert Cover's observation that institutions and prescriptions do not exist apart from the narratives that locate and give them meaning,[6] it is fair to say that the particular "peace" and the particular "justice" that serve to undergird conceptions of transitional justice in the twenty-first century matter a great deal. While Part I of this book was largely devoted to exploring the blind spots of the "justice" that transitional justice has traditionally entailed, Part II will explore concepts of peace and peacebuilding, with a particular focus on whether "transitional justice as peacebuilding" might serve as a more emancipatory foundation for the field than what came before. I will argue that (re)conceptualizing transitional justice as a form of peacebuilding has the *potential* to reinvigorate the field, upend long-standing blind spots and assumptions, and open the doors to more creative thinking, policies, and practices by helping to challenge the field's traditional foreground and background. However, this cannot be taken for granted.

But before developing this argument in full, it is important to consider what is meant by concepts like "peace" and "peacebuilding" in the first place. Neither concept is part of the daily working vocabulary of lawyers and human rights advocates – communities that have historically provided a great deal of intellectual capital to the transitional justice enterprise – and only a handful of transitional justice

---

[3] See UN Secretary-General, *The Rule of Law and Transitional Justice in Conflict and Post-conflict Societies*, ¶ 8, UN Doc. S/2004/616 (August 23, 2004) (arguing that "[j]ustice, peace and democracy are not mutually exclusive objectives, but rather mutually reinforcing imperatives").
[4] See generally Roland Paris, *At War's End: Building Peace after Civil Conflict* (Cambridge: Cambridge University Press, 2004).
[5] On "victor's peace," see Oliver Richmond, "Emancipatory Forms of Human Security and Liberal Peacebuilding," *International Journal* 62 (2007): 462.
[6] Robert Cover, "*Nomos* and Narrative," *Harvard Law Review* 97 (1983): 4.

scholars have thus far situated their work in the context of peace or peacebuilding.[7] This chapter will therefore be devoted to a brief exploration of the concept of post-conflict peacebuilding in particular as it has been operationalized at the international institutional level by organizations such as the United Nations.[8] After outlining its trajectory since the Cold War, I will explore the ways in which peacebuilding interventions have functioned in tandem with other associated global projects such as development, human rights, and rule-of-law programming as part of a liberalizing "post-conflict checklist." I will devote special attention to some of the critiques that have developed to what has become known as "liberal international peacebuilding." This will lay the predicate for work in subsequent chapters that will explore potential connections between peacebuilding and transitional justice, together with constructs from critical peacebuilding theory that that might inform the emerging "transitional-justice-as-peacebuilding" narrative, nudging it in a more emancipatory direction.

FROM PEACEKEEPING TO PEACEBUILDING

During the Cold War at least, the concept of peace in the West was often seen as not only vaguely and suspiciously subversive, leftist, and political, but hopelessly unrealistic as well.[9] The best that could be hoped for in Dr. Strangelove's mid-century world, it seemed, was "peace through strength" backed up by the threat of mutually assured destruction. At the United Nations, one did not yet speak of grandiose "peacebuilding" but the seemingly more modest "peacekeeping," a difference that has proved to be far more than pedantic. With the fall of the Berlin Wall and collapse of the Soviet Union, however, those associations began to ease and the concept has now forcefully entered the discourse and practices of policy makers accompanied by the tacit assumption that peace is an uncontested and non-ideological concept.[10]

To appreciate this change, it is first necessary to consider the limited notion of "peacekeeping" that prevailed during the Cold War. For the most part, peacekeeping actions of the Cold War era placed a premium on neutrality, consent,

---

[7] Andrieu, "Civilizing Peacebuilding," 539 (noting that "few transitional justice scholars have yet situated their research in the context of peacebuilding, seeing it instead through the dominant lens of legalism and human rights"); see Lambourne, "Transitional Justice and Peacebuilding," 29 (noting that "few researchers have analysed the relationship between justice, reconciliation and peacebuilding").

[8] I distinguish here between what I am calling peacebuilding at the "international institutional level," which emanates in large part from the United Nations, and the various types of interpersonal, community-level, and "track-two" peacebuilding that are done by individuals, religious groups, NGOs, etc.

[9] Laurent Goetschel and Tobias Hagmann, "Civilian Peacebuilding: Peace by Bureaucratic Means?," *Conflict, Security and Development* 9, no. 1 (2009): 56.

[10] Ibid.

and minimum force – notions all central to traditional Westphalian conceptions of sovereignty.[11] So-called first-generation[12] or consensual peacekeeping often involved interposition of forces for the monitoring of ceasefires geared toward containing conflicts and maintaining stability. Examples of this approach to peacekeeping include the UN Military Observer Group in India and Pakistan (established in 1949) designed to monitor a ceasefire, the UN Peacekeeping Force in Cyprus (established in 1964) established to prevent fighting between Turk and Cypriot communities, and the UN Disengagement Observer Force (established in 1974) after the disengagement of Israel and Syria from the Golan Heights. The ultimate goal of such actions was avoiding international conflict between states as opposed to the preoccupation with intrastate conflict and civil wars that we often associate with conflict interventions today.[13] Rather than attempting to address "root causes" or to resolve conflict, the driving idea was to contain instability and prevent isolated incidents from escalating in an era when a larger confrontation between great powers was to be avoided at all costs.

If the peacekeeping efforts of the Cold War were therefore relatively minimalist and (in theory, at least) involved the avoidance of domestic politics, the end of the Cold War brought about a huge shift in the approach to conflict management both in terms of the *means* that members of the "international community" were willing to employ in the name of peace and in terms of desired *ends*. In essence, this involved a shift from peacekeeping to what became known as peacebuilding. The term *peacebuilding* itself came into the modern international lexicon and policyscape thanks in part to Boutros Boutros-Ghali's 1992 *Agenda for Peace* report, which defined the term as: "action to identify and support structures which will tend to strengthen and solidify peace in order to avoid relapse into conflict."[14] Among other things, Ghali's definition is both sweepingly broad and hopelessly vague, begging the question of what exactly is meant by "peace." While the passage of time has not contributed greatly to precision in this regard, a more recent UN definition of peacebuilding shows no hint of diminished ambitions, making clear that the goal of UN peace operations is to "lay the foundation for sustainable peace *and* development."[15] Despite this breadth and looseness in definition, or perhaps

---

[11] See Simon Chesterman, *You, the People: The United Nations, Transitional Administration, and State-Building* (Oxford: Oxford University Press, 2004), 238.

[12] Some refer to three different generations of peacekeeping, which evolved in quick succession in the early 1990s. Others, such as Roland Paris, simply distinguish between "traditional" peacekeeping and "peacebuilding operations." See Roland Paris, "Peacekeeping and the Constraints of Global Culture," *European Journal of International Relations* 9, no. 3 (2003), 448–50.

[13] See Edward Newman, Roland Paris, and Oliver Richmond, "Introduction," in *New Perspectives on Liberal Peacebuilding*, ed. Edward Newman et al. (New York: United Nations University, 2009), 6.

[14] United Nations, *Agenda for Peace, Preventative Diplomacy, Peacemaking and Peace Keeping*, UN Doc. A/47/277–S/24111 at 6, ¶ 21 (1992).

[15] See United Nations, *United Nations Peacekeeping Operations: Principles and Guidelines* (United Nations 2008), 26, emphasis added, http://pbpu.unlb.org/pbps/library/Capstone_Doctrine_ENG.pdf, emphasis added.

precisely because of it, the concept of peacebuilding has in the last twenty-five years been institutionalized within the UN system (as well across a number of organizations outside of it) to frame and organize a wide variety of postconflict activities.[16]

At the most general level, this shift from peacekeeping to peacebuilding has involved a growing commitment on the part of the UN system (and beyond) to the idea of building "positive peace," rather than simply maintaining "negative peace"; to building peace *within* states rather than simply managing conflict *between* states. If the Cold War logic of peacekeeping was to prevent a larger conflagration between great powers, the shift to peacebuilding was bolstered in part by the belief that threats to security in the new era came not just from interstate wars, but also from weak, failing, and conflict-prone states, and, particularly in the post-9/11 world, nonstate actors.[17] In this way, concepts of peace and security have always been heavily (if implicitly) shaped by the felt peace and security needs of great powers.

Over time, international peacebuilding efforts have embraced a broad array of activities, ranging from democratization initiatives and the strengthening of civil society to development and free-market reforms. Despite such breadth, peace operations typically include a fairly established checklist of programs and initiatives, including efforts to disarm previously warring parties, reintegrate former soldiers into society, demine and destroy weapons, reform the formal "security sector," and repatriate or resettle refugees.[18] While the need for many such programs is clear, with the shift from peacekeeping to peacebuilding has also come a level of intrusiveness and, at times, heavy-handedness that would have been unthinkable in previous eras. Indeed, as seen in East Timor, Kosovo, and Liberia, for example, the UN has increasingly found itself called upon in these next generation initiatives to address underlying economic, social, cultural, political, and humanitarian problems that would have once been considered exclusive "sovereign" or "internal" affairs. Such efforts have included drafting new laws and constitutions, monitoring and certifying elections, and helping to run or reform various institutions of governance in ways that can only be likened, in some instances, to neotrusteeship.[19]

From a legal standpoint, this intrusiveness has often been reflected in the increasing use of Chapter VII of the UN Charter for the establishment of peacebuilding mandates, where the use of force is permitted in the name of peace without the consent of the host state.[20] Parallels of this willingness to go so far as to wage war in the name of peace can also be seen in concepts of "humanitarian intervention,"

---

[16] See Michael Barnett et al., "Peacebuilding: What Is in a Name?," *Global Governance* 13, no. 1 (2007): 45–48.

[17] See Newman et al., "Introduction," 9.   [18] See United Nations, *Principles and Guidelines*, 26.

[19] See Constanze Schellhaas and Annette Seegers, "Peacebuilding: Imperialism's New Disguise?," *African Security Review* 18, no. 2 (2009): 2; Philip Cunliffe, "Still the Spectre at the Feast: Comparisons between Peacekeeping and Imperialism in Peacekeeping Studies Today," *International Peacekeeping* 19, no. 4 (2012): 426.

[20] This stands in contrast to efforts under Chapter VI, involving so-called consensual peacebuilding.

which has been given a new lease on life in the post–Cold War context, and its sibling, the so-called responsibility to protect.[21] As seen in Côte d'Ivoire, the Democratic Republic of the Congo and Libya, a more activist and interventionist United Nations Security Council has demonstrated an increasing if inconsistent willingness to intervene militarily in conflict and postconflict environments under the aegis of peace, at times giving liberalism and the concept of peace an aggressive face. With these shifts in both norm development and practice over time, sovereignty has been rendered increasingly permeable and conditional, and the distinction between waging war and making peace elided.[22]

Military intervention aside, a more activist Security Council is also part of what has permitted a general explosion of UN peace operations over the past twenty-five years with significant peacebuilding components. Though the Security Council establishes the mandates, the direction and implementation of the vast majority of on-the-ground peacekeeping missions across the world have been carried out by the UN Department of Peacekeeping Operations (DPKO). Beyond DPKO, full implementation of peace operations around the world is also the work of many UN agencies, ranging from the Department of Political Affairs and the United Nations Development Programme (UNDP) to the Office of the High Commissioner for Human Rights (OHCHR), and the Office of the United Nations High Commissioner for Refugees. The number of acronyms involved might be seen to reflect the breadth of modern-day peacebuilding, and indeed, the UN has emphasized that "effective peacebuilding must involve the entire United Nations system."[23] While examples of expansive operations are not in short supply,[24] it is helpful to sketch at least one of them for illustrative purposes. Because it helps to showcase many of the concepts discussed above, from peacekeeping and peacebuilding to armed intervention, the peace process in Côte d'Ivoire will be the focus here.

From Peacekeeping to Peacebuilding in Côte d'Ivoire

The Ivorian civil war erupted in September 2002 when rebel soldiers attacked Côte d'Ivoire's economic capital, Abidjan, with the stated aim of military reforms, new elections, and an end to discrimination against Ivorians from the north. While the

---

[21] UN Secretary-General, *Report of the High-Level Panel on Threats, Challenges and Change*, UN Doc. A/59/565, ¶ 201 (December 2, 2004) (noting that there "is a growing acceptance that while sovereign Governments have the primary responsibility to protect their own citizens... when they are unable or unwilling to do so that responsibility should be taken up by the wider international community").

[22] Florian Kuhn, "The Peace Prefix: Ambiguities of the Word 'Peace,'" *International Peacekeeping* 19, no. 4 (2012): 397.

[23] United Nations Security Council Resolution No. 2282, UN Doc. S/RES/2282 (2016), ¶ 13.

[24] Examples include Cambodia, Angola, Burundi, Central African Republic, Liberia, Mozambique, Rwanda, Sierra Leone, Chad, Sudan, Côte d'Ivoire, Democratic Republic of the Congo, Somalia, Kosovo, El Salvador, Guatemala, Haiti, Timor-Leste, Bosnia and Herzegovina, Eastern Slavonia, and Croatia, among others.

rebels failed to capture Abidjan (thanks in large part to the positioning of French forces who had come to evacuate foreigners), they rapidly took control of the northern half of the country. Official hostilities did not last long, ending in May 2003 with the signature of a peace accord, but the country would retain a de facto division between a rebel-controlled north and a government-controlled south for nearly a decade.[25] Patrolling the buffer zone between (and presumably preventing a return to all-out war) was the task of a host of international forces: beginning with France, the former colonial power; followed by the Economic Community of West African States (ECOWAS), a regional integration organization that played a key role in facilitating a ceasefire; and finally the United Nations.[26] At their peak, foreign peacekeeping troops numbered around 12,000, and their relationship with the Ivorian government ranged from frosty to bellicose.[27]

In patrolling the buffer zone, known as the "zone of confidence," UN and French troops exercised a classic peacekeeping function echoing the work of numerous UN peacekeeping forces during the Cold War. However, the mandate of the UN mission in Côte d'Ivoire (initially known as MINUCI, or the Mission des Nations Unies en Côte d'Ivoire, and subsequently as ONUCI, or the Opération des Nations Unies en Côte d'Ivoire) would gradually evolve to take on more and more peacebuilding tasks over time. By 2009, the Security Council had given ONUCI a formal mandate to play a role in: the reform of the security sector (monitoring of national borders; disarmament, demobilization, and reintegration of armed forces and militia groups; repatriation of foreign ex-combatants; restructuring of Ivorian defense and security forces; monitoring of the arms embargo imposed by the Security Council; destruction of weapons surrendered by former combatants); the reform and redeployment of civilian governance (redeployment of Ivorian state administration; restoration of a civilian policing presence; reestablishment of the role of the judiciary); the media (promotion of the peace process via a UN radio station; monitoring of Ivorian mass media for hate speech); and the promotion of human rights and accountability (monitoring and investigation of human rights violations).[28]

In addition to these fairly typical peacebuilding tasks, ONUCI was charged with playing a key role in long-delayed presidential elections, helping to secure processes involving the identification of Ivorian citizens and the registration of voters; providing technical assistance regarding the organization of elections; and, perhaps

---

[25] While the buffer zone was formally dismantled prior to 2010 presidential elections, rebels continued to exercise effective control over the north until after well after the disputed elections and ensuing stalemate.

[26] ECOWAS troops were relieved in April 2004, leaving UN and French troops (with the latter remaining under French command).

[27] In 2004, Ivorian government forces bombed French peacekeepers in rebel-controlled Bouaké, pro-government demonstrators clashed with French peacekeepers in Abidjan, and French jets destroyed the entire Ivorian air force. In 2006, pro-government protestors attacked UN bases in Abidjan, Daloa, Guiglo, and San Pedro.

[28] United Nations Security Council Resolution No. 1880, UN Doc. S/RES/1880 (2009).

most controversially, acting to "certify" that all stages of the electoral process were open, free, fair, and transparent.[29] These tasks built upon a series of earlier highly interventionist moves into Ivorian presidential politics. In 2006, for example, the Security Council effectively renewed the mandate of President Gbagbo, which had expired under the terms of the Ivorian constitution, for another twelve months.[30] In addition, the Council extended the mandate of the prime minister, and granted him extraconstitutional powers to implement various provisions of a "road map" drawn up by an "international working group," including "necessary authority over the Defense and Security Forces of Côte d'Ivoire."[31] If pro-Gbagbo nationalists were predictably apoplectic at these measures, their robustness should give many pause to think about the relationship between sovereignty, self-determination, and peacebuilding.

Unfortunately, the hope that 2010 presidential elections (originally scheduled for 2005) would clinch the resolution of the nearly decade-long stalemate proved to be misplaced when President Gbagbo refused to concede defeat to former prime minister Alassane Ouattara (a victory "certified" by the UN with clear international consensus). The ensuing political stalemate and spiral of violence ultimately led to the deaths of over 3,000 Ivorians[32] and a new, more dramatic role for UN and French peacekeepers Côte d'Ivoire. In 2011, the Security Council invoked the spirit if not the letter of the responsibility to protect (R2P) in determining that crimes against humanity were taking place and underscoring ONUCI's mandate to use "all necessary means" to protect civilians "including to prevent the use of heavy weapons."[33] The fighting ended in April 2011 when Ouattara's forces, with a crucial assist by UN and French attack helicopters and armored columns, arrested Gbagbo. This was not without controversy since, as in Libya, UN and French forces operating under a civilian protection mandate essentially facilitated regime change (albeit, unlike Libya, regime change from an electoral loser). Five years after the 2010–11 crisis, ONUCI had drawn down, but continued to operate with a robust peacebuilding mandate, providing assistance with respect to 2015 presidential elections, demobilization and disarmament, security-sector reform, compliance with human rights law, combating sexual and gender-based violence, and supporting the return of refugees and internally displaced persons.[34]

Taken together, international intervention in Côte d'Ivoire's civil war highlights some of the strengths of modern-day peacekeeping and peacebuilding, but also raises some challenging questions. To begin with the questions, foreign intervention arguably prolonged the conflict in Côte d'Ivoire by facilitating a stalemate that

---

[29] Ibid.   [30] United Nations Security Council Resolution No. 1721, UN Doc. S/RES/1721 (2006), ¶ 5.
[31] Ibid., ¶¶ 7–9.
[32] Human Rights Watch, *"They Killed Them Like It Was Nothing": The Need for Justice for Côte d'Ivoire's Post-Election Crimes* (New York: HRW, 2011).
[33] United Nations Security Council Resolution No. 1975, UN Doc. S/RES/1975 (2011), ¶ 6.
[34] United Nations Security Council Resolution No. 2226, UN Doc. S/RES/2226 (2015).

elites on both sides found quite profitable.[35] It also became clear over time that the UN and France, if neither true neutrals nor belligerents, were certainly central protagonists to the prolonged crisis, highlighting that peacebuilding is never an apolitical or technocratic affair, particularly when a former colonial power is involved. The Ivorian crisis also showcases the extremely intrusive measures that are taken in the name of "peacebuilding," including effectively suspending a national constitution and taking an active role in combat. Finally, while supporting many aspects of the peace process, it is clear that international pressure from 2005 to 2010 focused most heavily and anxiously on elections as an exit strategy as donors and the French government fatigued from footing the significant peacekeeping bill. And yet ironically, it was not ultimately elections that brought "peace" to Côte d'Ivoire, but an internationally assisted armed victory by northern rebels, the very thing the French prevented at the outbreak of the war in 2002–3. One might well question whether this can then be counted as a victory for "peacebuilding." On the other hand, while it raises the typical problems associated with all counterfactuals, it is quite possible that – in a fragile region where neighboring civil wars in Sierra Leone and Liberia had killed hundreds of thousands – intervention in Côte d'Ivoire, even with all of the questions it raises, effectively prevented the worst from occurring.[36]

Future Directions: The Peacebuilding Commission and Sustaining Peace

As illustrated by the Ivorian case study, the mandates of peacekeeping missions across the world have broadened to include various aspects of peacebuilding and statebuilding.[37] These developments were not initially met with a significant evolution of the UN's institutional doctrine or structure, leading to redundant and ad hoc efforts and a general lack of coordination.[38] However, the seemingly inevitable involvement in increasingly complex postconflict initiatives eventually culminated in the 2005 creation of the UN Peacebuilding Commission (PBC), which has been tasked with facilitating integrated approaches to postconflict reconstruction throughout the UN system and beyond.[39] The creation of the PBC reflects the

---

[35] Global Witness, *Hot Chocolate – How Cocoa Fueled the Conflict in Côte d'Ivoire* (London: Global Witness, 2007).

[36] See Marco Chown Oved, "In Côte d'Ivoire, a Model of Successful Intervention," *The Atlantic*, June 9, 2011.

[37] In general, while *peacebuilding* is the more inclusive term, *statebuilding* tends to focus more narrowly on rebuilding the core institutions and apparatuses of a modern, liberal state in the aftermath of conflict. For a discussion of the evolution of peacebuilding and statebuilding discourse, see generally John Heathershaw, "Unpacking the Liberal Peace: The Dividing and Merging of Peacebuilding Discourses," *Millennium: Journal of International Studies* 36, no. 3 (2008): 597.

[38] Liliana Lyra Jubilut, "Towards a New Jus Post Bellum: The United Nations Peacebuilding Commission and the Improvement of Post-Conflict Efforts and Accountability," *Minnesota Journal of International Law* 9 (2011): 31.

[39] See General Assembly Res. No. 60/180, UN Doc. A/RES/60/180 (2005), ¶¶ 1–2; Security Council Res. No. 1645, UN Doc. S/RES/1645 (2005), ¶¶ 1–2. The UN's new peacebuilding architecture also

normalization and institutionalization of peacebuilding across the UN system and beyond.

Unfortunately, a ten-year review of the PBC's performance made clear that it has not lived up to the task of facilitating greater coordination.[40] This helped to precipitate in part a larger review of the UN's peacebuilding architecture.[41] In 2016, the General Assembly and Security Council issued identically worded resolutions that embrace a vision of "sustaining peace" as a unifying theme for much of the United Nations' global work. The concept of sustaining peace has been defined as: "activities aimed at preventing the outbreak, escalation, continuation, and recurrence of conflict, addressing root causes, assisting parties to conflict to end hostilities, ensuing national reconciliation, and moving towards recovery, reconstruction and development."[42] Perhaps the most significant aspect of the resolutions is that they are the first to explicitly (and emphatically) link peacebuilding and prevention, making clear that peacebuilding is not an exclusively postconflict phenomenon, and is relevant to all phases of conflict.[43] While one can hope that the measures articulated within the resolutions intended to reform and strengthen the PBC will prove positive, the addition of conflict prevention to the PBC's mandate, while conceptually cogent and important, may prove a tall order given the PBC's general weakness over the last decade when it comes to coordinating even postconflict peacebuilding. Beyond this key development, the resolutions also call for a long-term, inclusive, and holistic approach to peacebuilding, offering perhaps the most ambitious and comprehensive description yet as to what this should include

> the prevention of conflict and addressing its root causes, strengthening the rule of law at the international and national levels, and promoting sustained and sustainable economic growth, poverty eradication, social development, sustainable development, national reconciliation and unity including through inclusive dialogue and mediation, access to justice and transitional justice, accountability, good governance, democracy, accountable institutions, gender equality and respect for, and protection of, human rights and fundamental freedoms.[44]

---

includes a Peacebuilding Support Office (PBSO), which acts as a secretariat to the PBC and serves the UN Secretary-General in coordinating UN agencies in their peacebuilding efforts, as well as a Peacebuilding Fund, administered by the PBSO, intended to address immediate peacebuilding needs in countries emerging from conflict and thereby fill a critical gap in postconflict project financing.

[40] See generally United Nations General Assembly & Security Council, Resolutions A/69/674-S/2014/911, December 17, 2014 [PBC ten-year review].

[41] Report of the Advisory Group of Experts for the 2015 Review of the United Nations Peacebuilding Architecture, *The Challenge of Sustaining Peace*, www.un.org/pga/wp-content/uploads/sites/3/2015/07/300615_The-Challenge-of-Sustaining-Peace.pdf.

[42] United Nations Security Council Resolution No. 2282, preamble.

[43] IPI Global Observatory, "With New Resolutions, Sustaining Peace Sits at Heart of UN Architecture," April 29, 2016, https://theglobalobservatory.org/2016/04/sustaining-peace-peacebuilding-united-nations-sdg.

[44] United Nations Security Council Resolution No. 2282, preamble.

Without doubt, these are all important conceptual shifts and clarifications in terms of the nature and temporality of peacebuilding. And yet if the holism and breadth of "sustaining peace" has intellectual cogency and traction, the description above might also be seen to reflect "laundry list syndrome."[45] Historically speaking, such sweeping rhetorical commitments have not always been translated into consistent practice.[46]

PEACEBUILDING AND ITS ASSOCIATED GLOBAL PROJECTS

As I have illustrated, peacebuilding has, since the end of the Cold War, become an important "global project" and a critical component of liberal postconflict governance.[47] If such governance is at times exercised through the conceptual and programmatic lens of peacebuilding, it also operates in synergy with a host of closely related global (and globalizing) projects such development, human rights, and various forms of democracy, governance, and rule-of-law assistance. To appreciate the critiques of "liberal peacebuilding" that will be discussed in the following section, it is worth pausing briefly to consider the extent to which postconflict countries have become positively enmeshed in the collective web of these global projects. Each of these areas is of course still subject to at times vigorous debate, and yet they nevertheless assume the character of global projects based on their overall projection of a sense of momentum, inevitability, and consensus. In other words, the question among international donors, practitioners, and policy makers today is increasingly less *whether* these projects are useful or desirable to achieve broader goals of peace, justice, development, and security than *how* they should be implemented.

One could ask whether these associated projects should not be viewed separately, but as part and parcel of peacebuilding itself, especially given the particularly comprehensive list of activities provided under the above-quoted definition of "sustaining peace." Indeed, the sheer breadth of peacebuilding's conceptualization makes it difficult to decide what, if any, programs and projects in the postconflict context could *not* be assimilated into the peacebuilding framework. From postconflict justice and reconciliation to the arts in school and better public sanitation, nearly everything can be plausibly construed as contributing to peace. But whether viewed as separate fields or merely as various dimensions of peacebuilding, the underlying logics and teleologies of these projects share much in common, and they might best be viewed as intertwined narratives of progress the boundaries of which are largely socially and politically constructed. The key here is to appreciate their synergistic

---

[45] See Padraig McAuliffe, "The Marginality of Transitional Justice within Liberal Peacebuilding: Causes and Consequences," *Journal of Human Rights Practice* 9, no. 1 (2017).
[46] Ibid.
[47] In using the term "Global Project," I am of course indebted to Rosemary Nagy and her influential article "Transitional Justice as a Global Project: Critical Reflections," *Third World Quarterly* 29, no. 2 (2008): 275–89.

effects in postconflict environments, particularly from the perspective of the targets of such interventions.

Developing countries in general and postconflict countries in particular have been in the floodlights of these global projects, having been the scene of myriad interventions in the name of democratization, marketization, legal reform, justice and human rights, good governance, and so on since the end of the Cold War. Tracing the trajectory of these projects over the decades, one sees that the sphere for intervention is ever widening in ambition and scope. Where peace used to be "kept" – a notion that suggests the preexistence of a degree of peace – it is now must be "built," from scratch where necessary, and then "sustained." Where development used to build bridges, it now seeks to build democracy and the rule of law.[48] And taken to its most extreme, where human rights were once to be protected through documentation and naming and shaming, the "international community" now shows an occasional willingness to do so through bombing campaigns. Both individually and collectively, these projects have become key vectors for pushing norms and practices from global core to periphery as part of what some have called a modern-day civilizing mission,[49] with "LDCs," "failed states," and "mass atrocities" being the modern equivalent of the historical "uncivilized," prizing open the gateway to intervention – with the best of intentions, of course – into matters once protected under the aegis of sovereignty and self-determination.[50]

The net result is an ostensibly apolitical and nonideological liberal postconflict governance based on notions of expertise, the law, and social science. It is less a governance of elected legislatures than of global laws, indices, logframes, and "best practices."[51] It is a governance of measurement, criteria, and standards; most of it conceptualized, labeled, and packaged in the Global North.[52] It is a governance discourse and currency peppered with talk at times impenetrable to the uninitiated – full of PRSPs, RFPs, MDGs, SAPs, UPR, and R2P – yet facile for those fluent in the lingo of UN, NGO, and donorese.[53] The projection of technocratic neutrality is further sustained though the increasing pride of place given to "the law" in and through all of these projects, leading to what some have called the progressive colonization

---

[48] Sundhya Pahuja, "Global Poverty and the Politics of Good Intentions," in *Law in Transition*, ed. Ruth Buchanan and Peer Zumbansen (Oxford: Hart, 2014), 38.
[49] See generally Roland Paris, "International Peacebuilding and the 'Mission Civilisatrice,'" *Review of International Studies* 28, no. 4 (2002): 637–56.
[50] See Mark Mazower, *Governing the World: The History of an Idea, 1815 to the Present* (London: Penguin, 2012).
[51] See Sally Engle Merry, "Measuring the World: Indicators, Human Rights and Global Governance," in *Law in Transition*, 141; Kerry Rittich, "Governing by Measuring: The Millennium Development Goals in Global Governance," in *Law in Transition*, 165.
[52] See Merry, "Measuring the World," 149.
[53] Poverty Reduction Strategy Papers (PRSPs), Request for Proposals (RFPs), Millennium Development Goals (MDGs), Structural Adjustment Programs (SAPs), Universal Periodic Review (UPR), Responsibility to Protect (R2P).

of the political – or the realm of hard choices, pragmatism, and trade-offs – with the legal.[54] In the chaos of postconflict and transitional contexts, the imagined rationality, certainty, objectivity and uniformity of the law and the legal sector as contrasted with the unruliness and grubbiness of politics are particularly powerful.[55]

This façade of neutrality and universality serves to imbue the views of an international cadre of outside experts, consultants, and technocrats – who appear to operate across the decades as both arsonists and firefighters – with an aura of knowledge and objectivity (in other words, power) that tends to further shift the balance of agency and decision making in favor of the global rather than the local in matters of postconflict governance and beyond. While it is one thing to contest policy recommendations understood to be "political" or "discretionary," it is more difficult to object to those proffered by humanist lawyers and technocrats operating on the basis of international "best practices" and international law.[56] In the eyes of such "experts," for example, transitional justice is less a debate about "a particular conception of justice" – a bundle of essentially contested concepts on which reasonable people may and will often disagree – than it is "a technical approach to exceptional challenges."[57] Over time, the legalist and technocratic discourse and power asymmetries at the heart of these projects then have had a tendency to reduce the policy horizon of national and community actors, ultimately narrowing the range of permissible responses to the challenges of poverty and injustice. To put it simply, to obtain the international funding available for postconflict development, peacebuilding, and reconstruction – and it is hard to imagine doing successful reconstruction without it – one must follow the international blueprint. Adherence to the blueprint can be facilitated explicitly and coercively as through the structural adjustment programs of the past, or more implicitly through the governance generated by phalanxes of experts and the "best practices" they peddle.

Over time, these collective projects have come to represent a complex facet of global governance more generally, rich in promises and possibilities, and yet also in the extent to which they may reflect and reinforce rather than transcend prevailing constellations of power. Historically, international human rights and development, for example, have been largely palliative, intended to moderate some of the excesses of market fundamentalism and state-perpetrated physical violence, without fundamentally transforming systems in ways that would do more than establish a

---

[54] Anne-Marie Slaughter, "Pushing the Limits of Liberal Peace: Ethnic Conflict and the 'Ideal Polity,'" in *International Law and Ethnic Conflict*, ed. David Wippman (Ithaca, NY: Cornell University Press, 1998), 134.
[55] Rosemary Nagy, "Transitional Justice as a Global Project: Critical Reflections," in *Law in Transition*, 217.
[56] Vasuki Nesiah, "The Trials of History: Losing Justice in the Monstrous and the Banal," in *Law in Transition*, 299.
[57] UN Approach to Transitional Justice, address by Ms. Navanethem Pillay, United Nations High Commissioner for Human Rights, New York, 2009, 2–3, www.un.org/ruleoflaw/files/TJ%20panel%20discussion%20-%20HC%20statement.pdf.

minimum floor for decency.[58] In the development context for example, legal reform has historically focused more on laying the foundation for free markets and barrier-free trade than on social justice and human rights. For its part, the human rights community has done a good job calling attention to discrete acts of physical violence – the death of a journalist or a demonstrator, for example – but has struggled to address many of the larger structural factors – the global economy and its trade rules – that create tremendous injustice in the developing world and beyond. What are projected as projects of liberation are therefore to some fundamentally conservative and status quo enterprises. Thus, if these projects have at times led to checks on the most egregious abuses of power, they may have simultaneously normalized quotidian violence, to say nothing of larger patterns of economic and structural violence.[59]

When the activities of the full spectrum of key postconflict actors are viewed in their ensemble in and through these projects – United Nations, international financial institutions, regional organizations, bilateral donors, NGOs, and so on – peacebuilding and its associated projects suggest nothing less than an attempt to (re)construct the Westphalian state, both politically and economically, by installing new modes of liberal democratic governance.[60] As Roland Paris has noted, this constitutes "an enormous experiment in social engineering."[61]

At a deeper level, such efforts also express a particular faith. First, a faith that the world can be fashioned by liberal ideas and institutions, and that weak, failing, and conflict-prone states – now conceptualized as threats to global security – can be relocated from a sphere of conflict to a sphere of peace through a process of political, social, and economic liberalization. Second, a faith that so-called partners actually know how to do it – that peace is universal and attainable if only "the correct methods are concretely and consistently applied by a plethora of different actors working on the basis of an agreed peacebuilding consensus."[62] And finally, a faith that the particular peace being sought is agreed upon and accepted by all concerned. Some of the controversies surrounding these assumptions will be explored in the following section.

CRITIQUES OF LIBERAL PEACEBUILDING

Beyond vagueness, one problem with many definitions of peacebuilding such as the various ones quoted above from the United Nations (e.g., "action to identify and support structures which will tend to strengthen and solidify peace in order to avoid

---

[58] See Samuel Moyn, "Do Human Rights Increase Inequality?," *Chronicle of Higher Education*, May 26, 2015.
[59] See, e.g., Morag Goodwin, "Holding Up a Mirror to the Process of Transition? The Coercive Sterilisation of Romani Women in the Czech Republic Post-1991," in *Law in Transition*, 227–43.
[60] Oliver Richmond, *The Transformation of Peace* (New York: Palgrave Macmillan, 2007), 193.
[61] Paris, *At War's End*, 4.   [62] Richmond, *The Transformation of Peace*, 183.

relapse into conflict")[63] is that they appear to suggest that concepts like "peace," "development," and "sustainable" are straightforward, uncontested, and nonideological. It is worth recalling, however, that peace (like justice) is an essentially contested concept capable of carrying a broad array of meanings. If peace and justice have emancipatory dimensions, they have also been associated with colonial logics and dominant ideologies and power structures throughout history. While both concepts are often presented as neutral and apolitical, devoid of inherent ideological content, they have at times been used to legitimate a world order characterized by economic and structural violence enforced by military interventionism. In short, there are reductionist notions of peace, just as there are reductionist notions of justice. And there can be a victor's peace, just as there can be a victor's justice. The explosion of peacebuilding practice in postconflict states over the last twenty-five years therefore begs the question of just what kind of "peace" we are talking about.

By and large, the peace the "international community" has sought to build since the end of the Cold War has been a liberal peace. The concept of the liberal peace is rooted in the theory of democratic peace, often attributed to Immanuel Kant, which suggests that liberal democratic states do not go to war with one another (even if they seem to go to war with nondemocracies with some frequency). Ideas about the liberal peace are also closely tied to assumptions about the pacifying effects of trade and economic integration. As Shahrbanou Tadjbakhsh has explained, these assumptions about democracy and trade "have been translated into attempts at democratization as the legitimate end goal of peacebuilding, and marketization as the best way for development and prosperity."[64] In the 1990s at least, these goals were "portrayed as almost magical formulas for peace in war-torn states."[65] While the emphasis is perhaps less crude and simplistic today, ideas about democratization and marketization continue to heavily shape the postconflict policyscape for states around the globe. Taken together, such efforts have become known as "liberal international peacebuilding" (LIPB).

As should not be surprising, LIPB has been subjected to serious and sustained critique at the level of both concept and implementation. As with all critiques, there is a danger of painting with too broad a brush, homogenizing diversity and difference.[66] With that important caveat, the bird's eye view of the academic and policy literature makes clear that one broad stream of critique is of more of a

---

[63] United Nations, *Agenda for Peace*, ¶ 21.
[64] Shahrbanou Tadjbakhsh, "Open Societies, Open Markets: Assumptions and Illusions," in *Rethinking Liberal Peace; External Models and Local Alternatives*, ed. Shahrbanou Tadjbakhsh (New York: Routledge, 2011), 20.
[65] See Roland Paris, "Saving Liberal Peacebuilding," *Review of International Studies* 36, no. 2 (2010): 338.
[66] Jenny Peterson, "A Conceptual Unpacking of Hybridity: Accounting for Notions of Power, Politics and Progress in Analyses of Aid-Drive Interfaces," *Journal of Peacebuilding and Development* 7, no. 2 (2012): 9.

"problem solving," practitioner, or policy-oriented nature,[67] geared toward better implementation of postconflict peacebuilding interventions without fundamentally questioning the deeper premises or assumptions at the core of LIPB. Thus, peacebuilding missions have been vigorously criticized for: failure to communicate and coordinate across sectors owing to stovepiping and bureaucratic territorialism; for a lack of political will to commit to a realistic time horizon to accomplish the goals established; for failure to furnish adequate resources; for insufficient knowledge of local conditions, history, and culture; and for ignoring the importance of local ownership, and so on.[68] For the most part, such criticism has been amply warranted, and has no doubt been part of the reason that the peacebuilding efforts of today have grown in complexity, sophistication, resources, and longevity compared to their earlier predecessors.

Though the distinction is not always a clean one, a second stream of analysis arising more out of the domain of academic theory and "critical studies" traditions has focused less on problems of implementation than on a dissection of more foundational problems undergirding peacebuilding as a global project. While there are a number of variants within this stream, all have tended question the narrow and reductionist view that would see economic and political liberalization – free markets and Western-style democracy – as the unique pathway to peace around the world.[69] In other words, it is problematic to assume that key liberal goods necessarily bring peace and not the other way around, or some other way. And it is doubly problematic to imagine that such a peace can be successfully "built" through an internationally driven, hegemonic project with all of the gross power disparities this entails. Attempting to impose such a one-size-fits-all peace risks creating not a genuine, but a "virtual peace," where root causes are not so much addressed as swept under the proverbial rug.[70] Thus, for critical theorists, it is important to lay bare the political and ideological assumptions and blind spots of LIPB and to marry this with an understanding of what LIPB looks like "from below," where a sense of solidarity between locals and internationals is often is less palpable than a spirit of cooptation and resistance.[71] Taken together, these dynamics become key to understanding how peacebuilding serves to "construct, reproduce and maintain particular visions or order" around the world.[72] In these and other ways, critical theorists have sought to

---

[67] On the distinction between problem solving and critical theory, see generally Robert Cox, "Social Forces, States and World Orders: Beyond International Relations Theory," in *Neorealism and Its Critics*, ed. R. O. Keohane (New York: Columbia University Press, 1986).

[68] See Roland Paris, "Saving Liberal Peacebuilding," *Review of International Studies* 36, no. 2 (2010): 347.

[69] See Roland Paris, "Peacebuilding and the Limits of Liberal Internationalism," *International Security* 22, no. 2 (1997): 56.

[70] Richmond, *The Transformation of Peace*, 185.

[71] See generally Balakrishnan Rajagopal, *International Law from Below: Development, Social Movements and Third World Resistance* (Cambridge: Cambridge University Press, 2003).

[72] Alex Bellamy, "The 'Next Stage' in Peace Operations Theory?," in *Peace Operations and Global Order*, ed. Alex Bellamy and Paul Williams (New York: Routledge, 2005), 32.

question the fundamental legitimacy of LIPB as a global project and the supposed naturalness of the order that it helps to replicate.

One sobering problem that both "problem solving" and "critical studies" camps have had to contend with is that a significant number of conflicts reignite in the years following their apparent settlement.[73] While not all of this can be attributed to the supposed failures of LIPB, it is clear that the simplistic formula of markets + democracy = peace as pushed through experiments in international social engineering has had a rather rocky track record, having worked rather well except for when it has not. Thus, for example, the internationally assisted push for democracy did not bring peace in Angola, Bosnia, or Afghanistan. And rapid market liberalization has proven similarly destabilizing, with "shock therapy" having created huge dislocations in the former Soviet bloc, not to mention the economic violence that flowed from structural adjustment programs of the 1980s and 1990s, which made a gospel out of privatization, deregulation, and cutbacks to social welfare in postconflict countries and beyond.[74] As these examples illustrate, the push for elections, democracy, and neoliberal economic policies associated with the typical package of postconflict peacebuilding interventions may not always result in a liberal peace, and may actually contribute to instability and undermine human rights. One possible explanation for this is that rapid economic and political liberalization can give rise to grievances and political competition with which the often fragile or shattered institutions in postconflict countries are as yet too weak to cope.[75]

For the "problem solving," practitioner camp, the realization that rapid democratization and marketization may be destabilizing eventually led to a chastened liberal peacebuilding paradigm that places greater emphasis on institution building as a prelude to more robust liberalization.[76] In this way, the conceptual building blocks of LIPB are retained, but efficiencies are sought through better sequencing. Thus, the disastrous push for elections as a departure strategy that has been associated with some early UN peace operations was moderated in the early 2000s with an increased emphasis on broad categories of programming such as rule-of-law assistance and

---

[73] Paul Collier once famously argued that over 50 percent of civil wars reignite within a period of five years of their supposed settlement. See Paul Collier and Anne Hoeffler, "On the Incidence of Civil War in Africa," *Conflict Resolution* 46, no. 1 (2002): 17. However, both figures have been disputed by some, and revised by Collier himself. See, e.g., Astri Suhrke and Ingrid Samset, "What's in a Figure? Estimating Recurrence of Civil War," *International Peacekeeping* 14, no. 2 (2007): 197–98 (explaining how they and others have arrived at figures closer to 20 percent after using the Correlates of War data set, and citing Collier's 2006 working paper, which established a 23 percent war recurrence rate for the first four years after the cessation of conflict).

[74] See, e.g., Naomi Klein, *The Shock Doctrine: The Rise of Disaster Capitalism* (New York: Picador, 2008); M. Rodwan Abouharb and David Cingranelli, *Human Rights and Structural Adjustment* (Cambridge: Cambridge University Press, 2007); Joseph Stiglitz, *Globalization and Its Discontents* (New York: W. W. Norton, 2002).

[75] See Amy Chua, *World on Fire: How Exporting Free Market Democracy Breeds Ethnic Hatred and Global Instability* (New York: Random House, 2004).

[76] See Paris, "Peacebuilding and the Limits," 57–58.

security-sector reform.[77] For the more skeptical "critical studies" camp, programming modeled on this "institutionalization-before-liberalization" model nevertheless tends to focus almost exclusively on building formal, national-level liberal institutions required for the Western, Weberian state and its centralized monopoly on the use of force. While key national-level institutions of the state are showered with the attention and dollars of international reformers, the everyday security and needs that ordinary people need to survive – housing, water, jobs, electricity – are often shortchanged.[78] This focus on central state institutions seems to assume that peacebuilding and state building are essentially one and the same,[79] and that institutions induce liberalism and peace rather than the other way around, or some other way. The idea that stronger institutions lead to peace also appears to reflect a rather top-town model for change that critics have called "trickle-down" peace.[80]

More normatively, critics assert that international peacebuilding predicated on the institutionalization-before-liberalization model still often involves the imposition of Western institutional modalities and preferences. At their core, such preferences remain premised on neoliberal policies of open markets and Western conceptions of both state and governance.[81] Equally worrisome, the strongest critics argue, is that there is little space for meaningful dissent from the prevailing and hegemonic international peacebuilding paradigm that might help lead to genuine alternatives, no matter how much lip service might be paid to concepts like "inclusivity" and "local ownership."[82] Thus, to the extent that LIPB is implicitly predicated on the notion that "being peaceful," "doing justice," or building the "rule of law" is to be "just like us," one can surely ask whether this and other associated global projects have not stymied the potential to develop a more heterogeneous, mosaic, and cosmopolitan theory and praxis.

In recent years, the question has been raised as to whether some of the critics have not gone too far in their attempts to skewer LIPB, becoming "hypercritical,"

---

[77] For a critique of the rush to rapid elections, see Chesterman, *You, the People*, 204–35.
[78] See generally David Roberts, "Post-Conflict Peacebuilding, Liberal Irrelevance and the Locus of Legitimacy," *International Peacekeeping* 18, no. 4 (2011).
[79] See Oliver Richmond and Audra Mitchell, "Towards a Post-Liberal Peace: Exploring Hybridity via Everyday Forms of Resistance," in *Hybrid Forms of Peace: From Everyday to Post-Liberalism*, ed. Oliver Richmond and Audra Mitchell (New York: Palgrave Macmillan, 2012), 4–5.
[80] Carla Castaneda, "Trickle-Down Peace: How Liberal Peacebuilding May Be Failing Sierra Leone," in *When War Ends: Building Peace in Divided Communities*, ed. David Francis (New York: Routledge, 2016).
[81] See Neil Cooper, Mandy Turner, and Michael Pugh, "The End of History and the Last Liberal Peacebuilder: A Reply to Roland Paris," *Review of International Studies* 37, no. 4 (2011): 1995; Chandra Lekha Sriram, Olga Martin-Ortega, and Johanna Herman, "Promoting the Rule of Law: From Liberal to Institutional Peacebuilding," in *Peacebuilding and the Rule of Law in Africa: Just Peace?*, ed. Chandra Lekha Sriram, Olga Martin-Ortega, and Johanna Herman (Milton Park: Routledge, 2011), 1–2 (arguing that promoting institutionalization as a response to the critique of liberal international peacebuilding may also entail an imposition).
[82] See Cooper et al., "The End of History," 1995.

and potentially throwing the baby out with the bathwater by conflating liberalism writ large with the particular failures of implementation of LIPB as we have thus far known it.[83] From this perspective, the critics are due for a "reality check" and have done little to offer any kind of realistic alternative to the LIPB model that they find so problematic.[84]

Moreover, it is pointed out, the skeptics are not only long on critique and short on concrete alternatives, but the critiques themselves tend to be based on fundamentally liberal principles.[85] In this way, one might view the controversy surrounding LIPB as involving not so much a choice between liberal and some kind of illiberal peacebuilding as it does a contest between conflicting liberal commitments and competing visions of liberalism itself. Indeed, it is hard to imagine "sustaining peace," where that peace is understood to be more than negative peace, without some level of democracy and respect for human rights. It is therefore possible that the real clash is between the what we might call the "liberal localism" of the critical theorists and the "neoliberal internationalism" of mainstream LIPB.[86]

This is not to say that the critical literature of peacebuilding must somehow offer a concrete program for action to prove its value, or that pointing out the fundamentally liberal basis of much of the critical theory in the field somehow invalidates the incisiveness of the critiques themselves. It is now clear that the narrow and reductionist international peacebuilding model has tended to privilege certain forms of expertise and knowledge, has too often been associated with exogenous imposition and has not been sufficiently willing to question its deeper assumptions or role in promoting a neoliberal world order that may not be in the best interest of all concerned. That this is increasingly obvious to some is due in part to the work of critical theorists. And if it now seems clear that neoliberalism is not a unique pathway to grappling with legacies of violent conflict; that attempting to impose a liberal peace through illiberal means is contradictory and likely self-defeating; and that the liberal international peacebuilding project is less a natural and inevitable program, an escape from politics and ideology, than a means by which a particular form of post-conflict governance is exercised, then the mental "shake up" that critical theorists have provided was certainly welcome and long overdue.

Liberal peacebuilding is therefore a contested project from within and without and is likely to remain so for some time. Given the dynamics of ideology and

---

[83] Shahrbanou Tadjbakhsh, "Introduction: Liberal Peace in Dispute," in *Rethinking Liberal Peace; External Models and Local Alternatives*, ed. Shahrbanou Tadjbakhsh (New York: Routledge, 2011), 4–5.
[84] See generally Shahar Hameiri, "A Reality Check for the Critique of the Liberal Peace?," in *A Liberal Peace? The Problems and Practices of Peacebuilding*, ed. Susanna Campbell, David Chandler, and Meera Sabaratnam (London: Zed Books, 2011); Roland Paris, "Alternatives to Liberal Peace?," in *A Liberal Peace?*
[85] See Roland Paris, "Saving Liberal Peacebuilding," *Review of International Studies* 2 (2010): 354.
[86] I will develop the concept of "liberal localism" in Chapter 7.

imposition at the heart of LIPB, this push and pull of contestation and the fundamental search for legitimacy should be seen as not only welcome, but vital to the future of the field. Liberal postconflict governance is exercised not entirely without governments, but neither does it contain the checks and balances democratic theory would suggest are necessary to hold such a citadel of power accountable to those most affected by its considerable footprint on the postconflict landscape. The need for sustained examination, critique, and, yes, concrete proposals for reform will be particularly acute given what appears to be the expansionist and totalizing peacebuilding agenda, which continues to assimilate other global projects and discourses at a rapid pace: sustainable development, national reconciliation, access to justice, transitional justice, accountability, good governance, democracy, gender equality, respect for human rights and fundamental freedoms, and so on.[87] The task of evaluating how peacebuilding and each of these projects might be shaped through their encounter with one another is one that has not been sufficiently addressed in the literature. In Chapters 6 and 7, I will explore in greater depth the parallels between the various critiques and LIPB and transitional justice. I will also address the thorny question of "alternatives," taking inspiration from some of the critical and emancipatory peacebuilding literature for a glimpse of how "transitional justice as peacebuilding" might be conceptualized in the twenty-first century.

[87] United Nations Security Council Resolution 2282, preamble.

6

Transitional Justice and Liberal International Peacebuilding

Over the last twenty-five years, programs and interventions associated with both liberal international peacebuilding and transitional justice have increasingly followed in war's wake. From Côte d'Ivoire to Colombia, pick a postconflict country today, and there is good chance that at least some of the various programs and initiatives associated with both international peacebuilding and transitional justice are being implemented. Such initiatives often share the same temporal and geographic space, and several United Nations (UN) peace operations have been given a mandate to address transitional justice as well as more general peacebuilding activities.[1] Despite this, connections between peacebuilding and transitional justice have generally been "under-researched,"[2] and even with the proximities of time and space, there has historically been little coordination between traditional pillars of postconflict peacebuilding – such as the demobilization, disarmament, and reintegration (DDR) of ex-combatants and security-sector reform (SSR) – and transitional justice initiatives.[3]

In this chapter, I observe signs that this historic, separate-tracks approach to peacebuilding and transitional justice programs is beginning to change. In contrast with

---

[1] Examples include the UN Mission in Kosovo and the UN Transitional Authority in East Timor.
[2] See Paul van Zyl, "Promoting Transitional Justice in Post-Conflict Societies," in *Security Governance in Post-Conflict Peacebuilding*, ed. Alan Bryden and Heiner Hänggis (Geneva: DCAF, 2005), 210.
[3] See Lars Waldorf, "Introduction: Linking DDR and Transitional Justice," in *Disarming the Past: Transitional Justice and Ex-Combatants*, ed. Ana Cutter Patel, Pablo de Greiff, and Lars Waldorf (New York: ICTJ, 2009), 16 (discussing lack of coordination between transitional justice and DDR); Alexander Mayer-Rieckh and Roger Duthie, "Enhancing Justice and Development through Justice-Sensitive Security Sector Reform," in *Transitional Justice and Development: Making Connections*, ed. Pablo de Greiff and Roger Duthie (New York: ICTJ, 2009), 222 (noting that the practices of SSR and transitional justice "rarely interact, either in practice or in theory").

earlier decades where peace and justice were seen to be in some tension,[4] today they are identified as "mutually reinforcing imperatives."[5] At least rhetorically, the UN has now defined transitional justice as part and parcel of peacebuilding itself.[6] And there is growing interest in academic and policy communities in exploring potential theoretical and programmatic linkages between peace and justice initiatives.[7] Given mutually shared goals between peacebuilding and transitional justice, there are reasons to think that the breaking down of siloes at the level of both concept and implementation is a good thing. If nothing else, better coordination between programs might at least help avoid potential frictions and tensions.

At the same time, there are grounds for caution when it comes to better coordination (if not gradual convergence) between transitional justice and liberal international peacebuilding. In particular, there is a danger that as transitional justice is "mainstreamed" into the postconflict peacebuilding policyscape by UN policy organs, it will come to be seen as yet one more box to tick on the "postconflict checklist," a routine part of the template deployed in the context of postconflict peace operations.[8] This would be consistent with the gradual normalization and

---

[4] Scholars and policy makers have long examined the possibility for tensions between peace and justice initiatives, manifested in the so-called peace versus justice debate. See, e.g., Chandra Lekha Sriram, *Confronting Past Human Rights Violations: Justice vs Peace in Times of Transition* (Milton Park: Frank Cass, 2004), 1–2. In recent years, however, transitional justice advocates have tended to see the various and sometimes contradictory goals of transitional justice as complementary. See Bronwyn Anne Leebaw, "The Irreconcilable Goals of Transitional Justice," *Human Rights Quarterly* 30, no. 1 (2008): 98.

[5] UN Secretary-General, "The Rule of Law and Transitional Justice in Post-conflict Societies," UN Doc. S/2004/616 (August 23, 2004), 1.

[6] United Nations Security Council Resolution No. 2282, UN Doc. S/RES/2282 (2016), preamble.

[7] See generally, e.g., Chandra Sriram, Olga Martin-Ortega, and Johanna Herman, "Evaluating and Comparing Strategies of Peacebuilding and Transitional Justice," JAD-PbP Working Paper Series 1 (May 2009), 13 (discussing increasing linkages between transitional justice and a broader set of peacebuilding activities); Alan Bryden, Timothy Donais, and Heiner Hängi, *Shaping a Security-Governance Agenda in Post-Conflict Peacebuilding* (Geneva: DCAF, 2005) (examining policy linkages between SSR, DDR, rule-of-law initiatives, and transitional justice); see also van Zyl, "Promoting Transitional Justice," 210 (arguing that "[t]ransitional justice strategies should be understood as an important component of peacebuilding").

[8] The problem of template-based or one-size-fits-all peacebuilding initiatives is a frequent trope in both academic and policy literature. See, e.g., Roger Mac Ginty, "Indigenous Peace-Making versus the Liberal Peace," *Cooperation and Conflict: Journal of the Nordic Studies Association* 43, no. 2 (2008): 144 (observing the existence of "set templates" and a "formulaic path" in internationally sponsored peacebuilding); Edward Newman et al., "Introduction," in *New Perspectives on Liberal Peacebuilding*, ed. Edward Newman, Roland Paris, and Oliver Richmond (New York: United Nations University, 2009), 42 (noting that "[a] core problem of contemporary peacebuilding is its tendency to be formulaic"); International Crisis Group, *Liberia and Sierra Leone: Rebuilding Failed States*, Africa Report no. 87 (Dakar/Brussels: International Crisis Group, December 2004), 9 (criticizing a mechanistic "operational checklist" approach to postconflict peacebuilding in which the international community assumes it can safely withdraw after rote implementation of a series of initiatives: deployment of peacekeeping troops, disarmament, demobilization, and reintegration of ex-combatants, the repatriation and return of refugees and internally displaced persons, security sector and judicial reform, transitional justice initiatives, and, finally, a first election).

institutionalization of transitional justice around the world, but comes at a time when the field is in desperate need of renewed legitimacy and more creative and context-specific approaches.

Caution is also warranted in view of the fact that traditional international peacebuilding programs as well as a number of transitional justice initiatives have been subject to powerful, parallel critiques: that they are too often externally driven, being planned, and implemented in a top-down and state-centric manner that gives insufficient voice and agency to those most affected by the conflict;[9] that they are biased toward Western approaches, giving too little attention to local or indigenous peace and justice traditions;[10] that they are presented as technocratic, neutral, and apolitical solutions to highly contested or contestable political issues and choices;[11] and that they ultimately reflect not local needs and realities, but a dominant liberal international peacebuilding paradigm that seeks to foster Western, market-oriented democracies in the wake of conflict with little regard to context.[12] Considered together, therefore, there is reason to worry that better integration and coordination between peacebuilding and transitional justice might exacerbate some of the tendencies that have given rise to these parallel critiques rather than alleviate them.

As academics and policy makers begin to sound out linkages and synergies, I will argue that attentiveness to some of the parallel critiques leveled against both peacebuilding and transitional justice interventions could lead to shifts that would strengthen policy in both areas in the process of promoting linkages. The possibility of integrating local reconciliation practices into both transitional justice mechanisms and reintegration schemes for former combatants is one such possibility that will be briefly examined in this chapter.

---

[9] See, e.g., Oliver Richmond, "The Romanticisation of the Local: Welfare, Culture, and Peacebuilding," *International Spectator: Italian Journal of International Affairs* 44, no. 1 (2009), 161–63 (discussing the tendency toward top-down institution building in a variety of "liberal" interventions); Kora Andrieu, "Civilizing Peacebuilding: Transitional Justice, Civil Society and the Liberal Paradigm," *Security Dialogue* 41, no. 5 (2010): 54 (noting that "transitional justice seems to be strongly under the influence of [a] top-down state-building approach").

[10] See, e.g., Mac Ginty, "Indigenous Peace-Making," 144–45 (noting that Western approaches to peacebuilding "risk[] minimizing the space for organic local, traditional or indigenous contributions to peace-making"); Wendy Lambourne, "Transitional Justice and Peacebuilding after Mass Violence," *International Journal of Transitional Justice* 3, no. 1 (2009): 32–34 (calling for a revalorization of local and cultural approaches to justice and reconciliation).

[11] See, e.g., Newman, "'Liberal' Peacebuilding Debates," 42 (critiquing attempts to "'depoliticize' peacebuilding and present it as a technical task"); Patricia Lundy and Mark McGovern, "Whose Justice? Rethinking Transitional Justice from the Bottom Up," *Journal of Law and Society* 35, no. 2 (2008): 276–77 (arguing that "wider geo-political and economic interests too often shape what tend to be represented as politically and economically neutral post-conflict and transitional justice initiatives").

[12] See generally Roland Paris, *At War's End: Building Peace after Nationalist Conflict* (Cambridge: Cambridge University Press, 2004); Chandra Lekha Sriram, "Justice as Peace? Liberal Peacebuilding and Strategies of Transitional Justice," *Global Society* 21, no. 4 (2007): 579.

SIGNS OF CONVERGENCE BETWEEN PEACEBUILDING AND TRANSITIONAL JUSTICE

Like Shakespeare's true love, the relationship between concepts of peace, peacebuilding, and transitional justice has not always "run smooth."[13] Indeed, in the context of transitional justice debates, the concept of peace has at times been mobilized as one of resistance to the advance of particular transitional justice mechanisms and policies.[14] This is manifest most clearly in the so-called peace versus justice debate, in which some form of transitional justice, typically a prosecution, is imagined to undermine or preclude chances for a negotiated peace agreement.[15] The debate has also arisen when it comes to the choice as among different elements of the transitional justice "toolbox," including whether to have prosecutions or a truth commission and whether to have international prosecutions or mechanisms of accountability rooted in local tradition and custom.[16] While there are an increasing number of concrete examples in which prosecutions have arguably advanced the cause of peace, the "peace versus justice" the debate is resurrected at regular intervals, as reactions to the indictments by the International Criminal Court of Omar al-Bashir of Sudan and Joseph Kony of the Lord's Resistance Army in Uganda have demonstrated.[17]

---

[13] William Shakespeare, "A Midsummer Night's Dream," in *The Complete Works*, ed. G. B. Harrison (New York: Harcourt Brace Jovanovich, 1952), 517.

[14] See, e.g., Chandra Lekha Sriram, *Confronting Past Human Rights Violations: Justice vs Peace in Times of Transition* (New York: Frank Cass, 2004).

[15] As an example of this phenomenon, in 2003, the then chairman of the Economic Community of West African States, President John Kufuor of Ghana, urged the UN to set aside the indictment of Charles Taylor by the Special Court for Sierra Leone on the grounds that it was necessary to facilitate a negotiated settlement to Liberia's civil war. See IRIN Humanitarian News and Analysis, "Liberia: ECOWAS Chairman Urges UN to Lift Taylor Indictment," June 30, 2003.

[16] Increasingly, there is a recognition that no one mechanism of transitional justice can hope to fulfill the many aspirations ascribed to it, and multiple overlapping mechanisms are thought to be necessary. For an exploration of the "truth versus justice" debate, see generally Miriam Aukerman, "Extraordinary Evil, Ordinary Crimes: A Framework for Understanding Transitional Justice," *Harvard Human Rights Journal* 15 (2002): 39; Reed Brody, "Justice: The First Casualty of Truth?," *The Nation*, April 30, 2001, 25. For an argument that international prosecutions can subvert local judicial and reconciliation practices while unwittingly playing into national-level politics, see generally Adam Branch, "Uganda's Civil War and the Politics of ICC Intervention," *Ethics and International Affairs* 21, no. 2 (2007): 179.

[17] See, e.g., Jeffrey Gettleman and Alexis Okeowo, "Warlord's Absence Derails Another Peace Effort in Uganda," *New York Times*, April 12, 2008 (discussing the refusal of Joseph Kony, leader of a rebel group known as the Lord's Resistance Army that is responsible for widespread human rights abuses in Uganda and neighboring countries, to attend peace negotiations due in part to indictments from the International Criminal Court); Priscilla Hayner, *Negotiating Peace in Liberia: Preserving the Possibility for Justice* (Geneva: Centre for Humanitarian Dialogue, November 2007), 8–9 (arguing that the indictment of Charles Taylor advanced the peace process in Liberia, even though it was criticized at the time as potentially undermining peace negotiations); Louise Arbour, "Justice v. Politics," *New York Times*, September 16, 2008 (justifying her decision to indict Slobodan Milošević by showing that it ultimately advanced the cause of peace, even though it was criticized at the time for threatening the peace process).

Although rarely defined as such, the concept of peace that is put in opposition to justice in the context of such debates is typically that of "negative peace," meaning the absence of direct physical violence.[18] Thus, if the threat of prosecution is feared to prevent a group of rebels from signing a peace agreement, and the guns may keep firing, justice could be said to undermine (negative) peace. A similarly narrow view of peace can be found when Ruti Teitel expresses the fear that as transitional justice mechanisms become increasingly associated with nation building, they will give up on the "ambitious goals of establishing the rule of law and democracy" in favor of the more modest aims of "maintaining peace and stability."[19]

The notion of negative peace that has often been employed in such transitional justice discourse and debates is a much narrower concept of peace than the notion of "positive peace," which involves not just the silence of AK-47s and the absence of the direct violence of hot conflict, but also the absence of more indirect forms of violence, including forms of structural and economic violence such as poverty, corruption, discrimination, and other forms of social injustice.[20] Without making use of the term, transitional justice advocates often seem to assume that accountability will lead to a type of positive peace.[21] Thus, for example, the concept of peace might be marshaled by the advocates for transitional justice as part of an argument that a potential amnesty agreement will not secure "lasting peace" or that the particular type of justice to be meted out by transitional justice mechanisms is necessary to "long-term peace." It is perhaps then assumed that the transition that is set in motion will allow the type of social and economic development that may lead to a more robust positive peace. As Alexander Boraine has argued, "[t]he overall aim [of transitional justice] should be to ensure a sustainable peace, which will encourage and make possible social and economic development."[22] One can also see these dynamics in debates regarding whether transitional justice is a "backward looking" luxury that postconflict countries can ill afford, as opposed to the supposedly "forward looking" projects of education, health, infrastructure, and so on. In fact, transitional justice might more accurately be understood as both backward looking, insofar as it is closely associated with justice and accountability for historical human rights violations, and forward looking, insofar as its advocates often claim that justice is essential to prevent recurrence and to lay the groundwork for longer-term peace and stability.[23]

---

[18] See Johan Galtung, "Violence, Peace, and Peace Research," *Peace Research* 6, no. 3 (1969): 167; Lambourne, "Transitional Justice and Peacebuilding," 34.
[19] Ruti G. Teitel, "Transitional Justice in a New Era," *Fordham International Law Journal* 26, no. 4 (2002): 898.
[20] See generally Galtung, "Violence," 167 (discussing different constructions of "positive peace" and "negative peace").
[21] See Alexander L. Boraine, "Transitional Justice: A Holistic Interpretation," *Journal of International Affairs* 60, no. 1 (2006): 26.
[22] Ibid.
[23] See, e.g., Andrieu, "Civilizing Peacebuilding," 538 (noting that transitional justice has both forward and backward looking aspects); Mayer-Rieckh and Duthie, "Enhancing Justice and Development,"

For the most part, however, peace has not historically been a central pillar transitional justice discourse,[24] with advocates debating issues of amnesty and prosecutions in a more legalistic idiom, asking, for example, whether there is a duty to prosecute under international law, or whether amnesties are compatible with international law.[25] To many lawyers, it seems, "peace" remains a fuzzy concept that evokes notions of 1960s counterculture. Nevertheless, the notion of peace is no more or less nebulous than the concepts of "justice," "accountability," "reconciliation," and the "rule of law" that typically pepper transitional justice discourse and debates.

In spite of this uneven history, there are signs that peace and justice have begun to make friends, at least at the level of international rhetoric. In a landmark 2004 publication, then Secretary-General Kofi Annan declared that "[j]ustice, peace and democracy are not mutually exclusive objectives, but rather mutually reinforcing imperatives."[26] Given the UN's involvement in transitional justice programs across the globe over the past twenty-five years, perhaps it would be hard for it to assert otherwise. For example, the international criminal tribunals for the former Yugoslavia (ICTY) and Rwanda (ICTR) were both created by the Security Council as part of a response to a threat to international peace and security under Chapter VII of the UN Charter.[27] In Sierra Leone, East Timor, Cambodia, Bosnia, and Lebanon, the UN created hybrid international tribunals. The Office of the High Commissioner for Human Rights has supported transitional justice programs in some twenty countries around the world.[28] The Bureau of Crisis Prevention and Recovery at the UN Development Programme also works to support transitional justice efforts. That does not, of course, mean that transitional justice has been consistently embraced by the UN, and indeed it continues to be marginal or absent in the mandates of many peacekeeping missions.[29] Even so, the rhetorical embrace of transitional justice, coupled with emerging shifts in norms and practice, remain significant.

Tracing the trajectory of these programs over the years, one could note that as transitional justice practices have been embraced by key global institutions such as

224 (arguing that it would be a mistake to see transitional justice as solely backward looking); Andrew Valls, "Racial Justice as Transitional Justice," *Polity* 36, no. 1 (2003): 58 (arguing for a balanced approach to transitional justice that takes into account both forward and backward looking dimensions).

[24] Just as transitional justice has not been a central pillar of liberal peacebuilding.

[25] For a classic example, see, e.g., Diane F. Orentlicher, "Settling Accounts: The Duty to Prosecute Human Rights Violations of a Prior Regime," *Yale Law Journal* 100, no. 8 (1991): 2537 (discussing the duty to prosecute or grant amnesty under international law).

[26] UN Secretary-General, "The Rule of Law and Transitional Justice," 1.

[27] UN Charter, Chapter VII.

[28] See United Nations, *Message by Ms. Navanethem Pillay at the Special Summit of the African Union* (October 22, 2009).

[29] See Padraig McAuliffe, "The Marginality of Transitional Justice within Liberal Peacebuilding: Causes and Consequences," *Journal of Human Rights Practice* 9, no. 1 (2017).

the UN (contributing to normalization of the field), they have increasingly been implemented in a wider range of contexts around the globe, including those that do not involve a particularly liberal transition.[30] In such instances in particular, it certainly behooves the UN to call what is happening "peacebuilding" for want of some other justification such as democratization. In this way, the "peace versus justice" debate has been bridged in part through the institutionalization of transitional justice across the UN system and beyond.

As discussed in Chapter 5, the concept of "sustaining peace" that is in principle to serve as a theme for harmonization of efforts across the UN system has been defined to include strengthening the rule of law, access to justice, accountability, protection of human rights, and transitional justice.[31] As this definition suggests, the nascent paradigm shift to thinking of transitional justice as part and parcel of peacebuilding should be understood in the context of the overall legalization of both peacebuilding and transitional justice efforts. That is, peace and justice are no longer in apparent conflict because peacebuilding has been defined to include law, justice, accountability, and so on. In this same vein, if in earlier periods "peace" sounded to transitional justice advocates like some kind of suspicious code word for "amnesty," the legalization of both fields now requires us to see amnesties for certain crimes as contrary to international law and therefore inconsistent with peacebuilding.

Outside of the UN, there is a growing interest in both academic and policy communities in exploring potential theoretical and programmatic linkages between peacebuilding and transitional justice.[32] Thus, over the last ten years in particular there has been a push to broaden the parameters of transitional justice work to connect it up with other dimensions of peacebuilding, and to increase coordination in order to facilitate complementarity.[33] For example, arguments have been made that there should be greater linkages between transitional justice and

---

[30] Key examples include the UN's transitional justice work with regard to Cambodia and Rwanda.

[31] United Nations Security Council Resolution No. 2282, preamble.

[32] See generally, e.g., Chandra Sriram, Olga Martin-Ortega, and Johanna Herman, "Evaluating and Comparing Strategies of Peacebuilding and Transitional Justice," JAD-PbP Working Paper Series 1 (May 2009), 13 (discussing increasing linkages between transitional justice and a broader set of peacebuilding activities); Alan Bryden, Timothy Donais, and Heiner Hängi, *Shaping a Security-Governance Agenda in Post-Conflict Peacebuilding* (Geneva: DCAF, 2005) (examining policy linkages between SSR, DDR, rule-of-law initiatives, and transitional justice); see also van Zyl, "Promoting Transitional Justice," 210 (arguing that "[t]ransitional justice strategies should be understood as an important component of peacebuilding").

[33] See, e.g., Johanna Herman, Olga Martin-Ortega, and Chandra Lekha Sriram, "Beyond Justice versus Peace: Transitional Justice and Peacebuilding Strategies," in *Rethinking Peacebuilding: The Quest for Just Peace in the Middle East and the Western Balkans*, ed. Karin Aggestam and Annika Björkdahl (Milton Park: Routledge, 2013), 50 (observing the importance "to find commonalities between the transitional justice and peacebuilding processes, particularly since activities in the field often overlap").

development work,[34] anticorruption efforts,[35] security-sector reform,[36] the DDR of former combatants,[37] and other peacebuilding activities.[38] At a policy level, there are early indications that this is in fact taking place. For example, in 2006 the UN Department of Peacekeeping Operations set forth guidance encouraging greater linkages between DDR programming and transitional justice.[39] The UN has also developed guidelines noting that approaches to transitional justice should take into account "the root causes of conflict or repressive rule,"[40] an important addition to the individual accountability model that characterized many earlier transitional justice initiatives. At the same time, peacebuilding efforts have increasingly incorporated rule-of-law reform programming more generally,[41] and a growing number of humanitarian and peacebuilding organizations are framing their efforts in ways that draw upon transitional justice discourse.[42]

To a large extent, exploring coordination, complementarity, and convergence makes sense. Building peace with justice is a complex and long-term endeavor that calls for holistic solutions that address crosscutting challenges. While peacebuilding is ultimately a broader notion, both peacebuilding and transitional justice are open-ended concepts with substantial overlap that "are contrived to achieve a common purpose": long-term positive peace.[43] Both seek to rebuild social trust and social capital and attempt to address problems of governance, accountability, and

---

[34] See generally de Greiff and Duthie, *Transitional Justice and Development*; Roger Duthie, "Toward a Development-Sensitive Approach to Transitional Justice," *International Journal of Transitional Justice* 2, no. 3 (2008): 292; Rama Mani, "Dilemmas of Expanding Transitional Justice, or Forging the Nexus between Transitional Justice and Development: Editorial," *International Journal of Transitional Justice* 2, no. 3 (2008): 253.

[35] See generally Ruben Carranza, "Plunder and Pain: Should Transitional Justice Engage with Corruption and Economic Crimes?," *International Journal of Transitional Justice* 2, no. 3 (2008): 310.

[36] See generally Mayer-Rieckh and Duthie, "Enhancing Justice and Development"; Corey Barr, "Making Connections: Bridging Transitional Justice and Security Sector Reform to Confront Conflict-Related Sexual and Gender-Based Violence," *Praxis: Fletcher Journal of Human Security* 26 (2011): 5; Eirin Mobekk, *Transitional Justice and Security Sector Reform: Enabling Sustainable Peace*, Geneva Centre for the Democratic Control of Armed Forces Occasional Paper 13, November 2006.

[37] See generally Dustin Sharp, "Bridging the Gap: The United Nations Peacebuilding Commission and the Challenges of Integrating DDR and Transitional Justice," in *Transitional Justice and Peacebuilding on the Ground: Victims and Ex-Combatants*, ed. Chandra Lekha Sriram et al. (London: Routledge, 2012); Patel et al., *Disarming the Past*.

[38] See Sriram et al., "Evaluating and Comparing Strategies," 13 (discussing general linkages between transitional justice and a broad set of peacebuilding activities).

[39] United Nations Department of Peacekeeping Operations (DPKO), *Integrated Disarmament, Demobilization and Reintegration Standards (IDDRS)*, § 2.10 (DPKO 2006).

[40] United Nations, *Guidance Note of the Secretary-General: United Nations Approach to Transitional Justice*, March 2010, 7.

[41] Michael Schoiswohl, "What's Law Got to Do with It? The Role of Law in Post-conflict Democratization and Its (Flawed) Assumptions," in *Rethinking Liberal Peace: External Models and Local Alternatives*, ed. Shahrbanou Tadjbakhsh (New York: Routledge, 2011), 113.

[42] Sandra Rubli, *Transitional Justice: Justice by Bureaucratic Means?*, Swiss Peace Working Paper 4, 2012, 3–6.

[43] Gerhard Thallinger, "The UN Peacebuilding Commission and Transitional Justice," *German Law Journal* 8 (2007): 696.

the need for institutional reform. To these same ends, promoting synergies between peacebuilding and transitional justice programs and initiatives is a worthwhile goal for policy makers, academics, and practitioners alike. At the same time, together with this new enthusiasm, some have urged caution, pointing to the need to manage potentially significant tensions between peacebuilding and transitional justice projects and programs.[44] And as I explore in the following section, there are also deeper reasons to be concerned about greater coordination and convergence.

GROUNDS FOR CAUTION: (SOME) PARALLEL CRITIQUES OF PEACEBUILDING AND TRANSITIONAL JUSTICE

As postconflict peacebuilding and transitional justice have expanded, becoming more normalized, institutionalized, and legalized in the post–Cold War era, they have also been subject to trenchant critiques from academics, activists, and policy makers. What is striking is that although the programs associated with international peacebuilding assistance have historically had little connection to transitional justice initiatives, either in terms of theory or policy and practice, many of the critiques leveled against international efforts in both domains strongly echo each other. Particularly given calls for greater linkages between peacebuilding and transitional justice, these parallel critiques bear close examination.

I have grouped the critiques into three loose general categories below: the critique of liberal international peacebuilding; the critique of politics as neutral technology; and the critique of the marginalization of "the local." These groupings are not meant to be definitive, and the critiques explored below are in no way exhaustive. For some scholars, such as Roland Paris, these critiques should all be disentangled from each other and do not necessarily go hand in hand.[45] For others, many of the concerns raised below cannot be disassociated from what has become known as the critique of liberal international peacebuilding.[46] What can be fairly said is that the critiques discussed below often share substantial overlap but that the groupings nevertheless serve a useful role for purposes of discussion and analysis. Because many of these critiques have been explored in some depth in previous chapters, they will be addressed here in more summary fashion.

The Critique of Liberal International Peacebuilding

As explored in Chapter 5, the critique of liberal international peacebuilding posits that in practice, peacebuilding interventions have largely been premised on a model of liberal internationalism that conceives of market-oriented economies and

---

[44] See generally Herman, *Beyond Justice versus Peace* (discussing the potential tensions between transitional justice, rule-of-law assistance, DDR, and SSR).
[45] See Roland Paris, "Saving Liberal Peacebuilding," *Review of International Studies* 36, no. 2 (2010): 363.
[46] See generally Neil Cooper, Mandy Turner, and Michael Pugh, "The End of History and the Last Liberal Peacebuilder: A Reply to Roland Paris," *Review of International Studies* 37, no. 4 (2011): 1995.

Western-style liberal democracy as the unique pathway to peace.[47] The interventions contrived to bring about just such a liberal peace are seen to constitute a sort of modern-day *mission civilisatrice*.[48] Yet because many of the postconflict and developing countries in which peacebuilding interventions take place have a historical and cultural grounding that varies from that of the Occident, some argue that the emphasis on elections, democracy, and free markets associated with the typical package of postconflict peacebuilding interventions can be both dangerous and destabilizing.[49] The combined effects of peace operations and development assistance facilitated by liberalizing international financial institutions such as the World Bank and the International Monetary Fund may therefore be to create instability and even a return to conflict.

Applying the critique of liberal international peacebuilding to transitional justice, Chandra Sriram argues that mainstream justice strategies "share key assumptions about preferable arrangements, and a faith that other key goods – democracy, free markets, justice – can essentially stand in for, and necessarily create peace."[50] To the contrary, Sriram argues that transitional justice processes and mechanisms may, like liberal peacebuilding, destabilize postconflict and postatrocity countries because "calls for justice are likely to generate tensions and exacerbate conflicts that have the potential to undermine peacebuilding."[51] And as with the other components of liberal peacebuilding, transitional justice strategies are often rooted in Western modalities of justice imposed from the outside.[52]

While transitional justice processes have historically been linked to an emphasis on building Western-style democracies, these processes have not traditionally been associated with the push for free markets.[53] Sriram therefore notes that transitional justice might not be as subject to this aspect of the critique of liberal international peacebuilding.[54] However, it is worth recalling that, as developed in Chapter 2, trials and truth commissions around the world have tended to focus on accountability for violations of physical integrity (murder, rape, torture, disappearances) and civil and political rights more generally. Issues of economic and distributive justice and economic and social rights, on the other hand, have often been placed in the background of transitional justice practice and concern.[55] The effect has at times generated outrage over acts of physical violence conceived of as exceptional evils, while leaving the larger economic and social status quo intact, perhaps thereby obfuscating and legitimating patterns of economic violence that

---

[47] See Roland Paris, "Peacebuilding and the Limits of Liberal Internationalism," *International Security* 22, no. 2 (1997): 56.
[48] See generally Roland Paris, "International Peacebuilding and the 'Mission Civilisatrice,'" *Review of International Studies* 28, no. 4 (2002): 637.
[49] See generally Paris, *At War's End*.   [50] Sriram, "Justice as Peace?," 579.   [51] Ibid., 583.
[52] See ibid., 591.   [53] See ibid., 580.   [54] Ibid.
[55] See Zinaida Miller, "Effects of Invisibility: In Search of the 'Economic' in Transitional Justice," *International Journal of Transitional Justice* 2, no. 3 (2008): 275–76.

may be equally devastating.[56] In this sense, transitional justice has paralleled the neoliberal market orientation that is featured in the critique of liberal international peacebuilding.

Politics as Neutral Technology

A second criticism of both international peacebuilding and transitional justice that is related to but distinguishable from the critique of liberal international peacebuilding is the argument that that they are both presented as technocratic, neutral, and apolitical solutions to highly contested or contestable political issues and choices. In other words, the choice as to the modalities of better forms of governance and questions that arise out of a desire for justice (for example, justice for whom, for what, and to what ends?) are highly political choices that have important consequences for the distribution of political, economic, social, and cultural power in the postconflict context.[57] Yet, a perennial feature of the various components of postconflict peacebuilding, such as rule-of-law and democracy assistance, is that they are often imagined as fundamentally apolitical and neutral technologies – a misperception that obfuscates the difficult trade-offs that need to be made to further important postconflict objectives such as development, security, and human rights protection.[58] Thus, critics of both peacebuilding and transitional justice have argued that the fundamentally political nature of both enterprises needs to be brought to the surface.[59] In this regard, it is worth saluting that the 2016 "sustaining peace" resolutions adopted by the Security Council and General Assembly recognize that

---

[56] Dustin N. Sharp, "Addressing Economic Violence in Times of Transition: Toward a Positive-Peace Paradigm for Transitional Justice," *Fordham International Law Journal* 35 (2012): 781–82.

[57] See Nagy, "Transitional Justice as a Global Project," 280–86 (employing the categories of when, whom, and what in order to interrogate the limits of mainstreamed transitional justice).

[58] See Balakrishnan Rajagopal, "Invoking the Rule of Law in Post-Conflict Rebuilding: A Critical Examination," *William and Mary Law Review* 49 (2008): 1349 (arguing that renewed enthusiasm for building the rule of law in the postconflict context represents a "desire to escape from politics by imagining the rule of law as technical, legal, and apolitical"); Ole Sending, *Why Peacebuilders Fail to Secure Ownership and Be Sensitive to Context*, Security in Practice, NUPI Working Paper 755, 2009) (observing that the ends of liberal international peacebuilding are often imagined to be "a-historical and pre-political").

[59] See, e.g., Edward Newman, "'Liberal' Peacebuilding Debates," 42–43 (critiquing attempts to "'depoliticize' peacebuilding and present it as a technical task"); Patricia Lundy and Mark McGovern, "Whose Justice? Rethinking Transitional Justice from the Bottom Up," *Journal of Law and Society* 35, no. 2 (2008): 277 (arguing that the "rise in interventionism, based on Western conceptions of justice, has also been paralleled by reluctance on the part of many rule of law experts to acknowledge the political dimensions of such activities" and that "[e]xpressing transitional justice questions as a series of technical issues offsets this potentially troubling recognition"); Leebaw, "The Irreconcilable Goals," 98–106 (arguing that the seeming consensus as to the goals of transitional justice masks a deeper politicization and debate but that it has become difficult to assess the tensions, trade-offs, and dilemmas associated with transitional justice to the extent that they have been reconceptualized in apolitical terms).

"peacebuilding is an inherently political process."[60] How this is translated into an operational level remains to be seen.

The need to more openly assess the tensions, trade-offs, and debates that undergird peacebuilding and transitional justice interventions is all the more plain if we take seriously the notion that they serve to replicate essentially Western liberal economic and governance models. In this regard, it is important to examine the discourse of "the local" that has emerged in recent years in the critique of both peacebuilding and transitional justice.

The Marginalization of the "Local"

A third set of concerns leveled against both international peacebuilding and transitional justice broadly addresses the extent to which an appropriate balance has been struck between the "local" and the "international" in terms of agency, input, and authority over postconflict planning and programming. Concerns about striking the right balance take a number of rhetorical forms, and include the worry that postconflict agendas are "externally driven," that they are planned and implemented in a "top-down" matter, or otherwise fail to give sufficient agency to local actors with respect to core issues and choices.[61] A related concern is the extent to which mainstream peacebuilding and transitional justice initiatives are biased toward Western approaches, giving too little attention to local practices of promoting peace, justice, and reconciliation.[62] As explored in some depth in Chapter 3, at least as regards transitional justice, in recent years, exploration of the complexity of the discourse of the local has experienced renewed interest in academic and policy circles.[63] At rhetorical level at least, the importance of local or national ownership has now become a virtual UN mantra in official policy documents.[64] Yet despite all of the attention,

---

[60] United Nations Security Council Resolution No. 2282, preamble.
[61] See, e.g., Richmond, "The Romanticisation of the Local," 161–63 (discussing the tendency toward top-down institution building in a variety of "liberal" interventions); Andrieu, "Civilizing Peacebuilding," 541 (noting that "transitional justice seems to be strongly under the influence of [a] top-down state-building approach"); Sriram, "Justice as Peace?," 591 (noting that "[t]ransitional justice, and in particular trials, are frequently imported from the outside and occasionally externally imposed").
[62] See, e.g., Mac Ginty, "Indigenous Peacemaking," 144–45 (noting that Western approaches to peacebuilding "risk[] minimizing the space for organic local, traditional or indigenous contributions to peace-making"); Lambourne, "Transitional Justice and Peacebuilding," 30 (calling for a revalorization of local and cultural approaches to justice and reconciliation).
[63] See generally, for example, Timothy Donais, "Empowerment or Imposition? Dilemmas of Local Ownership in Post-Conflict Peacebuilding Processes," *Peace and Change* 34, no. 1 (2009): 3; Richmond, "The Romanticisation of the Local," 44; Simon Chesterman, "Ownership in Theory and in Practice: Transfer of Authority in UN Statebuilding Operations," *Journal of Intervention and Statebuilding* 1, no. 1 (2007): 3.
[64] See, e.g., United Nations, "The Rule of Law and Transitional Justice," ¶ 17 (arguing that the UN must "learn better how to respect and support local ownership, local leadership and a local constituency for reform"); United Nations, *Report of the Secretary General on Peacebuilding in the Immediate*

the precise meaning of the discourse of local ownership in peacebuilding remains imprecise and poorly understood.[65]

Broadly speaking, the mobilization of the concept of the local in the context of peacebuilding debates might be viewed as an argument over strategy in which context-specific solutions are pitted against a perceived standardization or a checklist approach to postconflict programming.[66] Yet the discourse of the local could also be thought of as one of resistance to the perceived hegemony of liberal international peacebuilding itself insofar as it is conceived of or forms part of a larger effort to reconstitute postconflict societies in the image of Western liberal democracies. At a deeper level, the local versus international debate might also be thought to capture one of the essential dilemmas and contradictory goals of postconflict interventions in general. That is, while such interventions must be responsive to local context, traditions, and political dynamics in order to be perceived as legitimate, they often seek to challenge and transform many of the dynamics that may have led to the conflict in the first place, which can include traditional practices and power structures.[67] Even were this not the case, in the immediate postconflict aftermath, the very local political and cultural structures that might have ordinarily served as an interface point between the local and the international have often broken down, making it that much more difficult to find the ideal balance between local and international agency. Indeed, the very notion of intervention is predicated on some idea of local failure, which may imply the need for something outside of the local to set things right again.

BUILDING LINKAGES BETWEEN PEACEBUILDING AND TRANSITIONAL JUSTICE

Peacebuilding and transitional justice efforts therefore parallel each other in many ways, ranging from shared historical and ideological origins in post–Cold War dynamics and political currents to similarities in the sharp critiques that these efforts have generated. If peacebuilding and transitional justice are in these ways "birds of a feather," this should make seeking greater coordination and complementarity all the more plausible and even natural. At the same time, given the historic "peace versus justice" frictions that continue to well up, together with the disturbing symmetry in the resistance and critique projects of liberal peacebuilding and transitional justice have managed to engender, a degree of caution is in order. With these

---

Aftermath of Conflict, UN Doc. A/63/881–S/2009/304 (2009), ¶ 7 (observing that "[t]he imperative of national ownership is a central theme of the present report").

[65] See Chesterman, "Ownership in Theory and Practice," 7–10 (reviewing the evolution of the concept of local ownership).

[66] See Lundy and McGovern, "Whose Justice?," 271 (criticizing the "one-size-fits-all" and "top-down" approaches to transitional justice).

[67] See Leebaw, "The Irreconcilable Goals of Transitional Justice," 117.

principles in mind, in this section I will explore the possibility of greater coordination between transitional justice and DDR programs. DDR has been chosen as a case study in part because it serves to vividly illustrate the possibility for both tensions and complementarity with transitional justice, together with the fact that, as a policy matter, the UN has explicitly encouraged the development of greater linkages between DDR and transitional justice.[68]

Acknowledging Both Tensions and Complementarity

Given many of the shared goals of peacebuilding and transitional justice – rebuilding social trust and social capital, addressing problems of governance and accountability, and fostering institutional reform, to name only a few – the desire to promote linkages and complementarity seems eminently sensible. And yet, a closer examination reveals that many of the traditional programmatic components of international postconflict peacebuilding have the potential to both complement and conflict with transitional justice initiatives.[69] I briefly outline here the potential for tension and complementarity between transitional justice and programs relating to the disarmament, demobilization, and reintegration of former combatants and security-sector reform more generally.

In the last twenty years, DDR programs have become a regular feature of postconflict peacebuilding.[70] Of recent peacekeeping missions, at least seven of those established by the UN Security Council included DDR in their mandate.[71] While programs vary in terms of their modalities, the basic goal of all such programs is to assure security and stability in the postconflict context by removing weapons from the hands of former combatants and helping them to integrate socially and economically into society.[72] If done well, DDR programs have the potential to contribute to the very stability that might be thought essential to getting larger development and justice initiatives off the ground. While few would therefore dispute the need for such programs, they have often been criticized for a short-term "guns for cash" approach that may shortchange some of the longer-term and more

---

[68] See *IDDRS*, § 2.1.
[69] See generally Herman, Martin-Ortega, and Sriram, *Beyond Justice versus Peace* (discussing the potential tensions between transitional justice, rule-of-law assistance, DDR, and SSR).
[70] Between 1994 and 2005, thirty-four different DDR programs were created around the world. Waldorf, "Linking DDR and Transitional Justice," 18. For a more detailed exploration of tensions and complementarities between DDR and transitional justice in broad comparative terms, see generally Chandra Lekha Sriram and Johanna Herman, "DDR and Transitional Justice: Bridging the Divide?," *Conflict, Security, and Development* 9, no. 4 (2009): 455.
[71] These are the United Nations Mission in the United Nations Assistance Mission in Sierra Leone (UNAMSIL, 1999), the Democratic Republic of Congo (MONUC, 1999), the United Nations Mission in Liberia (UNMIL, 2003), the United Nations Mission in Côte d'Ivoire (UNOCI, 2004), the United Nations Stabilization Mission in Haiti (MINUSTAH, 2004), the United Nations Operation in Burundi (UNOB, 2004), and the United Nations Mission in the Sudan (UNMIS, 2005).
[72] See *IDDRS*, § 1.2.

challenging goals of DDR, particularly the reintegration of former combatants back into the community.[73]

Despite increasingly global experience and expertise with DDR, it has been hard to overlook the disappointing results of many DDR programs, ultimately leading the UN and others to stress the need for a more "integrated" approach.[74] But while more integrated approaches sound laudable in the abstract, such efforts have the potential to create enormous challenges when dealing with fields such as DDR and transitional justice that, historically, have enjoyed few connections at the level of policy and practice.[75] The historical separation between DDR and transitional justice may in part reflect a perception that they are meant to serve different constituencies for different purposes. Thus, while transitional justice mechanisms are often viewed as victim oriented, DDR is seen to serve the needs of former perpetrators.[76] While transitional justice focuses on justice and accountability for past violations, traditional approaches to DDR focus on military and security objectives.[77]

With this backdrop in mind, it is not hard to imagine that the existence of robust accountability mechanisms might make some former combatants reluctant to come forward and lay down their arms. Moreover, to the extent that those who need to be disarmed are either embedded in state security forces or stand to be integrated into reconstituted state security forces as part of a larger SSR program, this too makes the prospects for restoration of the rule of law difficult since the very forces responsible for enforcing the law have the most to lose from the accountability measures that are part and parcel of transitional justice.[78] Beyond this, the provision of reinsertion and reintegration benefits to former combatants, a typical feature of many DDR programs, can be contrasted with the relative paucity and lack of generosity of reparations programs for victims.[79] The perception that former perpetrators

---

[73] United Nations Development Programme, *Practice Note: Disarmament, Demobilization and Reintegration of Ex-Combatants* (New York: UNDP, 2005), 18.
[74] See United Nations, *Report of the Secretary-General: Disarmament, Demobilization and Reintegration*, UN Doc. A/60/705 (2006), ¶ 9(b); Mark Knight and Alpaslan Özerdem, "Guns, Camps and Cash: Disarmament, Demobilization and Reinsertion of Former Combatants in Transitions from War to Peace," *Journal of Peace Research* 41, no. 4 (2004): 513. The felt need for better integration helped in part to spur the publication of the Integrated Disarmament, Demobilization and Reintegration Standards (IDDRS), a policy guide that sets forth best practices for DDR programming and the various ways in which it can and should be linked with other postconflict programmatic areas, including transitional justice. See generally *IDDRS*.
[75] See Waldorf, "Linking DDR and Transitional Justice," 16.
[76] The victim/perpetrator distinction can be problematic in several respects, particularly in the context of DDR where many former combatants are both perpetrators and victims at the same time. See Luisa Maria Dietrich Ortega, "Transitional Justice and Female Ex-Combatants: Lessons Learned from International Experience," in *Disarming the Past*, 169.
[77] Kimberly Theidon, "Transitional Subjects: The Disarmament, Demobilization and Reintegration of Former Combatants in Colombia," *International Journal of Transitional Justice* 1, no. 1 (2007): 69.
[78] Herman, *Beyond Justice versus Peace*.
[79] See Eric Witte, "Beyond 'Peace versus Justice': Understanding the Relationship between DDR Programs and the Prosecution of International Crimes," in *Disarming the Past*, 96.

are being rewarded for bad behavior while former victims are left to fend for themselves could ultimately make reintegration and reconciliation initiatives all the more difficult.[80]

Taken together, there is ample potential for tension between DDR programs and transitional justice initiatives. However, despite the potential to work at cross-purposes, DDR programs and transitional justice mechanisms also share common goals, including trust building, prevention of renewed violence, and reconciliation.[81] In terms of furthering these common goals, there are a number of areas of potential complementarity, particularly as regards the reintegration component of DDR programs. For example, while there is some evidence to suggest that parallel DDR and transitional justice initiatives might decrease former combatants willingness to come forward and engage in truth-telling and reconciliation activities, it can also be argued that sending a strong public signal that only the "big fish" will be put on trial might allow victims to feel justice is being done, while at the same time making it clear that most combatants were not among the worst offenders and can be reconciled to their community.[82] Beyond community-level reconciliation, which will be discussed in more detail in the next section, building stronger linkages between DDR and transitional justice would likely involve a greater focus on human rights vetting to ensure that abusive former combatants are not channeled into reconstituted security services.[83] This mechanism, along with other accountability mechanisms, could ultimately enhance the credibility and legitimacy of the new forces, while at the same time lowering the chances of recurrence of abuses by the reformed security forces, even if the potential for some short-term frictions cannot be eliminated.[84]

SSR is a process that could be thought to include DDR but which is at the same time much broader and more comprehensive. While definitions of SSR vary in scope, the UN generally understands it to comprise efforts to promote "effective

---

[80] See generally Jeremy Ginifer, "Reintegration of Ex-Combatants," in *Sierra Leone: Building the Road to Recovery*, ed. Mark Malan et al. (Pretoria: Institute for Security Studies, 2003), 39.

[81] According to one UN definition, the aims of transitional justice include ensuring accountability, serving justice, achieving reconciliation, and preventing human rights violations in the future. See United Nations, "The Rule of Law and Transitional Justice," ¶ 4. The IDDRS similarly underscores the centrality of DDR programs to preventing renewed violence, encouraging trust and confidence, and reconciliation. See *IDDRS*, § 1.2.

[82] In Sierra Leone, for example, the Special Court for Sierra Leone's outreach efforts included activities targeting ex-combatants to explain the meaning of the phrase those "who bear the greatest responsibility" for crimes within its mandate. The purpose of these efforts was to dispel rumors that the court intended to indict every fighter, from top to bottom. See Mohamed Gibril Sesay and Mohamed Suma, *Transitional Justice and DDR: The Case of Sierra Leone* (New York: ICTJ, 2009), 18–19.

[83] See Mobekk, *Transitional Justice and Security Sector Reform*, 68–71 (discussing the role of vetting in conducting reform of military forces, police services, the judiciary, intelligence services, and the governance sector).

[84] See ibid., 18 (discussing the role of SSR and transitional justice in engendering trust in critical state institutions).

and accountable security for the State and its peoples without discrimination and with full respect for human rights and the rule of law."[85] Similar to DDR programs, there exists a significant potential for tension between SSR programs and transitional justice initiatives.[86] The potential for conflict between members of the security sector, who risk possibly being downsized or excluded through vetting procedures, and transitional justice, which seeks to promote accountability and truth-telling for abusive members of those same security forces, is fairly straightforward and obvious. At the same time, without security and stability, accountability mechanisms associated with transitional justice will have difficulty functioning. Thus, the basic tension between the felt needs of stability and security on the one hand, and the exigencies of accountability and human rights on the other, renders the already complicated task of reforming or reconstituting the security sector all the more challenging. Perhaps in part due to this potential for tension, SSR and transitional justice "rarely interact, either in practice or in theory."[87]

Despite these tensions, it would be difficult to foster effective and accountable security "with full respect for human rights and the rule of law"[88] without some attention to issues of past abuses and impunity. In particular, attention to these issues through both transitional justice and SSR mechanisms has the potential to provide a much-needed sense of legitimacy for formerly abusive security forces.[89] This, together with other potential avenues of complementarity, has given rise to a small but growing literature exploring the possibility of a "justice-sensitive" approach to SSR that would include, among other things, more robust human rights training and vetting.[90] Thus, as with DDR, building better linkages between SSR and transitional justice could ultimately promote trust building, prevention of renewed violence, and reconciliation.

As defined by some global institutions, the "security sector" extends well beyond traditional security actors like the police and the military to management and oversight bodies, broader justice, and rule-of-law institutions and nonstatutory security forces.[91] It is particularly in this broader conception of security-sector reform, with its inclusion of the judicial sector and access to justice, that the potentially positive linkages between SSR and transitional justice might be more apparent. Therefore,

---

[85] See United Nations, *Securing Peace and Development: The Role of the United Nations in Supporting Security Sector Reform*, UN Doc. A/62/559-S/2008/39, ¶ 17 (January 23, 2008).
[86] See Herman et al., *Beyond Justice versus Peace*, 15.
[87] Mayer-Rieckh and Duthie, "Enhancing Justice and Development," 222.
[88] United Nations, *Securing Peace and Development*, ¶ 17.
[89] Herman et al., *Beyond Justice versus Peace*, 15–16.
[90] See, e.g., Mayer-Rieckh and Duthie, "Enhancing Justice and Development," 215; Barr, "Making Connections: Bridging Transitional Justice and Security Sector Reform," 5; Mobekk, *Transitional Justice and Security Sector Reform*, 1–7; Laura Davis, *Justice-Sensitive Security System Reform in the Democratic Republic of the Congo* (New York: Initiative for Peacebuilding, 2009), 24–26.
[91] Organization for Economic Cooperation and Development, *OECD DAC Handbook on Security System Reform: Supporting Security and Justice* (Paris: OECD, 2007), 5.

while not always thought of as being part of SSR, programs that ensure access to justice, particularly access to justice for those abused by security forces, could be one way of fostering accountability long term, and maintaining sustained "bottom-up" pressure for reform on the security sector as a whole.[92]

Building Linkages through the Lens of Critique

The potential for both conflict and complementarity between transitional justice and peacebuilding initiatives highlights the need for coordination sufficient to mitigate tensions and promote positive overlaps. Indeed, recognition of the need to promote coherence and integration while avoiding the fragmented and duplicative approaches of the past helped in part to inspire the creation of the Peacebuilding Commission (PBC) in 2005. The many challenges associated with building peace and justice in the postconflict context call for holistic solutions that address crosscutting challenges. For these reasons, this chapter has taken it as a starting point that promoting synergies between peacebuilding and transitional justice programs and initiatives is a worthwhile goal. At the same time, despite the seemingly unobjectionable nature of appeals for greater coordination, more integrated approaches to peace and justice issues in the postconflict context may also create problems and challenges of their own.

To begin, the UN's historic track record on coordination leaves ample room for improvement, and assessments of the PBC's ability to promote more integrated approaches to complex and multidimensional peacebuilding challenges have not been optimistic.[93] Further complicating the task of coordination is the fact that postconflict peacebuilding is a large and multifaceted task, with key roles being played by a variety of actors. Though this chapter has focused largely on the UN, the larger postconflict peacebuilding picture also includes actors over which the PBC has no direct authority, ranging from the World Bank and key bilateral donors such as the United States, the European Union, and Japan to national governments, civil society actors, and various local constituencies. Getting actors both in and outside of the UN system to work toward more integrated approaches to postconflict peacebuilding is an enormous task, especially given the stovepiping, overlapping mandates, and bureaucratic territorialism that have plagued such efforts in the past.[94] Of course,

---

[92] For a review of the potential for "bottom-up" access to justice initiatives to effect larger rule-of-law reforms, see generally Stephen Golub, "The Rule of Law and the UN Peacebuilding Commission: A Social Development Approach," *Cambridge Review of International Affairs* 20, no. 1 (2007): 47.

[93] See United Nations, *Review of the United Nations Peacebuilding Architecture*, UN Doc. A/64/868–S/2010/393 (2010), ¶ 57–59.

[94] See Herman et al., *Beyond Justice versus Peace*, 17 (observing that improving connections between peacebuilding and transitional justice requires a level of coordination that large bureaucracies are not very good at).

coordination difficulties stem not only from the magnitude of the task or difficulties of communication among all of the various players, but also because of underlying disagreements and uncertainties as to how to best accomplish peacebuilding objectives in the first place.[95]

Second, beyond the inherent challenges of large-scale coordination itself, there is a danger of over-standardization and bureaucratization as best practices for the coordination of transitional justice and peacebuilding initiatives are taken up by the global institutions associated with postconflict peacebuilding and development assistance that have the tendency to operate through standardized templates.[96] It has been argued that as transitional justice practices have spread around the world, they have done so not necessarily by adapting themselves de novo to each new context, but through a process of "acculturation" whereby a dominant script or practice is replicated again and again as a result of repeated information exchanges and consultations.[97] Once a dominant paradigm or script develops, modifying that script to suit new conditions or circumstances can be extremely challenging.[98] In the context of internationally driven peacebuilding initiatives more generally, the existence of "set templates" and a "formulaic path" has similarly been observed.[99] Given these tendencies, there is reason to worry that – notwithstanding paeans to national ownership and context-appropriate solutions – as transitional justice is mainstreamed into emerging best practices for postconflict reconstruction, transitional justice initiatives will come to be seen as yet another item on the "postconflict checklist," a mechanistic part of the template deployed in the context of postconflict peace operations.[100] That postconflict peacebuilding and transitional justice initiatives have frequently been criticized for being planned and implemented in a top-down, externally driven, and Western-biased manner, only serves to highlight the concern of standardization.

---

[95] See Roland Paris, "Understanding the 'Coordination Problem' in Postwar Statebuilding," in *The Dilemmas of Statebuilding: Confronting the Contradictions of Postwar Peace Operations*, ed. Roland Paris and Timothy D. Sisk (Milton Park: Routledge, 2009), 72.

[96] As Roland Paris has argued, this is particularly true insofar as efforts at coordination give impetus to centripetal forces in policy making. See ibid., 62.

[97] James Cavallaro and Sebastián Albuja, "The Lost Agenda: Economic Crimes and Truth Commissions in Latin America and Beyond," in *Transitional Justice from Below: Grassroots Activism and the Struggle for Change*, ed. Kieran McEvoy and Lorna McGregor (Portland: Hart, 2008), 125.

[98] See ibid.

[99] See Sending, "Why Peacebuilders Fail to Secure Ownership and Be Sensitive to Context," 7 (observing that "international organizations, such as the UN and the World Bank, are bureaucratic organizations that operate through standardized templates").

[100] See Elizabeth Stanley, "Transitional Justice: From the Local to the International," in *The Ashgate Research Companion to Ethics and International Relations*, ed. Patrick Hayden (Farnham: Ashgate, 2009), 276 (observing that, together with other international interventions, "transitional justice practices have commonly become part of a longer list of 'tickboxes' to attain peace and security").

Third, as explored earlier in this chapter, international peacebuilding programs, as well as a number of transitional justice initiatives, have frequently been subject to powerful, parallel critiques, including the critique of liberal international peacebuilding, the critique of politics as neutral technology, and concerns about striking the right balance between the local and the international in postconflict programming. Considered together with the danger of over-standardization, there is reason to worry that better integration and coordination between peacebuilding and transitional justice, especially insofar as it is carried out by the large bureaucracies traditionally associated with postconflict assistance, might actually exacerbate some of the tendencies that have given rise to these parallel critiques rather than alleviate them. At a minimum, given historic patterns, there is no reason to think that simply linking peacebuilding and transitional justice, without more, will do anything to counter these tendencies. With this perspective in mind, as scholars, practitioners, and policy makers begin to take a greater interest in sounding out potential linkages, viewing transitional justice and peacebuilding overlaps through the prism of the critiques and concerns outlined in this chapter should prove instructive. Attentiveness to some of the parallel critiques and concerns that have been raised could lead to shifts that would strengthen policy in both areas in the process of promoting linkages.

Ultimately, promoting linkages that reflect a cognizance of critique might involve more hybridized forms of peacebuilding and transitional justice that involve a mixture of conventional and local practices and models.[101] For example, as previously discussed, DDR programs and transitional justice initiatives have the potential to both conflict with and complement each other, and careful coordination is called for if synergies are to be exploited. One of the areas where DDR programs have had the least amount of success is in the community reintegration element, sometimes known as the forgotten "R" of DDR, or the "the weakest link in the DDR chain."[102] This is an area where the reconciliation components of transitional justice initiatives might serve as a potential bridge, strengthening both DDR and transitional justice goals in the process.[103] The potential use of local ritual and tradition in facilitating reconciliation generally and the reintegration of former combatants specifically might be one way of building linkages between transitional

---

[101] See Newman et al., "Introduction," 16.
[102] Sami Faltas, *DDR without Camps: The Need for Decentralized Approaches: Topical Chapter of the Conversion Survey* (Bonn: International Center for Conversion, 2005), 1; see also Macartan Humphreys and Jeremy M. Weinstein, "Demobilization and Reintegration," *Journal of Conflict Resolution* 51, no. 4 (2007): 549 (concluding that combatants who did not participate in DDR were reintegrated as successfully as those who did).
[103] For a longer elaboration of this argument, see Sharp, "Bridging the Gap," 34–36. For an exploration of the application of local ritual in the context of the reintegration of former child combatants, see Roger Duthie and Irma Specht, "DDR, Transitional Justice, and the Reintegration of Former Child Combatants," in *Disarming the Past*, 207–10.

justice and DDR programs that gives deference to the critiques and concerns that have in the past plagued both fields (including that they are Western-biased and externally driven).[104] Such approaches to reintegration have seen limited but intriguing use in Sierra Leone and Mozambique.[105] Similarly, in East Timor, a postconflict community reconciliation process combined aspects of arbitration and mediation grounded in local ritual in bringing former perpetrators and combatants into dialogue with their estranged communities and victims.[106] In the future, it might be possible for coordinating bodies like the PBC to encourage the use of local ritual and tradition to bridge the gap between DDR and transitional justice. This could, of course, be a difficult needle to thread since too much international involvement in such affairs might be seen to co-opt or corrupt the authenticity of local practices. Nevertheless, the PBC could play a helpful role even if only to brief local constituencies as to the range of local ritual that has been successfully used in other contexts.

A CALL TO FURTHER EXPLORATION

This chapter has explored but one example of what building creative linkages between peacebuilding and transitional justice might look like. There are other possibilities ripe for exploration. One such example might be the use of "bottom-up" approaches to rule-of-law assistance that attempt to effect reforms though grassroots legal empowerment.[107] Another could be more comprehensive approaches to transitional justice and SSR programs that give greater emphasis to accountability for economic crimes and economic violence perpetrated in the course of the conflict. Additional possibilities that would cut against the grain of long-standing critiques of transitional justice and peacebuilding need to be developed by academics, practitioners, and policy makers going forward.

As has been suggested, building linkages in creative ways that avoid the superficiality of simple "information sharing" between bureaucratic agents responsible for their respective programs; eschew one-size-fits-all approaches; and manage to cut against the grain of the historical critiques that have been leveled against both peacebuilding and transitional justice will be far from easy. Indeed, genuinely addressing

---

[104] Ministry of Foreign Affairs Sweden, *Stockholm Initiative on DDR*, Final Report 30, Stockholm, March 2006; see also Theidon, "Transitional Subjects," 90.
[105] See generally Roger Duthie, "Local Justice and Reintegration Processes as Complements to Transitional Justice and DDR," in *Disarming the Past*.
[106] See generally Patrick Burgess, "A New Approach to Restorative Justice: East Timor's Community Reconciliation Process," in *Transitional Justice in the Twenty-First Century*, ed. Naomi Roht-Arriaza and Javier Mariezcurrena (Cambridge: Cambridge University Press, 2006).
[107] See generally Golub, "The Rule of Law and the UN Peacebuilding Commission."

some of the historic critiques may cast doubt upon the prospects of more coordinated approaches to postconflict peacebuilding altogether. The types of locally owned, context-specific and bottom-up solutions frequently advocated in the literature may take us beyond the "postconflict checklist," but they also call into question the role of international organizations and international standards that are typically part and parcel of international postconflict assistance. On this note, I will explore visions of more "radical" or emancipatory transitional justice in the following chapter.

7

Toward a More Emancipatory Foundation for Transitional Justice

This book began by examining transitional justice foundations, with a particular focus on some of the cracks that have developed as those foundations – based largely on atrocity justice and (neo)liberal democracy building – have been questioned over time. Such an examination inevitably raises questions as to potential alternative visions and foundations for the future. In recent years, the increasingly close association between transitional justice and postconflict peacebuilding has called upon us to ask what it might mean to go beyond the type of coordination discussed in Chapter 6, and to more fundamentally (re)conceptualize the field of transitional justice itself as a form of peacebuilding. Answering this question in ways that go beyond the loose sloganeering of "no peace without justice" is no easy task. What, if any, difference might such a paradigm shift make in terms of theory, policy, and practice? Could a "transitional-justice-as-peacebuilding" paradigm prove more emancipatory than what came before, furthering long-term goals of social justice and positive peace? Might it help to remedy some of the deficits of the dominant script and shake up calcified mental maps?

Much of the answer to these questions depends on what we mean by "transition," by "justice," and by "peacebuilding." In the abstract at least, it seems clear that such concepts can be marshaled in ways that are both limiting and expansive; ways that can empower but also obfuscate hierarchies of power and further perpetuate inequalities. And yet as quasi-hegemonic global projects, both transitional justice and peacebuilding have come to take on an aura of naturalness and inevitability that can make it difficult to imagine something that goes beyond dominant understandings. After all, it might be said, how else should one respond to mass atrocities if not through the mechanisms of transitional justice? And how should the "international community" respond to violent intrastate conflict and civil war if not through traditional peacebuilding initiatives? Thus, if transitional justice has its own "toolbox," said to include, among other things, prosecutions, truth-telling, vetting and dismissals, and reparations, perhaps it can simply be subsumed into the larger post-conflict peacebuilding template without much more ado.

In previous chapters, I have therefore sought to deconstruct some of the assumptions undergirding these global projects in an attempt to disrupt the sense of normalcy that has accrued. In Chapter 2, for example, I questioned the notion that the "justice" of transitional justice should be limited to legal and atrocity justice for physical violence. In Chapter 4, I questioned the idea that "transition" should necessarily be understood as a narrow, democratic (neo)liberal teleology. And in Chapter 6, I cautioned against conflating "peacebuilding" with what has come to be known as "liberal international peacebuilding" (LIPB). Taken together, these chapters have suggested that dominant understandings of "transition," "justice," and "peacebuilding" are problematic building blocks with which to construct a better foundation for transitional justice in the future.

Previous chapters have also sought to set into relief the remarkable symmetries that that LIPB and transitional justice have exhibited over the last twenty-five years: symmetry in terms ideological and political origins; symmetry in terms of patterns and trajectories of practice; and symmetry in terms of the critiques and resistance they have generated. As I have argued, all of this should make us wary of any emerging "transitional-justice-as-peacebuilding" narrative. There are ample grounds to be skeptical that simply subsuming transitional justice into the broader field of peacebuilding will lead to greater "peace" or "justice" in the broader or even narrower senses of those terms.

And yet despite this, transitional justice and LIPB appear to be on a path of gradual association if not convergence.[1] The question then becomes whether we can hope for something better than a simple elision of mainstream transitional justice and LIPB. That is, if dominant understandings of peacebuilding are a poor foundation on which to generate a more emancipatory transitional justice project, what are the alternatives? It turns out that this is a surprisingly hard question to answer given the dominance of the LIPB model and the paucity of operational alternative paradigms "on the ground." Nevertheless, this chapter will focus on concepts from critical peacebuilding theory that do more than analyze and deconstruct LIPB, but which offer a glimpse of what it might mean to go beyond LIPB in practice.[2] While such concepts do not furnish a ready-made blueprint for action, they nevertheless provide pointers and insights that can help to reorient thinking and practice for both

---

[1] This does not, of course, mean that transitional justice has yet been embraced as a "core pillar" of mainstream liberal international peacebuilding. As McAuliffe notes, UN rhetoric may often outshine reality in this regard. See Padraig McAuliffe, "The Marginality of Transitional Justice within Liberal Peacebuilding: Causes and Consequences," *Journal of Human Rights Practice* 9, no. 1 (2017). Nevertheless, even if transitional justice remains marginal to the thinking of some peacebuilders, the emerging shifts in rhetoric, policy, and practice remain significant.

[2] By using the phrase "critical peacebuilding theory," I am not referring to any unitary school of thought. Rather, I use the phrase as a sort of shorthand umbrella term to refer to groups scholars of peacebuilding whose tone, methods, and approach generally mirror that of "critical studies" approaches familiar to many in the legal and justice communities such as the "critical legal studies"

peacebuilding and transitional justice in useful ways. In this, they might also serve as a bulwark against simple elision of transitional justice and LIPB and offer some hope for the construction of a more emancipatory "transitional-justice-as-peacebuilding" project.

The first step in imagining such a project, I will argue, is to (re)orient transitional justice thinking and praxis around the broad goal of progressively achieving "positive peace" over time. While positive peace is a broad and abstract notion, it provides a goal that is more holistic, open-textured, and contextually adaptable than classic transitional justice goals of atrocity justice and the facilitation of (neo)liberal democracy. In this, it might plausibly serve as the foundation for a global project where *global* is not a simple byword for *Northern* or *Western*. To avoid the potential for cooptation or being watered down, the concept of positive peace should be conjugated with several other concepts from critical peacebuilding theory – including "popular peace," "the everyday," and "hybridity." These concepts serve as useful correctives to the historically narrow assumptions that have dominated both peacebuilding and transitional justice, and give greater content to the question of *how* transitional justice should be used to pursue positive peace.

At the same time – and to be clear – concepts from critical peacebuilding theory do not require some kind of illiberal peacebuilding or that we jettison liberalism and the establishment of liberal principles as one of the goals of transitional justice. These concepts do, however, call into question our ability to privilege and sustain narrow, neoliberal understandings of "justice," "transition," and "peacebuilding" for one and all. Liberalism is a broad canvass, and the recovery of alternative liberalisms will be an important part of building a stronger foundation for transitional justice going forward. I will offer the idea of "liberal localism" as one potential means of threading constructs from critical peacebuilding theory together, and of shifting the center of gravity of transitional justice going forward.

POSITIVE PEACE

Originally developed by peace theorist Johan Galtung, the concept of "positive peace" is perhaps most easily understood in contrast with the notion of "negative peace."[3] A negative peace would be one what involves the absence of direct physical

---

movement of the late twentieth century together with so-called Third World Approaches to International Law (TWAIL) scholarship. While quite diverse, a common thread between these streams of scholarship is that they generally attempt to bring to the surface the politics and ideological assumptions of regimes and practices that are often presented as technocratic, apolitical, and nonideological and to examine the implicit trade-offs and distributional consequences that often go undiscussed. Some influential contributors to critical peacebuilding theory are more moderate, some more radical, but all have generally labored to the aforementioned ends. Representative scholars include Timothy Donais, Roger Mac Ginty, Edward Newman, Roland Paris, Oliver Richmond, and many others.

[3] See generally Johan Galtung, "Violence, Peace, and Peace Research," *Peace Research* 6, no. 3 (1969): 167.

violence, but little more. A ceasefire or peace agreement may have been signed and the shooting stopped, but society may still be wracked with racial and religious animus, systemic discrimination, radical economic inequality, poverty, pervasive corruption, marginalization, and exploitation of women, children, and minority groups, and so on. In other words, open combat has halted, but many of the flashpoints for future armed conflict likely remain. Far from being a hypothetical, this is the typical situation in nearly all countries in the immediate wake of conflict. From Guatemala and Liberia to Côte d'Ivoire and Cambodia, the postconflict landscape is often a virtual pockmarked moonscape of problems that need to be addressed if renewed conflict is to be averted.[4]

In contrast, a positive peace would be one where many of the aforementioned problems are comparatively absent. The concept of positive peace therefore helps to capture the idea that violence can be both direct and indirect, and that structural and economic violence do real harm and can even lay the groundwork for a return to conflict.[5] Even a moment's reflection makes clear that the goal of positive peace sets a very high bar, and one that few if any societies have fully achieved. After all, even many consolidated liberal democracies are rife with problems of marginalization, discrimination, radical inequality, and so on.[6] Considering the challenges and the limitations of transitional justice and peacebuilding practice as we have thus far known them, it would perhaps be tempting to fall back on thinner notions of "good enough justice" or "good enough peace" (echoing Merliee Grindle's idea of "good enough governance") in defense of much more limited and modest projects.[7] At the same time, if we think of "justice" as a broad social project and a condition in society[8] – not where everything is perfect – but where earnest and good faith efforts are being made by citizens, civil society and government to "progressively realize"[9]

---

[4] For these reasons, perhaps it is unsurprising that a significant number of conflicts reignite only a few years after their apparent cessation. Paul Collier once famously argued that over 50 percent of civil wars reignite within a period of five years of their supposed settlement.

[5] For more on this point, see generally Dustin Sharp (ed.), *Justice and Economic Violence in Transition* (New York: Springer, 2014).

[6] On this point there is perhaps no better example than the United States, which continues to struggle with radical and widening inequality, systemic racism, pervasive inequities in its criminal justice system, and marginalization of various minority groups well over 200 years after its first democratic elections. See, e.g., Human Rights Watch, "United States," in *World Report 2016* (New York: HRW, 2016), 609.

[7] See generally Merilee Grindle, "Good Enough Governance Revisited," *Development Policy Review* 25, no. 5 (2007): 533–74.

[8] See David Kennedy, "The International Human Rights Regime: Still Part of the Problem?," in *Examining Critical Perspectives on Human Rights*, ed. Rob Dickinson et al. (Cambridge: Cambridge University Press, 2012), 25.

[9] In choosing the phrase "progressively realize," I am of course echoing one of the standards for state-based duties under the International Covenant on Economic, Social, and Cultural Rights. See International Covenant on Economic, Social, and Cultural Rights, opened for signature December 16, 1966, 993 UNTS 3 (1978), Art. 2. Under the ICESCR, governments are required to do the maximum possible to achieve economic and social rights based on the resources available at any given time,

positive peace, then the journey toward positive peace may be as important as the destination. In this, transitional justice can and should play and important role in moving the ball forward.

As developed in previous chapters, the bedrock foundations of transitional justice are grounded in the twin goals of legal accountability and the facilitation of (neo)liberal political transitions. In this, the field has clearly aspired to do more than establish mere negative peace, but can be thought of as having worked toward a degree of positive peace. At the same time, the heavy focus on atrocity justice and physical violence to the exclusion of all else is not consonant with the more expansive vision of positive peace expounded by Galtung, which is intimately bound up with considerations of social and distributive justice.[10] In this way, explicitly reorienting transitional justice theory and practice around the goal of facilitating a more robust, Galtungian positive peace would involve more holistic sets of objectives, and would represent a broadening and a loosening of earlier paradigms and moorings, consistent with a fuller panoply of human rights.[11] Under this paradigm, the conception of justice shifts from "justice for transition" and "justice for atrocities" to "justice for positive peace." Grounding the field in such a conception would be a first step in helping to push past the boundaries of mainstream transitional justice and liberal international peacebuilding.

To elaborate in more detail, anchoring the field of transitional justice in the concept of positive peace could potentially have at least four specific, positive effects.

First, it would likely broaden the approach from a relatively narrow and legalistic one focused on physical violence and civil and political rights to one that would also grapple, where appropriate, with the socioeconomic underpinnings of conflict, including various forms of economic violence.[12] A paradigm shift in the direction of positive peace would not dictate a "thick" or "thin" approach to economic violence in transition, or even ensure that economic violence would be addressed at all. As with all transitional justice mechanisms and modalities, the needs and limits of the context would have to be considered. Depending on the context, addressing economic violence might not always be necessary, or even desirable. As Chandra Lekha Sriram argues, simply presuming that more justice necessarily generates or

---

with no backsliding. While the so-called right to peace has never been widely embraced by global powers, the progressive realization standard might be one way to make it more palatable to some. See generally Jeanne Woods, "Theorizing Peace as a Human Right," *Human Rights & International Legal Discourse* 7 (2013): 178.

[10] Galtung, "Violence, Peace, and Peace Research," 183.

[11] In effect, embracing positive peace would involve an emphasis on both civil and political as well as economic and social rights. This could be achieved though a more legalistic lens, with accountability for violations of the key representative legal covenants, or less legalistically through a focus on broader concepts of social justice. See International Covenant on Civil and Political Rights, opened for signature December 16, 1966, 999 UNTS 171 (1978); International Covenant on Economic, Social, and Cultural Rights.

[12] See generally Sharp, *Justice and Economic Violence in Transition*.

equates to more peace is potentially problematic.[13] The point, however, is that starting from the lens of positive peace calls upon one to examine whether the roots and drivers of the conflict suggest a need to address facets of economic violence through the modalities of transitional justice. In this, it would be a more searching and open-ended departure point than has been the case in the past.

Second, as the achievement of positive peace is a long-term endeavor, the notion of justice for positive peace implies that justice-oriented projects, even those formally relating to the past, should not be seen as an event that takes place primarily during a narrow window of opportunity immediately after conflict, but a process that will necessarily continue for many years. As discussed in Chapter 4, this has been amply clear in countries such as Argentina and Chile where vigorous victim and civil society coalitions have doggedly pursued transitional justice goals for decades after the immediate cessation of conflict. In many other societies, however, there has been a tendency for such efforts to slip into political oblivion after an initial burst of transitional justice activity. The critical questions during the immediate transitional period then relate to sequencing and how to kick-start this longer-term transitional process in ways that will be sustainable, even after international funding and interest have moved on. Along similar lines, the pursuit of positive peace suggests the need for preventative strategies that look beyond the confines of an unspecified political transition. In doing so, transitional justice mechanisms may be conceptualized more holistically to blend with ongoing development and peacebuilding initiatives associated with postconflict reconstruction, and may potentially be marshaled in an effort to address the *ongoing* violence and criminality that is typically associated with postconflict situations.[14] It is certainly an irony, for example, to focus almost exclusively on justice for conflict-related gender-based violence in a postconflict context where levels of sexual and domestic violence remain highly elevated.[15]

Third, because positive peace is a destination never fully arrived at, it means that even consolidated liberal democracies are not "off the hook" when it comes to grappling with historic injustices. Whether it focuses on justice for slavery and genocide against Indigenous peoples in North America or abuses under a recent dictatorship in North Africa, transitional justice could have a very important role to play. As discussed in Chapter 4, this of course requires us to conceptualize "transition" in ways

---

[13] Chandra Lekha Sriram, "Justice as Peace? Liberal Peacebuilding and Strategies of Transitional Justice," *Global Society* 21, no. 4 (2007): 580.

[14] For a more detailed look at potential connections between transitional justice and development, see generally Roger Duthie, "Toward a Development-Sensitive Approach to Transitional Justice," *International Journal of Transitional Justice* 2, no. 3 (2008): 292 (arguing that transitional justice measures should be designed and implemented in a way that focuses on a synergistic links between transitional justice and development); Pablo de Greiff and Roger Duthie (eds.), *Transitional Justice and Development: Making Connections* (New York: Social Science Research Council, 2009) (discussing the issues and considerations arising from the connection between transitional justice and development).

[15] See generally Doris Buss et al. (eds.), *Sexual Violence in Conflict and Post-Conflict Societies: International Agendas and African Contexts* (New York: Routledge, 2014).

that go beyond a narrow transition from war to (negative) peace or to liberal democracy. In opening to these possibilities, transitional justice becomes more of a truly global project that calls upon all societies to look in the mirror, and not a project that is seen as something for the "backward rest" rather than the liberal West.

Fourth, and finally, the notion of justice for positive peace suggests that the determination of the modalities and mechanisms of transitional justice should be grounded in a context-based inquiry into the particular roots and drivers of the conflict in question. This stands in contrast to a package of mechanisms drawn from a toolbox of "best practices"[16] with some sort of predetermined political endpoint, be it elections, democracy, or locking perpetrators up in jail. For example, Paige Arthur has speculated that while many of the dominant themes and responses to violence of mainstream transitional justice evolved out of the Latin American experience, these responses might not be optimal for countries with "different histories, cultures, and positions within the world economy."[17] Many countries in Africa with a history of neopatrimonial government, corruption, and very weak state institutions, she notes, might need to focus on a different set of issues through a different set of mechanisms.[18] While the denunciation of templates and one-size-fits-all solutions is a common theme in the academic and policy literature,[19] the LIPB paradigm with its implicit assumptions about what peace looks like and how it must be generated, often tends to bias practice toward the very cookie-cutter practices which are so often decried. Focusing on positive peace as the ultimate goal of the mechanisms of transitional justice could be one way to refocus attention on the context-specific interventions needed to move in that direction.

To be clear, the benefit of the positive-peace paradigm is not that it offers a goal more precise or less subject to being co-opted than "democracy," "accountability," "reconciliation," or the "rule of law," the historic pivots of transitional justice. In the end, these may all be "essentially contested concepts."[20] At the same time, because the very core import of the concept of positive peace calls upon one to attend to a broader set of concerns than has historically been the practice of both liberal international peacebuilding and mainstream transitional justice, it offers a better

---

[16] On so-called best practices, see generally Warren Feek, "Best of Practices?," *Development in Practice* 17 (2007): 653 (arguing that "best practices" tend to promote an undesirable uniformity and bias interventions toward the global rather than the local).

[17] Paige Arthur, "How 'Transitions' Reshaped Human Rights: A Conceptual History of Transitional Justice," *Human Rights Quarterly* 31, no. 2 (2009): 360.

[18] Ibid., 361.

[19] See, e.g., Roger Mac Ginty, "Indigenous Peace-Making versus the Liberal Peace," *Cooperation and Conflict: Journal of the Nordic Studies Association* 43, no. 2 (2008): 144 (observing the existence of "set templates" and a "formulaic path" in internationally sponsored peacebuilding); Ole Sending, *Why Peacebuilders Fail to Secure Ownership and Be Sensitive to Context*, Security in Practice, NUPI Working Paper 755, 2009, 7.

[20] Christine Bell, "Transitional Justice, Interdisciplinarity and the State of the 'Field' or 'Non-Field,'" *International Journal of Transitional Justice* 3, no. 1 (2009): 27.

starting point than existing paradigms for developing a more holistic and emancipatory vision.

CRITICAL THEORIES OF PEACEBUILDING

In attempting to ground the field of transitional justice in a paradigm of positive peace, it will be important to be wary of limiting constructions in which the notion of positive peace is simply reshaped to fit and support existing practices and paradigms. It would be very easy for the United Nations, for example, to develop an index of indicators for positive peace – perhaps echoing the Millennium Development Goals – together with a rote checklist of interventions thought best to boost those indicators. This is, after all, how most large bureaucracies operate, trundling over a variety of postconflict landscapes with the same elephantine footprints. The most likely scenario, in this case, would be a conflation of positive peace with the goals of liberal international peacebuilding (LIPB). After all, liberal peacebuilders, like transitional justice professionals, are surely working to establish more than negative peace. And yet liberal peacebuilding, with its faith in market economies and Western-style liberal democracy as the unique pathway to peace is a far cry from the more robust, Galtungian, and context-specific positive peace approach described above.[21]

While LIPB is therefore a dubious foundation for any emerging transitional justice narrative – and carries with it the potential to eclipse a goal of genuine positive peace – a key challenge has been that the sharpest critics of LIPB have tended to be long on critique and short on concrete alternatives. Thus, if LIPB does not involve the type of positive peace we are looking for, one might ask, then what does? At the end of the day, the liberal international peacebuilding model remains mainstream and dominant, and there is as yet no full-fledged, rival paradigm.[22] However, even if they do not provide a comprehensive solution, there are concepts from critical peacebuilding theory – including "popular peace," "the everyday," and "hybridity" that can serve as possible correctives to help address some of the more problematic aspects of the narrow LIPB model that has been the subject of such sustained critique, while providing additional clarity when it comes to how one should pursue the positive peace to which transitional justice should aspire. As will be evident, these concepts are overlapping and mutually supportive, lacking sharp edges and crispness, but this does not diminish their importance or utility.

Perhaps one of the most significant contributions of the concepts from critical peacebuilding theory discussed below is that they call for a shift in *perspective* that,

---

[21] See Roland Paris, "Peacebuilding and the Limits of Liberal Internationalism," *International Security* 22, no. 2 (1997): 56; see also Sriram, "Justice as Peace?," 580.

[22] Of course, it should be pointed out that one of the primary critiques of the liberal international peacebuilding model is that it has been applied in a template-based, one-size-fits-all manner. In this way, proposing a true "alternative paradigm" may risk self-contradiction.

if taken seriously, would prove to be a game changer for both peacebuilding and transitional justice practice. This perceptual shift occurs on at least two levels: first, a reprioritization of emphasis and resources from the state and its core security institutions to the needs of communities and individuals; and second (and relatedly), an increased emphasis on understanding and generating a sense of local legitimacy as one of the keys to long-term success. Taken together, such shifts help one to envision a peacebuilding process that goes well beyond the state-centric LIPB paradigm with its comparative emphasis on elections, restored courts, retrained, and reequipped security forces, and so on.

David Roberts, for example, invokes the concept of "popular peace" to emphasize the need for greater focus on everyday problems faced by ordinary individuals and communities as part of the peacebuilding process: social services delivery; economic and social rights; basic needs such as shelter, clean water, sanitation, electricity, jobs; and human security.[23] If LIPB tends to reflect a paradigm of peacebuilding as top-down, institutional engineering, or "trickle-down" peace,[24] Roberts argues that attention to local needs is key to generating a desperately needed sense of legitimacy for both local government and international peacebuilding initiatives in the postconflict context, which can in turn serve as a key to macro-level stability and peace.[25] This shift in emphasis offered by the concept of "popular peace" therefore involves a broader imagining of security and peace, one which "trickles up" from micro to macro rather than the other way around.[26] Given persistent critiques that LIPB has too often been imposed "from the outside" or by local elites and that the needs of ordinary citizens who suffered the brunt of the conflict are overlooked, the concept of "popular peace" could prove quite powerful if used as a prism for policy making. To be clear, it is not that the top-down, legal-institutional reforms that constitute the bread and butter of LIPB are not worthwhile, but that they are not sustainable and are prone to backlash, resistance, and cooptation without the popular sense of legitimacy that popular peace approaches might help to generate. In this sense, top-down and bottom-up approaches are mutually reinforcing.

The concept of "popular peace" is helpfully understood in tandem with the concept of "the everyday" found in critical peacebuilding literature.[27] In contrast with

---

[23] David Roberts, "Post-Conflict Peacebuilding, Liberal Irrelevance and the Locus of Legitimacy," *International Peacekeeping* 18, no. 4 (2011): 415.
[24] Shahrbanou Tadjbakhsh, "Liberal Peace in Dispute," in *Rethinking Liberal Peace; External Models and Local Alternatives*, ed. Shahrbanou Tadjbakhsh (New York: Routledge, 2011), 3.
[25] Roberts, "Post-Conflict Peacebuilding," 411.
[26] The concept of peacebuilding "from below" or transitional justice "from below" is a concept that has been developed and arrived at by many scholars. As but two examples, see, e.g., Kieran McEvoy and Lorna McGregor (eds.), *Transitional Justice from Below* (Portland: Hart, 2008); Timothy Donais and Amy Knorr, "Peacebuilding from Below vs. the Liberal Peace: the Case of Haiti," *Canadian Journal of Development Studies* 34, no. 1 (2013): 54–69.
[27] For a longer exposition of the concept, see David Roberts, *Liberal Peacebuilding and Global Governance: Beyond the Metropolis* (New York: Routledge, 2011), 89–91.

the dominant LIPB paradigm, an "everyday peace" is one "in which a population's preferences are recognized...beyond narrow liberal confines."[28] As many scholars and observers have noted, the sense that peacebuilding processes are remote or irrelevant to the everyday lives, preferences, and social reality of the very individuals those processes are ostensibly intended to benefit may spark resistance,[29] leading those affected by these programs to attempt to reconfigure them "so that they begin to reflect their own everyday lives rather than structural attempts at assimilation."[30] Thus, peacebuilding processes that ignore the lived realities and needs of "the everyday" in the postconflict context risk generating needless and counterproductive friction and struggle.

To harken back to the question of *Gacaca* in Rwanda discussed in Chapter 3, or the case of peacebuilding in Côte d'Ivoire discussed in Chapter 5, it is remarkable that only rarely are everyday people actually asked what they think is needed to consolidate peace and justice. All too often, peacebuilding and transitional justice initiatives end up being a show put on by elites (both local and national) for elites. It is a curious basis on which to attempt to (re)build a democracy, and is particularly ironic in societies such as Liberia or Sierra Leone where civil wars were sparked and sustained in large part due to frustration with corrupt elite rule.[31] Against this backdrop, shifting the focus of the peacebuilding binoculars to that of the problems, needs, and preferences of those who have to live with the success or failure of peacebuilding initiatives could be nothing short of revolutionary. Such an approach would need to go beyond the triviality of consultations, outreach, and participation, which in practice have often been shallow, technocratic exercises that fail to take the needs and preferences of nonelites seriously.[32]

If concepts such as "the everyday" and "popular peace" call for a shift in focus and perspective, the concept of "hybridity" provides an additional layer of complexity and critique, asking us to think about the intricate interaction between top-down and bottom-up forces and processes in peacebuilding. Simply put, outside of the

---

[28] Ibid., 90.

[29] See Andrea Talentino, "Perceptions of Peacebuilding: The Dynamic of Imposer and Imposed Upon," *International Studies Review* 8, no. 2 (2007): 253.

[30] Oliver Richmond, "Resistance and the Post-Liberal Peace," *Millennium – Journal of International Studies* 38 (2010): 677.

[31] See generally *Witness to Truth, Report of the Sierra Leone Truth and Reconciliation Commission* (2004), vol. I; Truth and Reconciliation Commission [Liberia], *Consolidated Final Report* (2009), Vol. I, 44.

[32] On the failures of "outreach," see, e.g., Peter Uvin and Charles Mironko, "Western and Local Approaches to Justice in Rwanda," *Global Governance* 9 (2003): 221; Stuart Ford, "How Special Is the Special Court's Outreach Section?," in *The Sierra Leone Special Court and Its Legacy: The Impact for Africa and International Law*, ed. Charles Jalloh (Cambridge: Cambridge University Press, 2013), 505. On the limitations of "consultation" programs, see, e.g., Sandra Rubli, *Transitional Justice: Justice by Bureaucratic Means?*, Swiss Peace Working Paper 4, 2012, 12. On problems with "participation" initiatives, see, e.g., Bill Cooke and Uma Kothari (eds.), *Participation: The New Tyranny?* (London: Zed Books, 2001).

academic and policy literature, there is really no such thing as pure "bottom-up" or "top-down." Rather, as described in the case study on Gacaca in Chapter 3, peacebuilding and transitional justice initiatives represent a mixture of both dynamics, making the end result more of a hybrid than anything else. The concept of hybridity therefore calls upon us to consider the ways in which peacebuilding initiatives are made and remade through a complex cocktail of local resistance, cooptation, and appropriation.[33] Thus, it suggests that peacebuilding does not involve a dynamic of external actors introducing new ideas and practices to static local societies,[34] but is in practice a "glocal" phenomenon.[35]

Hybridity often presents itself more as a description of the messy, awkward, and complex nature of internationally driven peacebuilding, of the heterogeneity and diversity in societies, than a conscious policy aim.[36] Even so, so-called hybrid tribunals described in Chapter 3 are a good example of the successes and failures of trying to engineer global-local hybridity into an initiative from the outset. While those experiments were in large part unsuccessful at striking a satisfactory global-local balance, that does not mean that the concept is not still worth pursuing in the future.[37] Nevertheless, as a descriptive lens, the concept of hybridity allows us to assess the prominence of liberalism in both peacebuilding and transitional justice without collapsing into a stereotype of an all-encompassing ideological behemoth;[38] to stand in a place where we neither romanticize the local, nor demonize the hegemonic, liberal West.[39] Taken together, hybridity helps to shift the focus in peacebuilding from efficiency to the need to generate a sense of local legitimacy that has often been sorely lacking.[40] It signals that international actors ignore dimensions of the local at their own peril. Thus, like the concept of "the everyday" and "popular peace," understanding the reality of hybridity calls upon us to move away from solely elite-level analysis – from the state and its institutions – and to take the

---

[33] See generally Roger Mac Ginty, *International Peacebuilding and Local Resistance. Rethinking Peace and Conflict* (Basingstoke: Palgrave, 2011).

[34] Roger Mac Ginty and Gurchathen Sanghera, "Hybridity in Peacebuilding and Development: An Introduction," *Journal of Peacebuilding and Development* 7, no. 2 (2012): 4.

[35] Bruce Mazlish, "The Global and the Local," *Current Sociology* 53, no. 1 (2005): 99.

[36] Necla Tschirgi, "Bridging the Chasm between Domestic and International Approaches to Peacebuilding," paper for presentation at the joint CISS/KEYNOTE conference "Between the Global and the Local: Actors, Institutions and Processes," Prague, June 24–26, 2012.

[37] See generally Padraig McAuliffe, "Hybrid Tribunals at Ten: How International Criminal Justice's Golden Child Became an Orphan," *Journal of International Law and International Relations* 7 (2011): 64; Chandra Sriram, "Post-Conflict Justice and Hybridity in Peacebuilding: Resistance or Cooptation," in *Hybrid Forms of Peace: From Everyday Agency to Post-Liberalism*, ed. Oliver Richmond and Audra Mitchell (New York: Palgrave Macmillan, 2012), 60.

[38] See Jenny Peterson, "A Conceptual Unpacking of Hybridity: Accounting for Notions of Power, Politics and Progress in Analyses of Aid-Drive Interfaces," *Journal of Peacebuilding and Development* 7, no. 2 (2012): 12 (noting the tendency of assessments of liberal interventions to homogenize).

[39] Kristoper Liden, Roger Mac Ginty, and Oliver Richmond, "Beyond Northern Epistemologies of Peace: Peacebuilding Reconstructed?," *International Peacekeeping* 16, no. 5 (2009): 594.

[40] Ibid.

CRITICAL PEACEBUILDING THEORY AND LIBERALISM

As has been pointed out by a number of scholars, ideas from critical peacebuilding theory such as "the everyday," "popular peace," and many others are often themselves based on fundamentally liberal principles.[41] After all, the ideals of greater toleration, participation, inclusion, pluralism, equality, and so on, on which critical peacebuilding theory is often explicitly or implicitly premised are certainly not illiberal values. In this way, what many critical scholars are envisioning, and indeed what is being suggested here is not that we must choose between liberal and some kind of illiberal peacebuilding. Rather, as discussed in previous chapters in greater detail, the tensions undergirding peacebuilding debates are often less between liberal and illiberal peacebuilding than they are: (1) between conflicting liberal commitments (say, between ideas of self-determination and universal human rights or between pluralism and the aspiration toward universalism); (2) conflicting human rights principles (for example, in the case of traditional legal practices, between access to justice and fair-trial rights); and (3) between competing visions of what makes a liberal society (between social-democratic, welfarist liberalism and the shock-therapy-with-a-structural-adjustment-cherry-on-top form of liberalism that has been pushed and peddled throughout the world with special vigor since the end of the Cold War).

In other words, liberalism is a broad canvass with a long tradition and many internal, perhaps irreconcilable tensions. If classical liberals (who would be called neoliberals today) such as Herbert Spencer and William Graham Sumner embraced notions of "negative liberty" – generally associated with free trade, laissez-faire economics, minimal government intervention and taxation, and so on – others who can lay equal claim to important strands of the broader liberal tradition such as Thomas Hill Green and L. T. Hobhouse[42] have promoted visions of "positive liberty" in which individuals have a duty to promote the common good and where more equitable social and economic conditions are seen as essential to both liberty and peace. In many ways, Thomas Hill Green's distinction between "negative" and "positive" liberty would later be echoed by distinctions between so-called negative (civil and political) rights and positive (economic and social) rights, as well as negative peace and positive peace. In general, the concepts in the negative column have been conceptualized as being more "hands-off" than those in the positive column, which have been thought, rather simplistically, to require more "hands-on"

---

[41] See, e.g., Roland Paris, "Saving Liberal Peacebuilding," *Review of International Studies* 2 (2010): 354.
[42] See, e.g., Thomas Hill Green, *Lectures on the Principles of Political Obligation* (Uxbridge: Cambridge Scholars Press, 2002); L. T. Hobhouse, *Liberalism and Other Writings* (Cambridge: Cambridge University Press, 1994).

affirmative intervention for consolidation and protection.[43] Just as transitional justice has traditionally focused on accountability for "negative" or "hands-off" civil and political rights, a shift in the direction of "positive peace" would entail a greater focus on "positive rights" and "positive liberty."

While both the "negatives" and the "positives" can lay claim to important historical strands of the liberal tradition, the curious fact is that LIPB has been largely premised on the vision of the classical (or neo) liberals and not the welfare liberalism of the social-democratic tradition. Given the ascendency of neoliberalism from the 1970s on through the birth of peacebuilding and transitional justice in the 1980s and 1990s, this was perhaps unsurprising, though hardly inevitable. After all, the diversity of democratic societies in the Western world alone suggests that there are many models of marketization and democratization that could have served as a model for peacebuilding and transitional justice (putting to side for one moment the problem of using Western models as the template). Thus, even if one accepts the rather simplistic "markets + democracy = peace" premise of the liberal peace thesis, the policy reductionism and tunnel vision of LIPB practice seems unwarranted.

From the bird's eye view then, it is not that most critical theorists are opposed to classical liberal goods such as democracy, the rule of law, and human rights, or that these are unworthy goals for the transitional justice and peacebuilding enterprises. If concepts like positive peace and peacebuilding should not be seen as synonymous with simplistic LIPB equations of free markets and liberal democracy, it is also hard to image a robust positive peace without some level of democracy and respect for human rights. In this way, the label "liberal international peacebuilding" used by so many critical scholars is actually problematic for at least two reasons. First, because it suggests that the alternatives being explored are not in fact liberal variants. And second, because it obfuscates the extent to which the problem being addressed is not liberalism writ large, but a narrow neoliberal variant that has been aggressively imposed around the world through illiberal means. What is needed in these debates is then to remember that there are multiple liberalisms, and that the critique of liberal international peacebuilding is, in large part, a critique of a particular kind of liberalism and a particular way of trying to induce it in postconflict countries.

Thus, there are certainly readings of the liberal tradition that would give greater weight to local autonomy, participation, and decision making, to everyday needs and distributive justice, and which would reflect greater contextual openness and adaptability – principles which would go a long way to addressing the various critiques leveled against liberal international peacebuilding. Along these same lines, it is possible to conceptualize a number of "liberal peaces" that are not so reductive, but which nevertheless retain a core of human rights, rule of law, pluralism, self-determination, democracy, and so on, with less of a neoliberal focus on theories of small government and free markets that aren't really even put into practice in the

---

[43] In reality, of course, "negative" rights such as freedom from torture, arbitrary arrest, unlawful detention, etc., all require significant resources and attention from the state if they are to be safeguarded.

liberal West. In this way, what is typically being proposed in the critical literature is not so much an alternative to liberalism and the broader goals of liberal international peacebuilding, but a counterweight to a neoliberal conception of peacebuilding that sees a veneer of electoral democracy and policies of laissez-faire capitalism as the unique pathway to peace; and where to be "peaceful" is too often conflated with being "like us."

It is therefore possible that the real clash is between what we might call the "liberal localism" of the critical peacebuilding theorists – which places greater weight on principles of self-determination, local agency, and social justice – and the neoliberal internationalism of mainstream liberal international peacebuilding which has too often been associated with arrogance, imposition, and a checkered history of success. That history calls upon us to be more attentive to the hypocrisy and self-defeating nature of promoting liberal ends through illiberal means. As a unifying theme, the concept of "liberal localism" is a helpful way to understand many of the varied critiques of liberal international peacebuilding and the attempt to shift the center of gravity and the perspective of liberal peacebuilders. Yet it also helpfully suggests the need to retain a global-local balance in matters of peacebuilding. While the "the local" is often good, it may at times also need a more global, liberal counterweight to avoid excessive parochialism.

Thus, "liberal localism" is intended to create space for a strong pluralism that, when allied with a robust "margin of appreciation," might help to strike a better balance between the classical pivots of liberalism – the rule of law and human rights, for example – and non-Western concepts and modalities of peace and justice. And because liberal ends must be pursued via liberal means, the desired endpoints of peacebuilding and transitional justice are to be achieved with a much greater emphasis on local autonomy, participation, decision making, and traditional practices as a means to get there. That does not make peacebuilding easier and may, if anything, render the process messier and more chaotic. But it should be borne in mind that the goal of "liberal localism" is less the promotion of what Stephan Hopgood has called "Human Rights" – with a capital "H" and capital "R," the formal, bureaucratic, and legalistic international human rights system – than securing "human rights," lowercase "h" and lowercase "r," meaning the ability of everyday people to find varied ways of living in freedom and dignity.[44] While the pathways to formal "Human Rights" may be limited, those leading toward "human rights" are more numerous and diverse.

CRITICAL PEACEBUILDING THEORY AND TRANSITIONAL JUSTICE

Given the parallel origins, ideological assumptions, and critiques of both liberal international peacebuilding and transitional justice, it would be dangerous to

---

[44] See Stephen Hopgood, *The Endtimes of Human Rights* (Ithaca: Cornell University Press, 2014).

assume that "transitional justice as peacebuilding" will come to reflect more holistic rather than more reductive concepts of peacebuilding. Thus, long-standing critiques relating to the inaccessibility, neocolonial undertones, and inappropriateness[45] of transitional justice to local wants and needs are unlikely to be addressed unless greater thought is given to the particular kind of peace and peacebuilding with which transitional justice should be associated: whether a kind of emancipatory peace resonant with critical peacebuilding theory ideals of "positive peace," "the everyday" and "popular peace," or a more classically narrow and reductionist (neo)liberal one. As discussed in Chapter 6, to the extent that there are emerging efforts to seek greater complementarity between the staples of liberal international peacebuilding programming and initiatives associated with transitional justice, building linkages and programming with a cognizance of the parallel critiques that have historically dogged both fields would also be an important step.[46]

Viewed in their ensemble, the concepts discussed throughout this chapter – including "positive peace," "the everyday," "popular peace," and "hybridity" – ask us to reconsider the priorities and praxis of both peacebuilding and transitional justice and provide a useful prism for helping to imagine what more emancipatory transitional justice as peacebuilding might entail. Their key value may be as a set of constructs or guiding principles that can help to facilitate an important perceptual and attitudinal shift. Thus, while not presented here as a panacea to the realities of narrow liberal international peacebuilding or the parallel problems that have bedeviled transitional justice, they at least call for greater attention to historic blind spots and assumptions and might be a first step in moving liberal international peacebuilding and transitional justice in the direction of greater pluralism, contextualism and global-local balance, bringing some of the historic peripheries of the field into the foreground:

Historic Foreground	Historic Background[47]
the global, the Western	the local, the non-Western "other"
the modern, the secular	the traditional, the religious
the legal	the political
civil and political rights	economic and social rights
physical violence	economic violence
the state, the individual	the community, the group
formal, institutional, "top-down" change	informal, cultural, social, "bottom-up" change

---

[45] Sriram, "Post-Conflict Justice and Hybridity," 60.
[46] Dustin Sharp, "Beyond the Post-Conflict Checklist: Linking Peacebuilding and Transitional Justice through the Lens of Critique," *Chicago Journal of International Law* 14, no. 1 (2013): 169–70.
[47] Chart adapted from Dustin Sharp, "Addressing Economic Violence in Times of Transition: Toward a Positive-Peace Paradigm for Transitional Justice," *Fordham International Law Journal* 35, no. 3 (2012): 799.

If the historic foreground remains important to the work of transitional justice, neither is it obvious that peace and justice are best advanced by heavily privileging those items while pushing others to the margins. Thus, while concepts from critical peacebuilding theory do not themselves provide a "roadmap" for negotiating the many complex questions, choices, and trade-offs involved in striking a better balance between historic foreground and background, the shift in perspective they afford, together with the emphasis on the need for multiple levels of legitimacy, suggest that they offer a starting point for thinking, policy, and action that stands in refreshing contrast to the preoccupation in the earlier years of the field of transitional justice with elite bargains and decision making.[48] Taken together, they allow us to imagine a world where those developing transitional justice programming and policy ask themselves, at the outset, how those items traditionally pushed to the margins might be given genuine importance, value, and, where needed, priority. It is thought provoking to imagine, for example, what a transitional justice process might look like that did *not* privilege international "expertise" at the expense of local agency; nation or capital-based justice at the expense of community and rural based justice; largely Western legal modes of justice at the expense of "traditional" or "local" modalities of justice; the prosecution of the so-called big fish at the expense of a focus on reparations and community needs; and physical violence and civil and political rights at the expense of economic violence and economic and social rights.[49] We have as yet few empirical examples of such "alternative" transitional justice approaches, though the Fambul Tok project in Sierra Leone, with its emphasis on community-based reconciliation grounded in traditional ritual and practice, provides an intriguing, if occasionally flawed, example.[50]

Perhaps less ambitiously, concepts of "positive peace," "popular peace," "the everyday," and "hybridity" might at least work together to serve as a sort of bulwark against the slide toward expediency that would continue to privilege the historical foreground of transitional justice work, answering sustained critique with only superficial appropriation. After all, even important themes evolving out of the critical studies literature like "participation" and "local ownership" intended to address some of the long-standing critiques of transitional justice and peacebuilding practice are easily co-opted by international institutions and donors who would turn them into a sort of ritualized mantra devoid of substance.[51] The concepts from

[48] See, e.g., Samuel P. Huntington, "The Third Wave: Democratization in the Late Twentieth Century," in *Transitional Justice: How Emerging Democracies Reckon with Former Regimes*, ed. Neil Kritz (Washington, DC: USIP, 1995); Guillermo O'Donnell and Philippe Schmitter, "Transitions from Authoritarian Rule: Tentative Conclusions about Uncertain Democracies," in Kritz, *Transitional Justice*, 57–64.

[49] Each of these pairings, of course, involves an extended debate and literature. They are presented here in broad-brush fashion for purposes of contrast.

[50] See generally Augustine Park, "Community-Based Restorative Transitional Justice in Sierra Leone," *Contemporary Justice Review* 13, no. 1 (2010): 95–119.

[51] See, e.g., Cooke and Kothari, *Participation: The New Tyranny?*

critical peacebuilding theory discussed in this chapter are then a reminder that we must resist these gravitational forces by continually asking whose peace (or whose justice) we are building, based on whose priorities, to what ends, and who gets to decide.[52]

AN AGENDA FOR TRANSITIONAL JUSTICE AND PEACEBUILDING GOING FORWARD

After some twenty-five years, it seems clear that transitional justice is gradually, if tentatively, moving beyond the peace versus justice debates of the past to be seen as a component of peacebuilding itself, even if it remains one component among many.[53] The import of any future transitional-justice-as-peacebuilding narrative will hinge to a large extent on our understanding of concepts of "transition," "justice," and "peacebuilding." This book has explored a number of problematic assumptions with regard to these three concepts that have historically enjoyed a great deal of privilege including: (1) the idea of "transition" as necessarily suggestive of a narrow (neo)liberal teleology; (2) ideas of "justice" as synonymous with legal and atrocity justice; and (3) the idea of "peacebuilding" as synonymous with what has come to be known as "liberal international peacebuilding." And while those assumptions have been painted with a fairly broad brush, it seems probable that they will in some form help to color our understanding of transitional justice as a form of peacebuilding going forward. This is especially true in a world where transitional justice and liberal peacebuilding have been mainstreamed and institutionalized, where the centripetal pull of dominant and mainstream practice is strong.[54]

Even so, there are emancipatory concepts of peace and peacebuilding that carry with them the potential to challenge long-standing blind spots and assumptions and to increase the possibility of a transitional-justice-as-peacebuilding project that is true to human rights ideals while becoming more open-textured and attuned to local needs and context. To these ends, I have argued that thinking of the transition of transitional justice as a transition to "positive peace" where the perspectives of "popular peace," "the everyday," and "hybridity" are paramount could be an important step in helping to emancipate the field from the bonds of the paradigmatic

---

[52] The question of "whose peace" is, of course, one asked by many peacebuilding scholars. See, e.g., Michael Pugh, Neil Cooper, and Mandy Turner (eds.), *Whose Peace? Critical Perspectives on the Political Economy of Peacebuilding* (New York: Palgrave Macmillan, 2008). This same refrain has also been asked in the context of transitional justice. See, e.g., Patricia Lundy and Mark McGovern, "Whose Justice? Rethinking Transitional Justice from the Bottom Up," *Journal of Law and Society* 35, no. 2 (2008): 265.
[53] United Nations Security Council Resolution No. 2282, UN Doc. S/RES/2282 (2016), preamble.
[54] See Roland Paris, "Understanding the 'Coordination Problem' in Postwar Statebuilding," in Roland Paris and Timothy D. Sisk (eds.), *The Dilemmas of Statebuilding: Confronting the Contradictions of Postwar Peace Operations* 62 (New York: Routledge, 2009).

transition and serve to resist a simple elision of transitional justice and liberal international peacebuilding. I have further offered the concept of "liberal localism" as a means of stitching the threads of these critical constructs together, while emphasizing the need for a better global-local balance than has been the case for transitional justice and peacebuilding practice in the past.

Some have worried that thinking of transitional justice more expansively (perhaps even along the lines suggested by this book) will somehow overburden the field – jeopardizing even the narrow aims of combating impunity for violations of physical integrity, for example.[55] The goal, however, is not to conflate transitional justice with social justice writ large or with the greater peacebuilding enterprise itself. Rather, by carefully considering and deconstructing assumptions implicit in the narratives of the field, both historic and emerging, it may be possible to liberate policy making from narrow pathways and paradigms that may stymie creativity and thinking, and possibly underserve the goal of the consolidation of a long-term, robust, and positive peace.

There is therefore a strong need for greater critical theoretical and empirical attention to the links between transitional justice, peace, and peacebuilding that take us beyond the "peace versus justice" debates and "no peace without justice" sloganeering of the past, and which build upon the work of pioneering scholars. To be clear, the claim is not that these ideas and questions cannot and have not been arrived at by constructs outside of critical peacebuilding theory. Indeed, critiques developed by transitional justice scholars and peacebuilding scholars, working in at times "splendid isolation," are often remarkably similar. At the same time, the concepts from critical peacebuilding theory discussed in this chapter carry with them special salience in a world where transitional justice is increasingly seen as part and parcel of the international peacebuilding enterprise. Greater collaboration by scholars in both areas would be welcome, and thinking in each area could serve as a source of insight and inspiration for the other.[56] This chapter, and indeed this book, have only sketched a few ideas in this regard as an attempt to stimulate further thinking and debate. The hope is that careful introspection and collaboration along these lines could lead to a conceptualization of "transitional justice as peacebuilding" that might serve to loosen moorings in the most rigid and narrow templates of Western neoliberalism, making transitional justice more of a true global project.

---

[55] Lars Waldorf, "Anticipating the Past: Transitional Justice and Socio-Economic Wrongs," *Social and Legal Studies* 21 (2012): 171–86.

[56] Compare, e.g., Laurent Goetschel and Tobias Hagmann, "Civilian Peacebuilding: Peace by Bureaucratic Means?," *Conflict, Security and Development* 9, no. 1 (2009): 56; and Rubli, *Transitional Justice: Justice by Bureaucratic Means?*, 11.

8

Conclusion

After the End of History, What Should Transitional Justice Become?

Like other works written in the critical studies tradition, much of this book has been devoted to deconstruction: breaking down the core narratives of peacebuilding and transitional justice and wrestling with their tensions and internal contradictions. In this, a key underlying question – the proverbial elephant in the room perhaps – has been whether transitional justice can be made into more of a truly global project, giving it greater legitimacy and adaptability to a broad range of contexts. For many, the value of such work needs no justification beyond the intellectual insights that it generates, or incisive questions that it manages to provoke. To others, these and other similar efforts are but a maelstrom of abstractions, a bramble of intractable academic debates of little use to communities of "real-world" policy and practice. From these latter quarters, one of the frequent frustrations is that works of critical theory do not do enough to explain how their ideas and critiques might be put into action.

And yet, even if critical theory does not offer the blueprint for change that some pragmatists might wish for, core narratives have a much greater impact on policy formulation than many would assume. Legal scholar Robert Cover put it even more starkly when he argued that institutions and prescriptions *do not exist* apart from the narratives that locate and give them meaning.[1] To take but one example, it is not hard to imagine that the policy implications for a United Nations peacebuilding agenda premised on the notion of advancing a sort of "popular peace" would be quite different than those that have flown from the narrower and more neoliberal conceptions of peace that have served to undergird what has become known as liberal international peacebuilding. In this respect, the fact that the core narrative of transition justice appears to be evolving to embrace notions of peacebuilding is a significant development not just for critical theorists, but for practitioners and policy makers as well. We all have a stake in the particular kinds of peacebuilding that are

---

[1] Robert Cover, "*Nomos* and Narrative," *Harvard Law Review* 97 (1983): 4.

ultimately embraced, and struggling with the implications of such shifting sands is the work of many hands.

Critical theory is also important to policy making to the extent that it helps to clear away some of the political and ideological static and debris that tends to cloud dominant practice in an aura of normalcy, leading to insufficient interrogation of "the way things are" or "the way things are done." At a time when the field is said to be in a state of crisis owing in part to questions about legitimacy,[2] critical theory may then be a useful tonic for helping to "clear the slate" and reimagine the field going forward. And even if the slate is not fully cleared, in placing assumptions about "the way things are" under a magnifying glass, it may at least become obvious that the writing on it was not made with a permanent pen.

So with all of that, what light does critical theory shed on the question of what transitional justice should look like in the twenty-first century, several decades after the "end of history" that so heavily shaped the earlier parameters? While the detailed architecture of a new paradigm would be the work of an entirely new book, the process of stripping down and laying bare, which has been the principle occupation of the current volume, nevertheless sets in relief a number of implications that may help to shape policy in useful ways. In this concluding chapter, I will attempt to sketch out a few of them, not as an NGO might draft its bullet points of detailed policy recommendations to various stakeholders, but at the level of very broad policy arcs. This exercise will also serve as a useful means of tying together analysis and conclusions from the preceding chapters, and drawing this work to a close.

In brief, I will argue that transitional justice policy in the twenty-first century should be (re)oriented around five broad themes: (1) it should embrace more extended concepts of peace, justice, and violence; (2) it should embrace the idea of "liberal localism"; (3) it should strike a better balance between retributive, restorative, and distributive justice; (4) it should embrace a paradigm of peacebuilding, of the emancipatory kind, supported by a broader range of liberalisms; and finally, (5) it should embrace a sense of "radical humility." These prescriptions are in many ways overlapping, but taken as a whole, their common thrust could prove transformative for the field. As will become clear, most of the directions I am calling for involve the need for deep-seated perceptual and attitudinal shifts as a prelude to down-in-the-weeds changes in policy and practice.

TRANSITIONAL JUSTICE SHOULD EMBRACE MORE EXTENDED CONCEPTS OF PEACE, JUSTICE, AND VIOLENCE

One consistent theme throughout this book has been a critique of the narrowness of dominant concepts of peace, justice, and violence at the heart of most transitional

---

[2] See Vasuki Nesiah, *Transitional Justice Practice: Looking Back, Moving Forward*, Scoping Study, Impunity Watch, May 2016, 5.

justice initiatives: "Peace" tends to be conceived of as a narrow (neo)liberal peace. "Justice" is typically understood in terms of legal and atrocity justice for a narrow if not egregious band of civil and political rights violations. And the "violence" that is to be condemned (and, hopefully, prevented) is understood as comprising physical violence, for the most part excluding violence of the economic, cultural, and structural kind. These are all, of course, social and political constructions, and there is a sense in which they are mutually reinforcing. That is, narrow constructions of justice and violence lead to a comparatively thin idea of peace, and vice versa.

The question going forward is whether such narrow conceptions can plausibly be sustained for a field increasingly tied to notions of prevention ("never again") and the consolidation of a durable peace. Without doubt, justice in its fullest and most expansive sense must necessarily remain a broader concept than transitional justice.[3] However, to the extent that questions of economic violence and distributive justice help to drive conflict, instability, and human rights abuses, their positioning at the periphery of transitional justice concern may ultimately be self-defeating. Thus, whatever the dividing line between abuses that will be addressed or go unaddressed by transitional justice mechanisms, it makes little sense as a matter of policy to draw a simplistic one that reifies historic dichotomies of civil and political versus economic and social rights.

As I have argued in previous chapters, (re)conceptualizing the transition of transitional justice as a transition to positive peace, which includes at its core a preoccupation with questions of resources and inequality, could be one way of helping to ensure that a greater balance is struck between a wider range of justice concerns. In this way, embracing a broader conception of peace naturally lends support toward broader understandings of both justice and violence. Such a paradigm shift would not of itself render transitional justice indistinguishable from broader projects of development and social justice or necessarily dictate radical resource redistribution. For this reason, I have argued against the misconception in some of the literature that addressing questions of economic violence will of itself overstretch the resources and intellectual coherency of the field. There are potentially narrow and broad approaches to questions of economic violence, just as there are narrow or more comprehensive approaches physical violence.

Much will depend on context, but whether issues of economic violence are addressed is a question largely bound up with practical and methodological challenges, not fundamental or structural impossibilities.[4] More cautious approaches might, for example, focus on those patterns of economic violence with the greatest negative impact on economic and social rights, or perhaps focus on a small group

---

[3] See Roger Duthie, "Transitional Justice, Development, and Economic Violence," in *Justice and Economic Violence in Transition*, ed. Dustin Sharp (New York: Springer, 2014), 195–97.
[4] Duthie, "Transitional Justice, Development, and Economic Violence," 191.

of those "bearing the greatest responsibility" for economic crimes. Another filtering device to render the inquiry more manageable might be temporal – limiting the investigation to a period of the last ten years, for example. In this, the embrace of economic violence would be little different than historical approaches to violations of civil and political rights, which have tended to be relatively limited and selective.

The question is therefore increasingly less *whether* facets of economic violence should be addressed than *how* they should be addressed in view of available resources and the roots and drivers of the conflict. This does not make the "how" question easy, and it will likely take years to work out, much like the methodological questions surrounding violations of civil and political rights continue to vex practitioners today. At the level of practice, an increasing number of truth commissions, including Chad, Ghana, Sierra Leone, Liberia, Kenya and East Timor have examined questions of economic violence more squarely, providing a small if useful series of case studies that can be mined to extract valuable lessons about practical and methodological challenges.[5] And there are ongoing experiments, such as Tunisia and its Truth and Dignity Commission, whose mandate includes corruption and abuses of economic rights, that should provide further grist for the mill to be refined over time.[6] With this ongoing work, together with the increasing recognition at the highest levels of policy that economic questions should be brought into the ambit of transitional justice, it is quite possible that in twenty years addressing both physical and economic violence will seem as natural as addressing only physical violence once seemed to some in earlier decades.

TRANSITIONAL JUSTICE SHOULD EMBRACE THE IDEA OF "LIBERAL LOCALISM"

In Chapter 3, I argued that the field's engagement with questions of "the local" and the "non-Western" has been both complex and clumsy, fraught with frictions and contradictions. Transitional justice has tended to privilege largely Western approaches to and understandings of what it means to "do justice." This has at frequent intervals sparked resistance and backlash, and diminished a sense of badly needed legitimacy and local support for many transitional justice initiatives. The sense that transitional justice is in essence a "Western" enterprise pushed, funded, and supported by the Global North is not entirely accurate, but contains an

---

[5] See generally Dustin Sharp, "Economic Violence in the Practice of African Truth Commissions and Beyond," in *Justice and Economic Violence in Transition*, ed. Dustin Sharp (New York: Springer, 2014).

[6] The commission's mandate has not been without controversy, spurring calls for amnesty for economic crimes. Human Rights Watch, "Tunisia: Amnesty Bill Would Set Back Transition; Would Replace Better Model for Handling Corruption," July 14, 2016, www.hrw.org/news/2016/07/14/tunisia-amnesty-bill-would-set-back-transition.

uncomfortable degree of truth that is ultimately corrosive to the very local ownership and support essential to long-term success.

Yet the choice going forward is not a simple one between dogmatic localism and strongly assertive if not imperious global justice. Rather, the dilemmas of "the local" reveal competing liberal principles and commitments that need to be balanced. In and of itself, there is nothing particularly illiberal, for example, in giving greater weight to local autonomy, participation, and decision making when it comes to deciding what justice is supposed to mean and what the appropriate mechanisms for delivering that justice should be. If taken seriously, principles of pluralism and concepts like the "margin of appreciation" worked out in historically liberal societies would also go a long way toward generating locally driven transitional justice practice reflective of greater contextual openness and adaptability. In sum, the clash between the global and the local, or between the Western and the non-Western in transitional justice may therefore flow in large part from a narrow and arrogant version of the liberal tradition associated with the 1990s and the triumphal spirit of the "end of history" that has come to undergird so many aspects of liberal postconflict governance.

There is no simple policy panacea for eliminating these tensions entirely. Even so, if managed better than in the past, a degree of tension might actually be a positive thing that could serve to spur innovation and creativity in transitional justice practice, perhaps generating new experiments in hybridity. To these ends, in Chapter 7, I proposed the concept of "liberal localism" as a useful lens for policy making that could serve as a reminder of several important principles. First, it serves to emphasize the importance of taking "the local" and the perspectives of nonelites seriously. Experience has shown that the center cannot hold, and projects tend to fall apart when this norm is not placed at the core of policy making. In contrast, in those countries where the transitional justice process was largely locally owned and driven, such as Argentina, efforts have proven more sustainable and enduring, inspiring work around the globe. While adopting a perspective of liberal localism might not sound like a very concrete policy prescription, the truth is that if taken seriously, it would be a huge perpetual and attitudinal shift from what has come in the past. In this sense, asking ourselves, from the outset, how "the local" might be brought from the background to the foreground of a particular transitional justice initiative could be nothing short of transformative.

Even with this increased emphasis on local perspectives, the concept of liberal localism is also a reminder that "the local" is not to be fetishized or romanticized, but must at times give way to a larger local. If the tipping point for such "giving way" will inevitably spark tension, the concept of liberal localism reminds us that the broader liberal tradition itself contains some of the keys, such as pluralism and the margin of appreciation, that can help to manage these tensions over time. Nothing about this will ever be easy or clean, and it is quite possible that the increased emphasis on "the local" will make things even messier. Yet it is equally true that staying the current course, continuing to think largely in terms of global justice with a local afterthought – often expressed in tokenistic projects of "consultation" – is not a recipe for generating genuine legitimacy and ownership.

TRANSITIONAL JUSTICE SHOULD STRIKE A BETTER BALANCE BETWEEN RETRIBUTIVE, RESTORATIVE, AND DISTRIBUTIVE JUSTICE

While it has not been explored in this volume to the same extent as some other debates, embracing broader concepts of peace, justice and violence and taking local perspectives on peace and justice seriously would likely lead to (and require) a better and more flexible balance between retributive, restorative, and distributive justice than has been the case in the past. At the same time, achieving a better balance may prove stubbornly difficult as it requires us to take a step back and question, as if from first principles, what it means to "do justice."

Considered most expansively, "justice" could be understood as a broad social project and a condition in society. To "do justice" with such a conception in mind would likely involve a wide spectrum of efforts involving components of retributive, restorative, and distributive justice.[7] Yet this holistic view of justice stands in contrast to a narrower human rights legalism often associated with transitional justice that has tended to see justice as a relationship to the state,[8] has tended see "accountability" for mass atrocities as synonymous with individual criminal accountability rather that a broader collective or institutional model, and which has imagined justice to be something that can, to some extent, be engineered and delivered through legal mechanisms and reforms. If this is the conception of justice animating the field, we can then ask whether "transitional justice" is not just a simple byword for "law," "legal justice,"[9] or "retributive justice." Thus, a necessary step in achieving a more holistic view of justice would be to question the bias of many in the field toward top-down retributivism as the "gold standard" response to mass atrocity. This assumption is particularly hardwired into lawyers for whom courtroom justice is often seen as the only form of "hard" or "real" justice that one should accept, with anything else being a second-best or compromise solution.[10]

One way to begin to relax such assumptions may be to take more of a peacebuilding perspective to what it means to "do justice." From this lens, one of the problems with what we might call the "retributivist forward" approach of mainstream transitional justice is that retributivism alone rarely addresses the root causes of

---

[7] See Rama Mani, *Beyond Retribution*, 5.
[8] David Kennedy, "The International Human Rights Regime: Still Part of the Problem?," in *Examining Critical Perspectives on Human Rights*, ed. Rob Dickinson et al. (Cambridge: Cambridge University Press, 2012), 25.
[9] Christine Bell, Colm Campbell, and Fionnuala Ni Aolain, "Transitional Justice: (Re)Conceptualising the Field," *International Journal of Law in Context* 3, no. 2 (2007): 86.
[10] See, e.g., Reed Brody, "Justice: The First Casualty of Truth?," *Nation*, April 30, 2001.

conflict. Indeed, given that most prosecutions involve a very small percentage of the perpetrators, it would be hard to image this being the case unless one somehow believes that mass atrocities are the exclusive work of only a few "bad apples." A second problem with the heavy emphasis on retributivism is that it tempts one to view justice not as a sustained process or a condition to be worked toward, but as a theatrical event. Of course, one might also accuse truth commissions of conflating justice with a public spectacle, and yet truth commissions also function to diagnose broad structural problems and issue recommendations for broader reforms that typically take the larger conflict landscape into account. A number of truth commissions have also attempted to lay the groundwork for the broader work of distributive justice, ranging from reparations programs to the need to address inequality and marginalization in order to secure a lasting peace.[11]

This is not to say that highly legalized approaches to transitional justice focusing on individual criminal responsibility are not valuable or that the advocates of such approaches are found only in the liberal West. It also seems clear that retributivist responses to mass atrocity do have a role to play when it comes to building positive peace in the long term. As the empirical literature on transitional justice suggests, they can play a helpful role in creating a climate of respect for human rights, especially when combined with other mechanisms such as truth commissions, selective amnesties, and so on.[12] One should also note that prosecutions have justifications beyond consequentialist logics, including giving victims a sense that justice of a sort has been done and broader publics a reminder that we live in a moral universe that must at times be set right, even if largely symbolically.

The problem lies in the conflation of retributivist justice with what it means to "do justice" in times of transition without considering the need for a more integrated and holistic approach that also includes elements of restorative and distributive justice. At first blush, an appeal to "strike a better balance" between retributive, restorative, and distributive might not seem like very actionable policy advice. However, the fact is that a transitional justice process that took as its starting point the notion that some kind of justice needs to meted out across each of these three axes would very likely lead to a more integrated agenda than what has often come before. This is particularly true when it comes to distributive justice, which has traditionally been the orphan step child of transitional justice. In this, transitional justice could likely prove more adaptable and culturally congruent to a range of non-Western contexts that place a greater premium on restorative and distributive elements of justice making.

---

[11] See, e.g., *Witness to Truth, Report of the Sierra Leone Truth and Reconciliation Commission* (2004), Vol. I.
[12] See Kathryn Sikkink, *The Justice Cascade* (New York: W. W. Norton, 2011), 183; Tricia Olsen, Leigh Payne, and Andrew Reiter, *Transitional Justice in Balance* (Washington, DC: USIP, 2010), 146–53.

TRANSITIONAL JUSTICE SHOULD EMBRACE PEACEBUILDING, THE EMANCIPATORY KIND, SUPPORTED BY A BROADER RANGE OF LIBERALISMS

Transitional justice has in several short decades become the "globally dominant lens"[13] through which we now grapple with legacies of violence and mass atrocity. That lens has not been an apolitical, acultural, or nonideological one, being most accurately viewed as a fairly narrow, mostly Western, (neo)liberal prism with all the reductive concepts of peace, justice, and violence that go with it. Seen through these optics, transitional justice is the harbinger and handmaiden of atrocity justice and liberal democracy. Previous chapters have sought to explore the ways in which these liberal optics have served to shape and stunt our sense of what it means to "do justice" in times of transition. As I have argued, they have contributed, at least in part, to some of the blind spots and frictions associated with transitional justice initiatives today, helping to push certain questions and modalities of justice into the foreground, while relegating others to the background of transitional justice concern:

Set in the Foreground	Set in the Background[14]
the global, the Western	the local, the non-Western "other"
the modern, the secular	the traditional, the religious
the legal	the political
civil and political rights	economic and social rights
physical violence	economic and structural violence
the state, the individual	the community, the group
formal, institutional, "top-down" change	informal, cultural, social, "bottom-up" change

A key question is what happens to the chart above if we come to conceptualize transitional justice not simply as a vector for the promotion of atrocity justice and liberal democracy, but as a broader component of peacebuilding. There are signs that this sort of narrative change is underfoot, but the implications have not been fully explored. What difference might this make for policy and practice? As a strong caution, I have argued that it may well make no difference at all. After all, what has become known has "liberal international peacebuilding" has tended to replicate the backgrounding and foregrounding in the chart above, and has suffered from the same withering critiques that have dogged transitional justice: too often externally driven, being planned and implemented in a top-down and state-centric manner; too often biased toward Western approaches, giving too little attention to local or

---

[13] Paul Gready and Simon Robins, "From Transition to Transformative Justice: A New Agenda for Practice," *International Journal of Transitional Justice* (2014) (Advance Access).
[14] Chart adapted from Dustin N. Sharp, "Addressing Economic Violence in Times of Transition: toward a Positive-Peace Paradigm for Transitional Justice," *Fordham International Law Journal* 35 (2012).

indigenous peace and justice traditions; too often presented as a technocratic, neutral, and apolitical solution to highly contested or contestable political issues and choices, and so on.

Even with that significant caveat, I have argued that there are also emancipatory concepts of peace and peacebuilding that carry with them the potential to challenge long-standing blind spots and assumptions and to significantly disrupt the backgrounding and foregrounding in the chart above, striking a better balance. Preventing simple elision of transitional justice and liberal international peacebuilding – and working toward a more emancipatory conception of transitional justice-as-peacebuilding in the process – can be facilitated in part through the use of several constructs from critical peacebuilding theory: positive peace, the everyday, popular peace, and hybridity. While they do not themselves create a program for action, these constructs, together with an effort to remember that liberalism is indeed a big tent capable of accommodating a great diversity of ideas and approaches, offer a very useful starting point for reimagining transitional justice going forward.

In more concrete terms, embracing a paradigm of emancipatory peacebuilding, buttressed by constructs from critical peacebuilding theory, would serve to support a number of the policy changes advocated above. For example, an embrace of positive peace would help to generate a default policy assumption that one should evaluate the need for both physical and economic violence, and consider the cocktail of retributive, restorative, and distributive most suited to the context. As another example, embracing a vision of peacebuilding informed by concepts of popular peace, the everyday and hybridity would help to generate a default policy assumption that justice initiatives should in most instances begin from the "bottom up," being planned and driven by local constituencies and cosmovision. In these ways, embracing emancipatory peacebuilding would involve perceptual shifts that could radically transform the historic background and foreground of the field.

In addition, such a vision of emancipatory peacebuilding is inherently holistic and long term, calling for greater coordination with broader postconflict initiatives and greater dialogue between peace and justice camps. While coordination can raise its own tensions and dilemmas, as I argued in Chapter 6, it might also be possible to coordinate in ways that cut against the grain of historic critiques, giving rise to new and innovative transitional justice and peacebuilding programs. The holistic nature of the peacebuilding lens makes it harder to take seriously the notion that justice has somehow been served by a handful of high-level prosecutions alone, underscoring the need for more comprehensive responses to mass atrocity that will require such coordination and innovation.

Finally, as it is not as narrowly wedded to the concept of democracy promotion, this kind of transitional justice as peacebuilding naturally extends itself to a greater range of contexts, ranging from consolidated democracies that have left historical abuses to fester, to countries emerging from civil war and authoritarian contexts where the wounds are still fresh. In this, transitional justice as peacebuilding becomes a global project, but without the ideological baggage of the "end of history" and dogmatic universalism and that has undermined the adaptability and perceived legitimacy of the field.

TRANSITIONAL JUSTICE SHOULD EMBRACE A SENSE OF RADICAL HUMILITY

Some will take arguments in this book for the expansion of transitional justice as reflecting a certain arrogance or naïveté as to what the field can reasonably be expected to accomplish. It is hard enough, one might say, to address physical violence, and yet here it is argued that questions of economic violence and distributive justice must be brought front and center. Surely, calls to expand the field reflect a misplaced faith in our ability to transform societies through transitional justice.

In fact, nearly the opposite is true. Historically, dominant transitional justice practice has been characterized by a sort of overconfidence in its abilities, predicated on the assumption that we know what concepts like "doing justice" and "accountability" actually mean, both in and beyond the West; and that mainstream understandings of such concepts are an unmitigated good for transitional societies and beyond. Dominant practice has also often reflected a lack of humility about the extent to which these concepts can be actualized by outsiders without robust local support.

In contrast, by interrogating "the way things are" and in opening to more extended conceptions of justice, violence, and peace, we are forced to confront the complexity and fundamental indeterminacy of these concepts. We recognize that the versions of them that we may have once embraced are not natural or inevitable, but largely socially and politically constructed. Such an exercise should lead to a sense of humility about the meaning of peace, justice, and peacebuilding, and humility about what we think we know is best for postconflict societies. And if after deep inquiry more flexible and extended concepts of justice, violence, and peace are indeed to be embraced as a policy matter, they must be accompanied by a sense of "radical humility" that accepts the need for their continued interrogation and contestation. Otherwise, the new boss may be the same as the old boss, the new paradigm as dogmatic and narrow in its own way as the old. And to be clear, whether the field of transitional justice is ultimately predicated on narrower or broader notions of justice, we should still be modest about the ability of transitional justice of whatever form to radically transform societies. Transitional justice initiatives are but a small part of a far larger constellation of postconflict initiatives operating at multiple levels. But if the transitional justice tail may not be able to wag the larger liberal peacebuilding dog, that does not mean that it should not seek to at least contest the postsettlement status quo.[15] To fail in this regard would indeed make transitional justice "part of the problem."[16]

Radical humility can be sustained in part through continued critical theory, which is newer to the field of transitional justice than some other fields of scholarship. But it also falls to scholars, practitioners, and policy makers to frequently step out of the bubble of their own epistemic communities of expertise – conferences, courtrooms, roundtables, UN dialogues, NGO strategy meetings, and so on – for a "reality check" that takes into account what the transitional justice machine looks like from the perspective of those who have often borne the brunt of the conflict, and for whom understandings of justice and peace may differ radically (or not) from the experts. With some time and repetition, our willingness to question the wisdom of templates and "best practices" may become more than rhetorical, leading to us to seek out, embrace, and perhaps even attempt to engineer opportunities for more vigorous dialogue and contestation at all levels of transitional justice intervention. Such debates about the varied meanings of peace and justice and the varied understandings of how to actualize them should not be seen as distractions, but one of the most fundamental elements of carrying out any kind of transitional justice.

---

[15] See Padraig McAuliffe, "The Marginality of Transitional Justice within Liberal Peacebuilding: Causes and Consequences," *Journal of Human Rights Practice* 9, no. 1 (2017).

[16] David Kennedy, "The International Human Rights Movement: Part of the Problem?," *Harvard Human Rights Journal* 15 (2002): 101.

Bibliography

Aguila, Gaby Oré, and Felipe Gómez Isa, eds. 2011. *Rethinking Transitions: Equality and Social Justice in Societies Emerging from Conflict*. Cambridge: Intersentia.

Airault, Pascal. 2013. Côte d'Ivoire – CPI: Gbagbo ou le Bénéfice du Doute. *Jeune Afrique*, June 14, 2013.

Allen, Tim. 2006. *Trial Justice: The International Criminal Court and the Lord's Resistance Army*. London: Zed Books.

Ameh, Robert. 2006. Doing Justice after Conflict: The Case for Ghana's National Reconciliation Commission. *Canadian Journal of Law and Society* 21.

Andrieu, Kora. 2010. Civilizing Peacebuilding: Transitional Justice, Civil Society and the Liberal Paradigm. *Security Dialogue* 41(5).

An-Na'im, Abdullahi Ahmed. 2013. Editorial Note: From the Neocolonial "Transition" to Indigenous Formations of Justice. *International Journal of Transitional Justice* 7(2).

Arbour, Louise. 2003. The Rule of Law and the Reach of Accountability. In *The Rule of Law*, ed. Cheryl Saunders and Katherine Le Roy. Annandale, VA: Federation Press.

— 2007. Economic and Social Justice for Societies in Transition. *New York University Journal of International Law and Politics* 40(1).

— 2008. Justice v. Politics. *New York Times*, September 16, 2008.

Argentine National Commission on the Disappeared. 1986. *Nunca Más*. New York: Farar, Strauss, and Giroux.

Arriaza, Laura, and Naomi Roht-Arriaza. 2008. Social Reconstruction as Local Process. *International Journal of Transitional Justice* 2(2).

Arthur, Paige. 2009. How "Transitions" Reshaped Human Rights: A Conceptual History of Transitional Justice. *Human Rights Quarterly* 31(2).

Ash, Timothy Garton. 1998. The Truth about Dictatorship. *New York Review of Books*, February 19.

Aukerman, Miriam. 2002. Extraordinary Evil, Ordinary Crimes: A Framework for Understanding Transitional Justice. *Harvard Human Rights Journal* 15.

Baines, Erin. 2010. Spirits and Social Reconstruction after Mass Violence: Rethinking Transitional Justice. *African Affairs* 109(436).

Barnett, Michael, Hunjoon Kim, Madalene O'Donnell, and Laura Sitea. 2007. Peacebuilding: What Is in a Name? *Global Governance* 13(1).

Barr, Corey. 2011. Making Connections: Bridging Transitional Justice and Security Sector Reform to Confront Conflict-Related Sexual and Gender-Based Violence. *Praxis: Fletcher Journal of Human Security* 26.

Bass, Gary. 2002. *Stay the Hand of Vengeance: The Politics of War Crimes Tribunals.* Princeton, NJ: Princeton University Press.

BBC News. 2009. African Union in Rift with Court. July 3. http://news.bbc.co.uk/2/hi/africa/8133925.stm.

  2013. ICC Delays Cases of William Ruto and Laurent Gbagbo. June 3. www.bbc.co.uk/news/world-africa-22762283.

Bell, Christine. 2009. Transitional Justice, Interdisciplinarity and the State of the "Field" or "Non-Field." *International Journal of Transitional Justice* 3(1).

Bell, Christine, Colm Campbell, and Fionnuala Ni Aolain. 2007. Transitional Justice; (Re)Conceptualising the Field. *International Journal of Law in Context* 3(2).

Bellows, John, and Miguel Edward. 2006. War and Institutions: New Evidence from Sierra Leone. *The American Economic Review* 96.

Bendix, Daniel, and Ruth Stanley. 2010. Deconstructing Local Ownership of Security Sector Reform: A Review of the Literature. *African Security Review* 17(2).

Bergsmo, Morten, Cesar Rodriguez, Pablo Kalmanovitz, and Maria Paula Saffon (eds.). 2010. *Distributive Justice in Transitions.* Oslo: PRIO.

Betts, Alexander. 2005. Should Approaches to Post-conflict Justice and Reconciliation Be Determined Globally, Nationally, or Locally? *European Journal of Development Research* 17.

Bigi, Giulia. 2007. The Decision of the Special Court for Sierra Leone to Conduct the Charles Taylor Trial in The Hague. *The Law and Practice of International Courts and Tribunals* 3.

Bingham, Laura. 2009. Trying for a Just Result? The Hissène Habré Affair and Judicial Independence in Senegal. *Temple International and Comparative Law Journal* 23.

Bond, Patrick. 2006. Reconciliation and Economic Reaction: Flaws in South Africa's Elite Transition. *International Affairs* 60(1).

Boraine, Alexander. 2006. Transitional Justice: A Holistic Interpretation. *Journal of International Affairs* 60(1).

Bosire, Lydiah. 2006. Overpromised, Underdelivered: Transitional Justice in Sub-Saharan Africa. *Sur International Journal on Human Rights* 5(5).

Botes, Lucius, and Dingie van Rensburg. 2000. Community Participation in Development: Nine Plagues and Twelve Commandments. *Community Development* 35.

Branch, Adam. 2007. Uganda's Civil War and the Politics of ICC Intervention. *Ethics and International Affairs* 21(2).

Brody, Reed. 2001. Justice: The First Casualty of Truth? *The Nation*, April 30.

Bryden, Alan, Timothy Donais, and Heiner Hängi. 2005. *Shaping a Security-Governance Agenda in Post-Conflict Peacebuilding.* Geneva: DCAF.

Buckley-Zistel, Susanne, Teresa Koloma Beck, Christian Braun, and Friederike Mieth (eds.). 2014. *Transitional Justice Theories.* New York: Routledge.

Burgess, Patrick. 2008. A New Approach to Restorative Justice: East Timor's Community Reconciliation Process. In *Transitional Justice in the Twenty-First Century*, ed. Naomi Roht-Arriaza and Javier Mariezcurrena. Cambridge: Cambridge University Press.

Burnet, Jennie. 2008. The Injustice of Local Justice: Truth, Reconciliation, and Revenge in Rwanda. *Genocide Studies and Prevention* 3(2).

Carothers, Thomas. 2002. The End of the Transition Paradigm. *Journal of Democracy* 13.

Carranza, Ruben. 2008. Plunder and Pain: Should Transitional Justice Engage with Corruption and Economic Crimes? *International Journal of Transitional Justice* 2(3).

Cavallaro, James, and Sebastián Albuja. 2008. The Lost Agenda: Economic Crimes and Truth Commissions in Latin America and Beyond. In *Transitional Justice from Below, Grassroots Activism and the Struggle for Change*, ed. Kieran McEvoy and Lorna McGregor. Oxford: Hart.

Chesterman, Simon. 2002. Walking Softly in Afghanistan: The Future of UN Statebuilding. *Survival* 44.

2004. *You, the People: The United Nations, Transitional Administration, and State-Building*. Oxford: Oxford University Press.

2007. Ownership in Theory and in Practice: Transfer of Authority in UN Statebuilding Operations. *Journal of Intervention and Statebuilding* 1(1).

Clark, Janine. 2011. Peace, Justice and the International Criminal Court: Limitations and Possibilities. *Journal of International Criminal Justice* 9.

Clark, Phil. 2010. *The Gacaca Courts, Post-Genocide Justice and Reconciliation in Rwanda; Justice without Lawyers*. Cambridge: Cambridge University Press.

2010. Law, Politics and Pragmatism: The ICC and Case Selection in the Democratic Republic of Congo and Uganda. In *Courting Conflict? Peace, Justice and the ICC in Africa*, ed. Phil Clark and Nichola Waddell. London: Royal African Society.

Clark, Phil, and Zachary Kaufman (eds.). 2009. *After Genocide: Transitional Justice, Post-Conflict Reconstruction and Reconciliation in Rwanda and Beyond*. New York: Columbia University Press.

Cockayne, James. 2004. Operation Helpem Fren: Solomon Islands, Transitional Justice and the Silence of Contemporary Legal Pathologies on Questions of Distributive Justice. NYU School of Law Center for Human Rights and Global Justice, Working Paper Series, No. 3.

Cohen, David. 2007. "Hybrid" Justice in East Timor, Sierra Leone, and Cambodia: "Lessons Learned" and Prospects for the Future. *Stanford Journal of International Law* 43.

Cohen, Ronald. 1989. Human Rights and Cultural Relativism: The Need for a New Approach. *American Anthropologist* 91(4).

Cohen-Jonathan, Gérard. 2003. Universalité et Singularité des Droits de l'Homme. *Revue Trimestrielle des Droits de l'Homme* 53.

Collier, Paul, and Anne Hoeffler. 2002. On the Incidence of Civil War in Africa. *Conflict Resolution* 46(1).

Collier, Paul, et al. 2003. *Breaking the Conflict Trap: Civil War and Development Policy*. Washington, DC: World Bank and Oxford University Press.

Cooke, Bill, and Uma Kothari (eds.). 2001. *Participation: The New Tyranny?* London: Zed Books.

Cooper, Neil, Mandy Turner, and Michael Pugh. 2011. The End of History and the Last Liberal Peacebuilder: A Reply to Roland Paris, *Review of International Studies* 37(4).

Cover, Robert. 1983. Nomos and Narrative. *Harvard Law Review* 97.

Cunliffe, Philip. 2012. Still the Spectre at the Feast: Comparisons between Peacekeeping and Imperialism in Peacekeeping Studies Today. *International Peacekeeping* 19(4).

Davis, Laura. 2009. *Justice-Sensitive Security System Reform in the Democratic Republic of the Congo*. The Initiative for Peacebuilding.

de Carvalho, Benjamin, and Niels Nagelhus Schia. 2011. Local and National Ownership in Post-Conflict Liberia: Foreign and Domestic Inside Out? NUPI Working Paper 787.

de Greiff, Pablo, and Roger Duthie (eds.). 2009. *Transitional Justice and Development: Making Connections*. New York: ICTJ.

2006. Repairing the Past: Reparations for Victims of Human Rights Violations. In *The Handbook on Reparations*, ed. Pablo de Greiff. Oxford: Oxford University Press.

de Guevara, Berit Bliesemann, and Florian Kuhn. 2011. "The International Community Needs to Act": Loose Use and Empty Signaling of a Hackneyed Concept. *International Peacekeeping* 18(2).

Des Forges, Alison, and Timothy Longman. 2004. Legal Responses to Genocide in Rwanda. In *My Neighbor, My Enemy: Justice and Community in the Aftermath of Mass Atrocity*, ed. Eric Stover and Harvey Weinstein. Cambridge: Cambridge University Press.

Donais, Timothy. 2009. Empowerment or Imposition? Dilemmas of Local Ownership in Post-Conflict Peacebuilding Processes. *Peace and Change* 34(1).

2009. Haiti and the Dilemmas of Local Ownership. *International Journal* 64.

Donais, Timothy, and Amy Knorr. 2013. Peacebuilding from Below vs. the Liberal Peace: The Case of Haiti. *Canadian Journal of Development Studies* 34(1).

Dube, Siphiwe Ignatius. 2011. Transitional Justice beyond the Normative: Towards a Literary Theory of Political Transitions. *International Journal of Transitional Justice* 5(2).

Dugard, John. 1997. Obstacles in the Way of an International Criminal Court. *Cambridge Law Journal* 56(2).

Duthie, Roger. 2008. Toward a Development-Sensitive Approach to Transitional Justice. *International Journal of Transitional Justice* 2(3).

2009. Enhancing Justice and Development through Justice-Sensitive Security Sector Reform. In *Transitional Justice and Development: Making Connections*, ed. Pablo de Greiff and Roger Duthie. New York: ICTJ.

2009. Local Justice and Reintegration Processes as Complements to Transitional Justice and DDR. In *Disarming the Past: Transitional Justice and Ex-Combatants*, ed. Ana Cutter Patel, Pablo de Greiff, and Lars Waldorf. New York: Social Science Research Council.

2014. Transitional Justice, Development, and Economic Violence. In *Justice and Economic Violence in Transition*, ed. Dustin Sharp. New York: Springer.

Elster, Jon. 2004. *Closing the Books: Transitional Justice in Historical Perspective*. Cambridge: Cambridge University Press.

Faltas, Sami. 2005. *DDR without Camps: The Need for Decentralized Approaches: Topical Chapter of the Conversion Survey*. Bonn: International Center for Conversion.

Feek, Warren. 2007. Best of Practices? *Development in Practice* 17.

Fletcher, Laurel, and Harvey Weinstein. 2004. A World unto Itself? The Application of International Justice in the Former Yugoslavia. In *My Neighbor, My Enemy: Justice and Community in the Aftermath of Mass Atrocity*, ed. Eric Stover and Harvey Weinstein. Cambridge: Cambridge University Press.

Ford, Stuart. 2013. How Special Is the Special Court's Outreach Section? In *The Sierra Leone Special Court and Its Legacy: The Impact for Africa and International Law*, ed. Charles Jalloh. Cambridge: Cambridge University Press.

Freeman, Mark, and Veerle Opgenhaffen. 2005. *Transitional Justice in Morocco: A Progress Report*. New York: ICTJ.

Fukuyama, Francis. 1992. *The End of History and the Last Man*. New York: Avon Books.

Galtung, Johan. 1969. Violence, Peace, and Peace Research. *Peace Research* 6(3).

Gberie, Lansana. 2008. Truth and Justice on Trial in Liberia. *African Affairs* 107.

Gettleman Jeffrey, and Alexis Okeowo. 2008. Warlord's Absence Derails Another Peace Effort in Uganda. *New York Times*, April 12.

Ginifer, Jeremy. 2003. Reintegration of Ex-Combatants. In *Sierra Leone: Building the Road to Recovery*, ed. Mark Malan et al. Pretoria: Institute for Security Studies.

Glasius, Marlies. 2009. What Is Global Justice and Who Decides? Civil Society and Victim Responses to the International Criminal Court's First Investigations. *Human Rights Quarterly* 31(2).
    2012. Do International Criminal Courts Require Democratic Legitimacy? *European Journal of International Law* 23(1).
Goering, Curt. 2006. Amnesty International and Economic, Social, and Cultural Rights. In *Ethics in Action; The Ethical Challenges of International Human Rights Nongovernmental Organizations*, ed. Daniel Bell and Jean-Marc Coicaud. Cambridge: Cambridge University Press.
Goetschel, Laurent, and Tobias Hagmann. 2009. Civilian Peacebuilding: Peace by Bureaucratic Means? *Conflict, Security and Development* 9(1).
Golub, Stephen. 2007. The Rule of Law and the UN Peacebuilding Commission: A Social Development Approach. *Cambridge Review of International Affairs* 20(1).
Goodale, Mark. 2007. Locating Rights, Envisioning Law between the Global and the Local. In *The Practice of Human Rights: Tracking Law between the Global and the Local*, ed. Mark Goodale and Sally Engle Merry. Cambridge: Cambridge University Press.
Gready, Paul. 2005. Reconceptualizing Transitional Justice: Embedded and Distanced Justice. *Conflict, Security, and Development* 5(1).
Gready, Paul, and Simon Robins. 2014. From Transition to Transformative Justice: A New Agenda for Practice. *International Journal of Transitional Justice* 8(3).
Greenawalt, Alexander. 2009. Complementarity in Crisis: Uganda, Alternative Justice, and the International Criminal Court. *Virginia Journal of International Law* 50(107).
Hansen, Thomas Obel. 2011. Transitional Justice: Toward a Differentiated Theory. *Oregon Review of International Law* 13.
    2012. A Critical Review of the ICC's Recent Practice Concerning Admissibility Challenges and Complementarity. *Melbourne Journal of International Law* 13.
    2013. Kenya's Power-Sharing Arrangement and Its Implications for Transitional Justice. *International Journal of Human Rights* 17.
    2014. The Horizontal and Vertical Expansions of Transitional Justice: Explanations and Implications for a Contested Field. In *Transitional Justice Theories*, ed. Susanne Buckley-Zistel et al. Milton Park: Routledge.
Hayner, Priscilla. 1994. Fifteen Truth Commissions – 1974 to 1994: A Comparative Study. *Human Rights Quarterly* 16.
    2007. *Negotiating Peace in Liberia: Preserving the Possibility for Justice*. Geneva: Centre for Humanitarian Dialogue.
    2011. *Unspeakable Truths: Confronting State Terror and Atrocity*. New York: Routledge.
Hazan, Pierre. 2010. Transitional Justice after September 11. In *Localizing Transitional Justice: Interventions and Priorities after Mass Violence*, ed. Rosalind Shaw and Lars Waldorf. Stanford: Stanford University Press.
Healy, Paul. 2006. Human Rights and Intercultural Relations. *Philosophical and Social Criticism* 32.
Heathershaw, John. 2008. Unpacking the Liberal Peace: The Dividing and Merging of Peacebuilding Discourses. *Millennium: Journal of International Studies* 36(3).
Hellum, Anne. 1999. Women's Human Rights and African Customary Laws: Between Universalism and Relativism – Individualism and Communitarianism. In *Development and Rights; Negotiating Justice in Changing Societies*, ed. Christian Lund. New York: Frank Cass.
Herman, Johanna, Olga Martin-Ortega, and Chandra Lekha Sriram. 2013. Beyond Justice versus Peace: Transitional Justice and Peacebuilding Strategies. In *Rethinking*

Peacebuilding: The Quest for Just Peace in the Middle East and the Western Balkans, ed. Karin Aggestam and Annika Björkdahl. Milton Park: Routledge.

Hickey, Sam, and Giles Mohan. 2004. Towards Participation as Transformation: Critical Themes and Challenges. In *Participation: From Tyranny to Transformation?*, ed. Samuel Hickey and Giles Mohan. New York: Zed Books.

Higonnet, Etelle. 2006. Restructuring Hybrid Courts: Local Empowerment and National Criminal Justice Reform. *Arizona Journal of International and Comparative Law* 23.

Hinton, Alexander (ed.). 2010. *Transitional Justice: Global Mechanisms and Local Realities after Genocide and Mass Violence.* Newark: Rutgers University Press.

Human Rights Watch. 2002. US: "Hague Invasion Act" Becomes Law. Press Release, August 4.

———. 2004. *Some Transparency, No Accountability: The Use of Oil Revenue in Angola and Its Impact on Human Rights.* New York: Human Rights Watch.

———. 2007. *Chop Fine: The Human Rights Impact of Local Government Corruption and Mismanagement in Rivers State, Nigeria.* New York: HRW.

———. 2011. *Justice Compromised: The Legacy of Rwanda's Community Based Gacaca Courts.* New York: HRW.

———. 2013. *Turning Rhetoric into Reality: Accountability for Serious International Crimes in Côte d'Ivoire.* New York: HRW.

Humphreys, Macartan, and Jeremy Weinstein. 2007. Demobilization and Reintegration. *Journal of Conflict Resolution* 51(4).

Huntington, Samuel. 1991. *The Third Wave: Democratization in the Late Twentieth Century.* Norman: University of Oklahoma Press.

Hussain, Varda. 2005. Sustaining Judicial Rescues: The Role of Judicial Outreach and Capacity-Building Efforts in War Crimes Tribunals. *Virginia Journal of International Law* 45.

Huyse, Luc. 2008. Introduction: Tradition-Based Approaches in Peacemaking, Transitional Justice, and Reconciliation Policies. In *Traditional Justice and Reconciliation after Violent Conflict*, ed. Luc Huyse and Mark Salter. Stockholm: IDEA.

Iliff, Andrew. 2012. Root and Branch: Discourses of "Tradition" in Grassroots Transitional Justice. *International Journal of Transitional Justice* 6(2).

Ingelare, Bert. 2008. The Gacaca Courts in Rwanda. In *Traditional Justice and Reconciliation after Violent Conflict: Learning from African Experiences*, ed. Luc Huyse and Mark Salter. Stockholm: IDEA.

International Commission on Intervention and State Sovereignty. 2001. *The Responsibility to Protect.*

International Crisis Group. 2001. *International Criminal Tribunal for Rwanda: Justice Delayed.* Africa Report 30. Brussels: ICG.

———. 2004. *Liberia and Sierra Leone: Rebuilding Failed States.* Africa Report 87. Dakar/Brussels: ICG.

IRIN Humanitarian News and Analysis. 2003. Liberia: ECOWAS Chairman Urges UN to Lift Taylor Indictment. June 30.

Isser, Deborah (ed.). 2011. *Customary Justice and the Rule of Law in War-Torn Societies.* Washington, DC: USIP.

Jalloh, Charles. 2013. What Makes a Crime against Humanity a Crime against Humanity? *American University Law Review* 28(2).

James-Allen, Paul, Aaron Weah, and Lizzie Goodfriend. 2010. *Beyond the Truth and Reconciliation Commission: Transitional Justice Options in Liberia.* New York: International Center for Transitional Justice.

Joseph, Edward. 2007. Ownership Is Over-rated. *SAIS Review* 27.
Jubilut, Liliana Lyra. 2011. Towards a New Jus Post Bellum: The United Nations Peacebuilding Commission and the Improvement of Post-Conflict Efforts and Accountability. *Minnesota Journal of International Law* 9.
Kelsall, Tim. 2005. Truth, Lies, Ritual: Preliminary Reflections on the Truth and Reconciliation Commission in Sierra Leone. *Human Rights Quarterly* 27.
Kennedy, David. 2002. The International Human Rights Movement: Part of the Problem? *Harvard Human Rights Journal* 15.
    2006. The "Rule of Law," Political Choices and Development of Common Sense. In *The New Law and Economic Development*, ed. David M. Trubek and Alvaro Santos. Cambridge: Cambridge University Press.
    2012. The International Human Rights Regime: Still Part of the Problem? In *Examining Critical Perspectives on Human Rights*, ed. Rob Dickinson et al. Cambridge: Cambridge University Press.
Kennedy, Duncan. 1976. Form and Substance in Private Law Adjudication. *Harvard Law Review* 89.
Knaus, Gerald, and Felix Martin. 2003. Travails of the European Raj. *Journal of Democracy* 14(3).
Knight, Mark, and Alpaslan Özerdem. 2004. Guns, Camps and Cash: Disarmament, Demobilization and Reinsertion of Former Combatants in Transitions from War to Peace. *Journal of Peace Research* 41(4).
Kritz, Neil (ed.). 1995. *Transitional Justice: How Emerging Democracies Reckon with Former Regimes, Volume I. General Considerations*. Washington, DC: United States Institute of Peace.
Kuhn, Florian. 2012. The Peace Prefix: Ambiguities of the Word "Peace." *International Peacekeeping* 19(4).
Lambourne, Wendy. 2009. Transitional Justice and Peacebuilding after Mass Violence. *International Journal of Transitional Justice* 3(1).
Laplante, Lisa. 2007. On the Indivisibility of Rights: Truth Commissions, Reparations, and the Right to Development. *Yale Human Rights and Development Law Journal* 10.
    2008. Transitional Justice and Peace Building: Diagnosing and Addressing the Socioeconomic Roots of Violence through a Human Rights Framework. *International Journal of Transitional Justice* 2.
Leebaw, Bronwyn Anne. 2008. The Irreconcilable Goals of Transitional Justice. *Human Rights Quarterly* 30(1).
Le Mon, Christopher. 2007. Rwanda's Troubled Gacaca Courts. *Human Rights Brief* 14.
Liden, Kristoffer, Roger Mac Ginty, and Oliver Richmond. 2009. Introduction: Beyond Northern Epistemologies of Peace: Peacebuilding Reconstructed? *International Peacekeeping* 16(5).
Longman, Timothy, et al. 2004. Connecting Justice to Human Experience: Attitudes toward Accountability and Reconciliation in Rwanda. In *My Neighbor, My Enemy: Justice and Community in the Aftermath of Mass Atrocity*, ed. Eric Stover and Harvey Weinstein. Cambridge: Cambridge University Press.
Lundy, Patricia. 2009. Exploring Home-Grown Transitional Justice and Its Dilemmas: A Case Study of the Historical Enquiries Team, Northern Ireland. *International Journal of Transitional Justice* 3(3).
    2011. Paradoxes and Challenges of Transitional Justice at the "Local" Level: Historical Enquiries in Northern Ireland. *Contemporary Social Science* 6(1).

Lundy, Patricia, and Mark McGovern. 2008. Whose Justice? Rethinking Transitional Justice from the Bottom Up. *Journal of Law and Society* 35(2).

Mac Ginty, Roger. 2008. Indigenous Peace-Making versus the Liberal Peace. *Cooperation and Conflict: Journal of the Nordic Studies Association* 43(2).

——— 2011. *International Peacebuilding and Local Resistance: Rethinking Peace and Conflict*. New York: Palgrave Macmillan.

Mac Ginty, Roger, and Gurchathen Sanghera. 2012. Hybridity in Peacebuilding and Development: An Introduction. *Journal of Peacebuilding and Development* 7(2).

Mani, Rama. 2002. *Beyond Retribution: Seeking Justice in the Shadows of War*. Cambridge: Blackwell.

——— 2005. Rebuilding an Inclusive Political Community after War. *Security Dialogue* 36(4).

——— 2008. Dilemmas of Expanding Transitional Justice, or Forging the Nexus between Transitional Justice and Development. *International Journal of Transitional Justice* 2(3).

Martin-Ortega, Olga, and Johanna Herman. 2012. Hybrid Tribunals: Interaction and Resistance in Bosnia and Herzegovina and Cambodia. In *Hybrid Forms of Peace: From Everyday Agency to Post-Liberalism*, ed. Oliver Richmond and Audra Mitchell. New York: Palgrave Macmillan.

Mazlish, Bruce. 2005. The Global and the Local. *Current Sociology* 53(1).

McAuliffe, Padraig. 2011. Hybrid Tribunals at Ten: How International Criminal Justice's Golden Child Became an Orphan. *Journal of International Law and International Relations* 7.

——— 2011. Transitional Justice's Expanding Empire: Reasserting the Value of the Paradigmatic Transition. *Journal of Conflictology* 2(2).

McEvoy, Kieran. 2007. Beyond Legalism: Towards a Thicker Understanding of Transitional Justice. *Journal of Law and Society* 34(4).

McEvoy, Kieran, and Lorna McGregor (eds.). 2008. *Transitional Justice from Below*. Portland: Hart.

Mead, Walter Russell. 2014. The Return of Geopolitics; the Revenge of Revisionist Powers. *Foreign Affairs*, May/June.

Mendeloff, David. 2004. Truth-Seeking, Truth-Telling, and Postconflict Peacebuilding: Curb the Enthusiasm? *International Studies Review* 6(3).

Merry, Sally Engle. 1997. Global Human Rights and Local Social Movements in a Legally Plural World. *Canadian Journal of Law and Society* 12.

——— 1997. Legal Pluralism and Transnational Culture: The Ka Ho'okolokolonui Kanaka Maoli Tribunal, Hawai'i, 1993. In *Human Rights, Culture and Contest; Anthropological Perspectives*, ed. Richard Wilson. London: Pluto Press.

Millar, Gearoid, Jair Van DerLijn, and Willemijn Verkoren. 2013. Peacebuilding Plans and Local Reconfigurations: Frictions between Imported Processes and Indigenous Practices. *International Peacekeeping* 20(2).

Miller, Zinaida. 2008. Effects of Invisibility: In Search of the "Economic" in Transitional Justice. *International Journal of Transitional Justice* 2(3).

Ministry of Foreign Affairs Sweden. 2006. *Stockholm Initiative on DDR*. Final Report 30. Stockholm.

Mobekk, Eirin. 2006. *Transitional Justice and Security Sector Reform: Enabling Sustainable Peace*. Occasional Paper 13. Geneva: DCAF.

Murithi, Tim. 2006. African Approaches to Building Peace and Social Solidarity. *African Journal on Conflict Resolution* 6.

Musila, Godfrey. 2009. Options for Transitional Justice in Kenya: Autonomy and the Challenge of External Prescriptions. *International Journal of Transitional Justice* 3(3).

Mutua, Makau. 1996. The Ideology of Human Rights. *Virginia Journal of International Law* 36.
   1997. Never Again: Questioning the Yugoslav and Rwanda Tribunals. *Temple International and Comparative Law Journal* 11.
   2001. Savages, Victims, and Saviors: The Metaphor of Human Rights. *Harvard International Law Journal* 42.
   2004. Republic of Kenya, Report of the Task Force on the Establishment of a Truth, Justice and Reconciliation Commission. *Buffalo Human Rights Law Review* 10.
Nagy, Rosemary. 2008. Transitional Justice as a Global Project: Critical Reflections. *Third World Quarterly* 29(2).
Newman, Edward, Roland Paris, and Oliver Richmond. 2009. Introduction. In *New Perspectives on Liberal Peacebuilding*, ed. Edward Newman, Roland Paris, and Oliver Richmond. New York: United Nations University.
O'Donnell, Guillermo, and Philippe Schmitter. 1995. Transitions from Authoritarian Rule: Tentative Conclusions about Uncertain Democracies. In *Transitional Justice: How Emerging Democracies Reckon with Former Regimes, Volume I. General Considerations*, ed. Neil Kritz. Washington, DC: United States Institute of Peace.
Okello, Moses Chrispus. 2010. Afterword: Elevating Transitional Local Justice or Crystallizing Global Governance? In *Localizing Transitional Justice: Interventions and Priorities after Mass Violence*, ed. Rosalind Shaw and Lars Waldorf. Stanford: Stanford University Press.
Olsen, Tricia, Leigh Payne, and Andrew Reiter. 2010. *Transitional Justice in Balance: Comparing Processes, Weighing Efficiency*. Washington, DC: USIP.
Oomen, Barbara. 2005. Donor-Driven Justice and Its Discontents: The Case of Rwanda. *Development and Change* 36(5).
Orentlicher, Diane. 1991. Settling Accounts: The Duty to Prosecute Human Rights Violations of a Prior Regime. *Yale Law Journal* 100(8).
Organization for Economic Cooperation and Development. 2007. *OECD DAC Handbook on Security System Reform: Supporting Security and Justice*. Paris: OECD Publishing.
Ortega, Luisa Maria Dietrich. 2009. Transitional Justice and Female Ex-Combatants: Lessons Learned from International Experience. In *Disarming the Past: Transitional Justice and Ex-Combatants*, ed. Ana Cutter Patel, Pablo de Greiff, and Lars Waldorf. New York: ICTJ.
Otim, Michael, and Marieke Wierda. 2008. Justice at Juba: International Obligations and Local Demands in Northern Uganda. In *Courting Conflict? Justice, Peace and the ICC in Africa*, ed. Nicholas Waddell and Phil Clark. London: The Royal African Society.
Paris, Roland. 1997. Peacebuilding and the Limits of Liberal Internationalism. *International Security* 22(2).
   2002. International Peacebuilding and the "Mission Civilisatrice." *Review of International Studies* 28(4).
   2003. Peacekeeping and the Constraints of Global Culture. *European Journal of International Relations* 9(3).
   2004. *At War's End: Building Peace after Civil Conflict*. Cambridge: Cambridge University Press.
   2009. Understanding the "Coordination Problem" in Postwar Statebuilding. In *The Dilemmas of Statebuilding: Confronting the Contradictions of Postwar Peace Operations*, ed. Roland Paris and Timothy D. Sisk. Milton Park: Routledge.
   2010. Saving Liberal Peacebuilding. *Review of International Studies* 2.

Paris, Roland, and Timothy Sisk. 2007. *Managing Contradictions: The Inherent Dilemmas of Postwar Statebuilding*. New York: International Peace Academy/Research Partnership on Postwar Statebuilding.
Park, Augustine. 2010. Community-Based Restorative Transitional Justice in Sierra Leone. *Contemporary Justice Review* 13(1).
Perriello, Tom, and Marieke Wierda. 2006. *The Special Court for Sierra Leone Under Scrutiny*. New York: ICTJ.
Peskin, Victor. 2005. Courting Rwanda: The Promises and Pitfalls of the ICTR Outreach Programme. *Journal of International Criminal Justice* 3.
Peterson, Jenny. 2012. A Conceptual Unpacking of Hybridity: Accounting for Notions of Power, Politics and Progress in Analyses of Aid-Drive Interfaces. *Journal of Peacebuilding and Development* 7(2).
Pham, Phuong, and Patrick Vinck. 2007. Empirical Research and the Development and Assessment of Transitional Justice Mechanisms. *International Journal of Transitional Justice* 1(2).
Posner, Eric, and Adrian Vermeule. 2003. Transitional Justice as Ordinary Justice. *Harvard Law Review* 117(3).
Pugh, Michael, Neil Cooper, and Mandy Turner (eds.). 2008. *Whose Peace? Critical Perspectives on the Political Economy of Peacebuilding*. New York: Palgrave Macmillan.
Pupavac, Vanessa. 2002. Pathologizing Populations and Colonizing Minds: International Psychosocial Programs in Kosovo. *Alternatives: Global, Local, Political* 27.
Rajagopal, Balakrishnan. 2008. Invoking the Rule of Law in Post-Conflict Rebuilding: A Critical Examination. *William and Mary Law Review* 49.
Ramji-Nogales, Jaya. 2010–11. Designing Bespoke Transitional Justice: A Pluralist Process Approach. *Michigan Journal of International Law* 21.
Reiger, Caitlin. 2006. Hybrid Attempts at Accountability for Serious Crimes in Timor Leste. In *Transitional Justice in the Twenty-First Century: Beyond Truth versus Justice*, ed. Naomi Roht-Arriaza and Javier Mariezcurrena. Cambridge: Cambridge University Press.
Republic of Chad. 1990. Decree Creating the Commission of Inquiry into the Crimes and Misappropriations Committed by ex-President Habré, His Accomplices and/or Accessories, Decree 014/P.CE/CJ/90. December 29.
1993. *Les Crimes et Détournements de l'ex-Président Habré et de ses Complices*. Paris: L'Harmattan.
Republic of East Timor. 2005. *Chega!, The Report of the Commission for Reception, Truth and Reconciliation in Timor Leste*. Final Report.
Republic of Ghana. 2004. *National Reconciliation Commission Report*.
Republic of Kenya. 2008. *The Truth, Justice and Reconciliation Act*.
Republic of Liberia. 2005. *An Act to Establish the Truth and Reconciliation Commission for Liberia*. May 12.
2009. *Truth and Reconciliation Commission*. Consolidated Final Report.
Republic of Sierra Leone. 2000. *The Truth and Reconciliation Act*.
2004. *Witness to Truth, Report of the Sierra Leone Truth and Reconciliation Commission*.
Richmond, Oliver. 2007. Emancipatory Forms of Human Security and Liberal Peacebuilding. *International Journal* 62.
2007. *The Transformation of Peace*. New York: Palgrave Macmillan.
2009. The Romanticisation of the Local: Welfare, Culture, and Peacebuilding. *International Spectator: Italian Journal of International Affairs* 44(1).

2010. Resistance and the Post-Liberal Peace. *Millennium – Journal of International Studies* 38.

2011. *A Post-Liberal Peace*. Milton Park: Routledge.

Richmond, Oliver, and Audra Mitchell. 2012. Towards a Post-Liberal Peace: Exploring Hybridity via Everyday Forms of Resistance. In *Hybrid Forms of Peace: From Everyday to Post-Liberalism*, ed. Oliver Richmond and Audra Mitchell. New York: Palgrave Macmillan.

Roberts, David. 2011. *Liberal Peacebuilding and Global Governance: Beyond the Metropolis*. New York: Routledge.

2011. Post-Conflict Peacebuilding, Liberal Irrelevance and the Locus of Legitimacy. *International Peacekeeping* 18.

Roht-Arriaza, Naomi. 2004. Reparations in the Aftermath of Repression and Mass Violence. In *My Neighbor, My Enemy*, ed. Eric Stover and Harvey Weinstein. Cambridge: Cambridge University Press.

2006. The New Landscape of Transitional Justice. In *Transitional Justice in the Twenty-First Century: Beyond Truth versus Justice*, ed. Naomi Roht-Arriaza and Javier Mariezcurrena. Cambridge: Cambridge University Press.

Rome Statute of the International Criminal Court. 1998. 2187 UNTS 90 (July 2002).

Roth, Kenneth. 2004. Defending Economic, Social and Cultural Rights: Practical Issues Faced by an International Human Rights Organization. *Human Rights Quarterly* 26(1).

Rothberg, Michael. 2012. Progress, Progression, Procession: William Kentridge and the Narratology of Transitional Justice. *Narrative* 20(1).

Rubli, Sandra. 2012. *Transitional Justice: Justice by Bureaucratic Means?* Swiss Peace Working Paper 4. Geneva: Swiss Peace.

Saul, Matthew. 2012. Local Ownership of the International Criminal Tribunal for Rwanda: Restorative and Retributive Effects. *International Criminal Law Review* 12.

Schabas, William. 2007. *An Introduction to the International Criminal Court*. Cambridge: Cambridge University Press.

2013. The Banality of International Justice. *Journal of International Criminal Justice* 11(3).

Scharf, Michael. 1997. The Case for a Permanent International Truth Commission. *Duke Comparative and International Law Journal* 7.

Schellhaas, Constanze, and Annette Seegers. 2009. Peacebuilding: Imperialism's New Disguise? *African Security Review* 18(2).

Schmid, Evelyne. 2011. War Crimes Related to Violations of Economic, Social and Cultural Rights. *Heidelberg Journal of International Law* 71(3).

Schoiswohl, Michael. 2011. What's Law Got to Do with It? The Role of Law in Post-conflict Democratization and Its (Flawed) Assumptions. In *Rethinking Liberal Peace; External Models and Local Alternatives*, ed. Shahrbanou Tadjbakhsh. New York: Routledge.

Sending, Ole. 2009. Why Peacebuilders Fail to Secure Ownership and be Sensitive to Context. Security in Practice, NUPI Working Paper 755.

Sesay, Mohamed Gibril, and Mohamed Suma. 2009. *Transitional Justice and DDR: The Case of Sierra Leone*. New York: ICTJ.

Sharp, Dustin. 2003. Prosecutions, Development, and Justice; The Trial of Hissein Habré. *Harvard Human Rights Journal* 16.

2011. Requiem for a Pipedream; Oil, the World Bank, and the Need for Human Rights Assessments. *Emory International Law Review* 25.

2012. Addressing Economic Violence in Times of Transition: Toward a Positive-Peace Paradigm for Transitional Justice. *Fordham International Law Journal* 35.

2012. Bridging the Gap: The United Nations Peacebuilding Commission and the Challenges of Integrating DDR and Transitional Justice. In *Transitional Justice and Peacebuilding on the Ground: Victims and Ex-Combatants*, ed. Chandra Lekha Sriram et al. London: Routledge.

2013. Beyond the Post-Conflict Checklist: Linking Peacebuilding and Transitional Justice Through the Lens of Critique. *Chicago Journal of International Law* 14(1).

2013. Interrogating the Peripheries; The Preoccupations of Fourth Generation Transitional Justice. *Harvard Human Rights Journal* 26.

(ed.). 2014. *Justice and Economic Violence in Transition*. New York: Springer.

Shaw, Rosalind. 2005. *Rethinking Truth and Reconciliation Commissions; Lessons from Sierra Leone*. United States Institute for Peace Special Report 130. Washington: USIP.

Shaw, Rosalind, and Lars Waldorf (eds.). 2010. *Localizing Transitional Justice: Interventions and Priorities after Mass Violence*. Stanford: Stanford University Press.

Sikkink, Kathryn. 2011. *The Justice Cascade: How Human Rights Prosecutions Are Changing World Politics*. New York: W. W. Norton.

Solomon Islands. 2008. *Truth and Reconciliation Act*.

Sriram, Chandra Lekha. 2007. Justice as Peace? Liberal Peacebuilding and Strategies of Transitional Justice. *Global Society* 21(4).

2004. *Confronting Past Human Rights Violations: Justice vs Peace in Times of Transition*. New York: Frank Cass.

2012. Post-Conflict Justice and Hybridity in Peacebuilding: Resistance or Cooptation. In *Hybrid Forms of Peace*, ed. Oliver Richmond and Audra Mitchell. New York: Palgrave Macmillan.

Sriram, Chandra Lekha, and Johanna Herman. 2009. DDR and Transitional Justice: Bridging the Divide? *Conflict, Security, and Development* 9(4).

Sriram, Chandra, Olga Martin-Ortega, and Johanna Herman. 2009. Evaluating and Comparing Strategies of Peacebuilding and Transitional Justice. JAD-PbP Working Paper Series 1. May.

2011. Promoting the Rule of Law: From Liberal to Institutional Peacebuilding. In *Peacebuilding and the Rule of Law in Africa: Just Peace?*, ed. Chandra Lekha Sriram, Olga Martin-Ortega, and Johanna Herman. Milton Park: Routledge.

Stahn, Carsten. 2004–5. Justice under Transitional Administration: Contours and Critique of a Paradigm. *Houston Journal of International Law* 27.

Stanley, Elizabeth. 2009. Transitional Justice: From the Local to the International. In *The Ashgate Research Companion to Ethics and International Relations*, ed. Patrick Hayden. Farnham: Ashgate.

Steinberg, Jonny. 2009. Liberia's Experiment with Transitional Justice. *African Affairs* 109.

Stensrud, Ellen. 2009. New Dilemmas in Transitional Justice: Lessons from the Mixed Courts in Sierra Leone and Cambodia. *Journal of Peace Research* 46(1).

Straus, Scott. 2012. Wars Do End! Changing Patterns of Political Violence in Sub-Saharan Africa. *African Affairs* 111(43).

Suhrke, Astri, and Ingrid Samset. 2007. What's in a Figure? Estimating Recurrence of Civil War. *International Peacekeeping* 14(2).

Tadjbakhsh, Shahrbanou. 2011. Liberal Peace in Dispute. In *Rethinking Liberal Peace; External Models and Local Alternatives*, ed. Shahrbanou Tadjbakhsh. New York: Routledge.

Talentino, Andrea. 2007. Perceptions of Peacebuilding: The Dynamic of Imposer and Imposed Upon. *International Studies Review* 8(2).

Tamanha, Brian. 2008. Understanding Legal Pluralism: Past to Present, Local to Global. *Sydney Law Review* 30.

Teitel, Ruti. 2000. *Transitional Justice*. New York: Oxford University Press.
  2002. Transitional Justice in a New Era. *Fordham International Law Journal* 26(4).
  2003. Transitional Justice Genealogy. *Harvard Human Rights Journal* 16.
  2008. Transitional Justice Globalized. *International Journal of Transitional Justice* 2(1).
Thallinger, Gerhard. 2007. The UN Peacebuilding Commission and Transitional Justice. *German Law Journal* 8.
Theidon, Kimberly. 2007. Transitional Subjects: The Disarmament, Demobilization and Reintegration of Former Combatants in Columbia. *International Journal of Transitional Justice* 1(1).
Thoms, Oskar, et al. 2010. State-Level Effects of Transitional Justice: What Do We Know? *International Journal of Transitional Justice* 4(3).
Thomson, Susan, and Rosemary Nagy. 2010. Law, Power and Justice: What Legalism Fails to Address in the Functioning of Rwanda's Gacaca Courts. *International Journal of Transitional Justice* 5(1).
Triponel, Anna, and Stephen Pearson. 2010. What Do You Think Should Happen? Public Participation in Transitional Justice. *Pace International Law Review* 22.
Tschirgi, Necla. 2012. Bridging the Chasm between Domestic and International Approaches to Peacebuilding. Paper for presentation at the joint CISS/KEYNOTE conference "Between the Global and the Local: Actors, Institutions and Processes," Prague, June 24–26.
United Nations, 2009. Message by Ms. Navanethem Pillay at the Special Summit of the African Union. October 22. www.unhchr.ch/huricane/huricane.nsf/0/110E705F1034E048C1257657005814CE?opendocument.
  Review of the United Nations Peacebuilding Architecture. UN Doc. A/64/868–S/2010/393.
United Nations. 1992. *Agenda for Peace, Preventative Diplomacy, Peacemaking and Peace Keeping*. UN Doc. A/47/277–S/24111.
United Nations Department of Peacekeeping Operations. 2006. *Integrated Disarmament, Demobilization and Reintegration Standards (IDDRS)*. New York: United Nations.
  2008. *United Nations Peacekeeping Operations: Principles and Guidelines*. New York: United Nations.
United Nations Development Programme. 2005. *Practice Note: Disarmament, Demobilization and Reintegration of Ex-Combatants*. New York: UNDP.
United Nations General Assembly. 2000. Resolution 55/2, "Millennium Declaration." UN Doc. A/RES/55.2. September 18.
  2005. Resolution 60/180. UN Doc. A/RES/60/180.
  2005. Resolution A/60/L.1. September 15.
United Nations Peacebuilding Commission. 2008. *Strategic Framework for Peacebuilding in Burundi*. UN Doc. PBC/1/BDI/4.
United Nations Secretary-General. 2004. *Report of the High-level Panel on Threats, Challenges and Change*. UN Doc. A/59/565. December 2.
  2004. *The Rule of Law and Transitional Justice in Post-conflict Societies*. UN Doc. S/2004/616. August 23.
  2009. *Report of the Secretary-General on Peacebuilding in the Immediate Aftermath of Conflict*. UN Doc. A/63/881-S/2009/304. June 11.
  2010. *Guidance Note of the Secretary-General: United Nations Approach to Transitional Justice*.
  2011. *The Rule of Law and Transitional Justice in Conflict and Post-Conflict Societies*. UN Doc. S/2011/634. October 12.

2011. *Strengthening and Coordinating United Nations Rule of Law Activities*, UN Doc. A/66/133. August 8.
United Nations Security Council. 1994. Resolution 955.
2005. Resolution 1645.
United Nations World Conference on Human Rights. 1993. *Vienna Declaration and Programme of Action*. UN Doc. A/CONF.157/23. July 12.
United States American Service-Members Protection Act of 2002, 22 USC § 7427.
United States Department of Justice. 2013. *Lawfulness of a Lethal Operation Directed Against a U.S. Citizen Who Is a Senior Operational Leader of Al-Qa'ida or An Associated Force*. White paper. Leaked copy available at http://msnbcmedia.msn.com/i/msnbc/sections/news/020413_DOJ_White_Paper.pdf.
Uvin, Peter. 2001. Difficult Choices in the New Post-Conflict Agenda: The International Community in Rwanda after the Genocide. *Third World Quarterly* 22(2).
Uvin, Peter, and Charles Mironko. 2003. Western and Local Approaches to Justice in Rwanda. *Global Governance* 9.
Valji, Nahla. 2006. *Ghana's National Reconciliation Commission: A Comparative Assessment*. International Center for Transitional Justice, Occasional Paper Series. New York: ICTJ.
Valls, Andrew. 2003. Racial Justice as Transitional Justice. *Polity* 36(1).
van Boven, Theo. 2005. Basic Principles and Guidelines on the Right to a Remedy for Victims of Gross Violations of International Human Rights Law and Serious Violations of International Humanitarian Law, Introductory Note. December 16. http://legal.un.org/avl/ha/ga_60-147/ga_60-147.html.
van der Merwe, Hugo, Victoria Baxter, and Audrey Chapman (eds.). 2009. *Assessing the Impact of Transitional Justice*. Washington, DC: USIP.
van Zyl, Paul. 2005. Promoting Transitional Justice in Post-Conflict Societies. In *Security Governance in Post-Conflict Peacebuilding*, ed. Alan Bryden and Heiner Hänggis. Geneva: DCAF.
Vaughan, Jenny, and Aude Genet. 2013. Africa Closes Ranks to Condemn "Racist" ICC on Kenya Cases. Associated France Press, May 27.
Venter, Christine. 2007. Eliminating Fear through Recreating Community in Rwanda: The Role of the Gacaca Courts. *Texas Wesleyan Law Review* 13.
Viaene, Lieselotte, and Eva Brems. 2010. Transitional Justice and Cultural Contexts: Learning from the Universality Debate. *Netherlands Quarterly of Human Rights* 28.
Vielle, Stephanie. 2012. Transitional Justice: A Colonizing Field? *Amsterdam Law Forum* 4(3).
von Carlowitz, Leopold. 2011. *Local Ownership in Practice: Justice System Reform in Kosovo and Liberia*. DCAF Occasional Paper 23. Geneva: DCAF.
Waldorf, Lars. 2006. Mass Justice for Mass Atrocity: Rethinking Local Justice as Transitional Justice. *Temple Law Review* 79.
2009. Introduction: Linking DDR and Transitional Justice. In *Disarming the Past: Transitional Justice and Ex-Combatants*, ed. Ana Cutter Patel, Pablo de Greiff, and Lars Waldorf. New York: ICTJ.
2012. Anticipating the Past: Transitional Justice and Socio-Economic Wrongs. *Social and Legal Studies* 21.
Weinstein, Harvey, et al. 2010. Stay the Hand of Justice: Whose Priorities Take Priority? In *Localizing Transitional Justice: Interventions and Priorities after Mass Violence*, ed. Rosalind Shaw and Lars Waldorf. Stanford: Stanford University Press.

Witte, Eric. 2009. Beyond "Peace versus Justice": Understanding the Relationship between DDR Programs and the Prosecution of International Crimes. In *Disarming the Past: Transitional Justice and Ex-Combatants*, ed. Ana Cutter Patel, Pablo de Greiff, and Lars Waldorf. New York: ICTJ.

Yacoubian, George. 2003. Evaluating the Efficacy of the International Tribunals for Rwanda and the Former Yugoslavia: Implications for Criminology and International Criminal Law. *World Affairs* 165.

Index

9/11, 99

Aborigines, 81–82
academic theory, 110
access to justice, 42, 101, 114, 131–32, 148
accountability, 21–22, 114, 120, 121, 141, 143–44, 164
acculturation, 9, 133
Acholi, 10, 50, 53
ad hoc tribunals, 7, 48
affirmative action, 26, 28–29
Afghanistan, 111
African Union, 50
agency, 66, 150, 152
  control, 42–43, 66
  process, 42–43, 66
  substance, 42–43, 66
Agenda for Peace report, 98
al-Bashir, Omar, 51, 118
Albuja, Sebastián, 12–13, 56
Alfonsín, Raúl, 84
alternative liberalisms, 139
American Service-Members Protection Act of 2002, 51
amnesty, 6, 8, 53, 84, 85, 88, 119, 120, 121, 137, 161
Amnesty International, 27–28
Angola, 111
An-Na'im, Abdullahi, 8, 71
Annan, Kofi, 40, 71, 120
apartheid, 20, 25, 30
Argentina, 3, 6, 33, 77, 78, 84–85, 86, 142, 159
arms trade, 24
Arthur, Paige, 9, 10–11, 143
Aspen Institute, 9
atrocity justice, 4, 20
Australia, 81–82, 86, 90

authoritarianism, 76, 78, 84, 163
autonomy, 149–50, 159

barbarism, 76
basic needs, 20, 145
Bendix, Daniel, 58
Berlin Wall, x–xi, 97
Berman, Paul, 72
blanket amnesty, 8, 84
blind spots, 5, 12–13, 15, 21, 22, 75, 89, 96, 110, 151, 154, 163
Boraine, Alex, 119
Bosnia, 111, 120
Bosnia-Herzegovina, 100
Boutros-Ghali, Boutros, 98
Brazil, 86
Bringing them Home Report, 81
Burundi, 51, 100
Bush, George W., 51

Cambodia, 7, 48, 62, 100, 120, 140
Canada, 81–82, 86
capitalism, 2, 149–50
Carothers, Thomas, 78, 87
Carranza, Ruben, 32
Cavallaro, James, 12–13, 56
Central African Republic, 50, 100
Chad, 7, 35, 36, 37, 79, 83, 87, 100, 158
Chesterman, Simon, 57
Chile, 4, 77, 85–86, 142
China, 24
civil and political rights, 3, 20, 21, 26, 33, 124, 141, 148, 152, 158. *See also* human rights
civil war, 23, 53, 60, 146, 163
Cold War, viii–ix, 2, 5, 21, 23, 27, 45, 79, 96–98, 105, 106, 109

183

Colombia, 115
colonialism, 71
Comisión Nacional sobre la Desaparición de Personas (CONADEP), 84
Commission for Reception, Truth, and Reconciliation in East Timor, 36
Commission of Inquiry into the Disappearance of People in Uganda, 80
communism, 76
community outreach, 46
Community Reconciliation Process (East Timor), 69
complementarity, 51–53, 128–32, 151
conflicts, 23–26
  causes of, 24
  human rights violations in, 26
  violence in, 25
Congo, 50, 100
consultants, 7, 12, 55–56
consultations, 9, 56, 67, 104, 133, 146
context-sensitive approach, xi, 4, 5, 8, 12, 25–26, 29–30, 31–32, 35, 41, 42–43, 54–55, 57, 58–59, 61, 67, 77, 82, 86–87, 88, 96–97, 99, 105, 116, 120–21, 126–27, 133, 139, 141, 143, 149–50, 155, 159, 163
corruption, 24, 32, 140
Côte d'Ivoire, 7, 50, 54, 80–81, 100, 140, 146
  civil war, 100–01
  peacekeeping to peacebuilding in, 100–03
  presidential election, 101–02
  zone of confidence, 101
coup d'état, 79
Cover, Robert, 96, 155
crimes against humanity, viii, 2, 3, 54, 80–81, 83
criminal justice, 11
critical legal studies, 138
critical studies, 111, 112, 113, 138
critical theory, 14, 113, 138, 139, 150–53, 154, 155–56, 165
Croatia, 100
cultural relativism, 41–42, 72, 73
cultural violence, 20
Cyprus, 98

Dada, Idi Amin, 80
Davenport, Christian, 82
Déby, Idriss, 79
decision making, 149–50, 159
demobilization, disarmament, and reintegration (DDR), 115, 121–30, 134–35
democracy, 87–88, 110, 114, 124, 143–44, 149
Democratic Republic of Congo, 50, 100
democratic transitions, 4–5, 22, 76, 78, 87, 89, 90
democratization, 78, 87–88

developing countries, 106
development, xi, 3, 5, 23, 29, 97, 105, 109
  broad-based, 31–32
  democracy and, 106
  economic, 119, 121–35
  participatory, 57, 67
  peace operations and, 124, 125
  peacebuilding and, 133, 142, 155
  rule of law and, 106
  social, 104–05, 119
  social justice and, 157
  sustainable, 98–99, 104–05, 114
dictatorship, 86, 88–89, 142–43
direct violence, 20
disappearances, 3, 25, 33, 80, 84, 85, 124
distributive justice, 10, 21–22, 28–29, 31–32, 89, 90, 124, 141, 149–50, 157, 160–61. See also justice
divisionism, 79
dominant liberal script, 15, 39–41
Donais, Timothy, 58, 139
donors, 58, 103
  bilateral, 104, 108, 132
  international, 12, 55–56, 64–66, 96, 103, 152
  security sector reform, 58
Due Obedience law (Argentina), 84

East Timor, 7, 35, 36, 48, 56, 62, 69, 70, 99, 120, 158
Eastern Europe, viii–ix, 22
Eastern Slavonia, 100
economic, social, and cultural (ESC) rights, 3, 20, 21, 27, 33, 124, 145, 148, 152. See also human rights
Economic Community of West African States (ECOWAS), 101
economic crime, 36
economic justice, 12–13, 22, 28–29. See also justice
economic violence, 21, 22, 36–37, 152, 157–58. See also violence
  human rights and, 33
  legal/conceptual filtering device, 33–34
  marginalization of, 26–29
  narrow and broad approaches to, 29–30, 36–37
  positive peace and, 141–42
  poverty and, 22, 24
  in transitional justice, 29–34
    cost and complexity, 31
    political backlash, 30–31
education, 21, 24, 57, 119
Egypt, 78
El Salvador, 100
elections, 3, 56, 80, 99, 100–02, 103, 111, 124, 140, 143

electoral democracy, 149
elites, 41, 145
emancipatory peacebuilding, 96, 108, 110, 138, 151, 153–54, 162–64
embezzlement, 32
end of history, viii–ix, x–xi, 2, 5, 76, 90, 163
environment, 35, 71, 106
Etchecolatz, Miguel, 85
European Convention on Human Rights (ECHR), 73
European Court of Human Rights (ECtHR), 73
European Union, 132
everyday peace, 146–47, 148, 151, 152, 154
Extraordinary Chambers in the Courts of Cambodia, 48

failed states, 106
Fambul Tok, 69, 152
First Nations, 81
first-generation rights, 27
Ford Foundation, 9
France, 101, 103
free markets, 110, 124
free trade, 3, 148
Freedom House, 78, 79
Fukuyama, Francis, viii–ix, 2
Full Stop law (Argentina), 84

Gacaca, 62, 64–69, 70, 146
Galtung, John, 20, 21, 89, 90, 139, 141
Gambia, 51
Gbagbo, Laurent, 51, 80–81, 101–02
gender equality, 114
genocide, viii, 64, 65–66, 79, 142–43
Germany, 44
Ghana, 35, 36, 158
global ("the global"), 69–74
Global North, 24, 41–42, 106
Global South, 8–9, 24, 28, 41–42, 59, 71, 104–05, 106, 114
globalization, 5
glocality, 63, 66, 70, 146–47
Golan Heights, 98
good governance, 3, 8, 114
Goodale, Mark, 63
governance, 140
Gready, Paul, 90
Green, Thomas Hill, 148
Greenawalt, Alexander, 54–55
Grindle, Merliee, 140
Guatemala, 31, 100, 140

Habré, Hissène, 83, 85
Hague Invasion Act, 51

Haiti, 100
Hansen, Thomas, 82
Hayner, Priscilla, 6
Hazan, Pierre, 52
health, 21, 51, 119
Hobbs, Harry, 88
Hobhouse, L.T., 148
Hopgood, Stephen, 150
human rights, vii–viii, xi, 3, 5, 11, 28, 29–30, 87–88, 95, 113, 114, 148, 149, 150, 161, 162
    abuses or violations of, viii–ix, 1, 2, 3, 6, 22, 25, 26, 28, 36–37, 51, 55, 75, 81, 85, 86, 88, 118, 119
    advocates, 96–97
    civil and political rights, 3, 20, 21, 26, 33, 124, 141, 148, 152, 158
    cultural relativism and, 41–42
    economic, social, and cultural (ESC) rights, 3, 20, 21, 27, 33, 124, 145, 148, 152
    economic violence and, 33
    first generation, 27
    international standards, 62
    legalism, 21–22
    liberal internationalism and, 69–70
    monitoring organizations, 78
    movements, 27–28
    pluralistic approach to, 72
    prosecutions, 7, 50
    protection of, 104–05, 106, 121, 125
    second generation, 27
    universality debate in, 69–70
Human Rights Watch, 27–28, 64
human security, 89, 145
humanitarian intervention, 99
hunger, 21, 101
Huntington, Samuel, 2, 83–84
Hussein, Saddam, 62
Huyse, Luc, 65
hybrid tribunals, 7, 43, 48–49, 147
    evaluation of, 49
    spaceship phenomenon, 49
    theoretical model, 49
hybridity, 70–71, 139, 144, 146–47, 151, 152, 154, 163

illiberal, 4–5, 69–70, 80, 82, 87, 113, 139, 148, 150
impunity, 6, 8–9, 19–20, 26, 36, 51, 153–54
inclusivity, 112
India, 98
indigenous people, 81–82, 142–43
inequality, 137, 140
injustice, 82–83
Instance Équité et Réconciliation (IER), 56
institutionalization-before-liberalization model, 112

186 Index

Inter-American Commission on Human Rights, 84
internally displaced persons (IDPs), 102, 115
International Center for Transitional Justice, 56
international community, 109, 137
International Criminal Court (ICC), 7, 43, 50, 51, 53, 54–55, 61, 80–81, 118
  Office of the Prosecutor, 35
international criminal justice, 43
International Criminal Tribunal for Rwanda (ICTR), 7, 43, 45–46, 47–48, 67–68, 79, 81, 83, 120
International Criminal Tribunal for the Former Yugoslavia (ICTY), 7, 43, 45–46, 47–48, 61, 120
international financial institutions (IFIs), 108, 124
international humanitarian law, 3, 46, 47–48
International Journal of Transitional Justice (IJTJ), x–xi, 58, 63
international law, 6, 11, 20, 21, 27, 33, 36, 41, 48, 54–55, 73, 120, 121
International Monetary Fund (IMF), 124
intrastate conflict, 137
Israel, 24, 98

Japan, 132
justice, viii, 21–22, 137, 139, 140, 157
  access to, 42, 101, 110, 131–32, 148
  for atrocities, 141
  community-based, 152
  distributive, 21–22, 28–29, 31–32, 89, 90, 124, 141, 149–50, 157, 160–61
  economic, 12–13, 22, 28–29
  local, 152
  for positive peace, 141
  rectificatory, 10
  reparative, 75, 89
  restorative, 21–22, 43, 53, 82, 160–61
  retributive, 10, 21–22, 50, 53, 89, 160–61
  rural-based, 152
  social, 119, 150
  traditional, 152
  transitional. *See* transitional justice
justice cascade, 20–21
justice-sector reforms, 8

Kagamé, Patrick, 79
Kant, Immanuel, 109
Kennedy, David, 8–9
Kennedy, Duncan, 14
Kenya, 30, 35, 50, 51, 158
Kenyatta, Uhuru, 50
Kony, Joseph, 118

Kosovo, 48, 62, 99, 100
Kritz, Neil, 76, 83

laissez-faire, 148, 149–50
Lambourne, Wendy, 90
land, 24, 29, 30, 35, 36, 86
land-tenure reforms, 10–11, 26, 28–29, 30, 37
Laplante, Lisa, 36
Latin America, viii–ix, 22
laundry list syndrome, 104–05
lawyers, 10, 11, 12, 27, 72, 76, 83, 96, 120
least-developed countries (LDCs), 106
Lebanon, 120
legal pluralism, 42–43, 69–70, 71–72, 73, 88, 148, 149, 151
legalism, 3, 11, 21–22, 96
liberal democracy, 2, 139, 142–43
liberal international peacebuilding (LIPB), 90, 97, 109, 115–36, 138–39, 143, 144–45, 149, 153, 155, 162
  associated global projects, 105–08
  core pillar, 138
  critical peacebuilding theory, 138, 139, 154, 155
  critiques of, 108–14, 123–25
  overview, 115–17
  problems in, 149
  transitional justice and
    convergence signs, 118–23
    critiques of, 132–35
    linkages, 121–35
    marginalization of the local, 126–27
    over-standardization and bureaucratization, 133
    politics as neutral technology, 125–26
    tensions and complementarity in, 128–32
liberal internationalism, 69–70, 113, 124, 150
liberal localism, 113, 139, 150, 154, 159–60
liberal peace, 96, 109, 111, 113, 124, 149
liberalism, 5
  alternative, 139
  critical peacebuilding theory and, 148–50
Liberia, 7, 24, 33, 35, 36, 37, 60, 99, 100, 140, 146, 158
Libya, 50, 78, 100, 102
Lisan, 70
local ("the local"), marginalization of, 126–27
local ownership, 39–69, 74, 112, 152
  agency and control, 61
  complementarity principle, 52–53
  constituent parts of, 42–43, 66
  dilemmas of, 41–43
  elites and, 41
  global-local balance in, 69–71, 72–73, 74
  international involvement in, 61–62

multidimensionality of, 67
normative questions on, 59
overview, 39–41
post-conflict, 60–61
promises and pitfalls of, 57–63
significance of, 58–59
Longman, Timothy, 58
Lord's Resistance Army, 10, 50, 53, 80–81, 118
Loyle, Cyanne, 82
lustration, 19

Mac Ginty, Roger, 139
Mali, 50
Mandela, Nelson, 7
Mani, Rama, 10, 55, 56, 75, 89
margin of appreciation, 73, 159
market democracy, viii, 2, 22
marketization, 106, 109, 111, 149
mass atrocities, 3, 8, 10, 11, 14, 37–38, 106, 163
mass murderers, 8–9
Mazlish, Bruce, 62
McAuliffe, Padraig, 49, 86–87
Menem, Carlos, 84, 85
Merry, Sally Engle, 16
Middle East, viii–ix
Millennium Development Goals (MDGs), 106, 144
Miller, Zinaida, 22, 25–26
Mironko, Charles, 46
mission civilisatrice, 124
Mission des Nations Unies en Côte d'Ivoire (MINUCI), 101
money laundering, 24
moral imagination, viii
Moreno-Ocampo, Luis, 53, 54
Moroccan Equity and Reconciliation Commission, 56
Mothers of the Plaza de Mayo, 85
Mozambique, 56, 100, 135
murder, 8–9, 10–11, 19–20, 25, 28, 65, 85, 124
Museveni, Yoweri, 54, 80

nation building, vii–viii, 119
National Socialist (Nazi) party, 44
natural resources, 21, 25, 33, 35, 36
Nazi, 1, 2
negative liberty, 148–49
negative peace, 26, 89, 90, 99, 119, 139. *See also* positive peace
Neier, Aryeh, 27
neocolonialism, 8
neoliberal internationalism, 113, 150
neoliberalism, ix, 5, 148, 149, 157, 162
Newman, Edward, 138

non-governmental organizations (NGOs), 108
North Africa, 142–43
North America, 142–43
Northern Uganda, 53
Nunca Más, 6, 84
Nuremberg International Military Tribunal, 2, 44

Office of the High Commissioner for Human Rights (OHCHR), 7, 100
Olsen, Tricia, 88
Oomn, Barbara, 64–65
Opération des Nations Unies en Côte d'Ivoire (ONUCI), 101–02
Ouattara, Alassane, 54, 80, 102
outreach, 46–47, 49, 50, 146

Pakistan, 98
paradigmatic transitions, 5, 10–11, 28–29, 76, 77, 81, 82–83, 86–87, 88, 90, 95, 153–54
Paris, Roland, 108, 123, 138
participation, 149–50, 152
participatory development, 67
particularism, 69–70
Payne, Leigh, 88
peace
   everyday, 146–47, 148, 151, 152, 154
   liberal, 96, 109, 111, 113, 124, 149
   negative, 26, 89, 90, 99, 119, 139
   popular, 145, 146–47, 148, 151, 152, 154, 155
   positive, 26, 89, 90–91, 99, 119, 139–44, 151, 152, 154, 157
   sustaining, 105, 120–21, 125
   trickle-down, 112, 145
   virtual, 110
peace agreement, 8, 118, 119, 139
peace versus justice, 6, 30, 115, 118, 120–21, 153, 154
peacebuilding, 29, 47–48, 58, 59–60, 90, 95–114, 120, 137, 139
   activities, 99
   agenda for, 153–54
   associated global projects, 105–08
   in Côte d'Ivoire, 100–03
   critical theories of, 144–48
   DDR in, 128
   emancipatory, 96, 108, 110, 138, 151, 153–54, 162–64
   legalization of, 121
   liberal international. *See* liberal international peacebuilding (LIPB)
   liberal vs. illiberal, 148
   overview, 95–97
   peacekeeping to, 97–100
   UN definition of, 98–99

peacebuilding (*cont.*)
  United Nations Peacebuilding Commission (PBC), 103–05, 135
Peacebuilding Fund (PBF), 103
Peacebuilding Support Office (PBSO), 103
peacekeeping, 58
  consensual, 98
  elections and, 3
  first-generation, 98
  legitimacy of, 58
  mandates, 120, 128
  peacebuilding and, 97–100
periphery, 5, 7, 22, 25–26, 106
physical violence, 20–21, 22, 36–37, 152
Pinochet, Augusto, 51, 85
plunder, 21, 30, 33
pluralism, 71–72, 148, 149, 159
political rights. *See* civil and political rights
politics, as neutral technology, 125–26
popular peace, 145, 146–47, 148, 151, 152, 154, 155
positive liberty, 148–49
positive peace, 26, 89, 90–91, 99, 119, 139–41, 144, 151, 152, 154, 157. *See also* negative peace
  achievement of, 142
  benefits of, 143–44
  economic violence and, 141–42
  justice for, 142, 143
  liberal democracy and, 142–43
Posner, Eric, 13
posttransitional justice, 85
postconflict checklist, 97, 116, 133
postconflict justice, vii–viii, 9, 27, 54–55, 59–61, 68, 69–70, 105
postconflict reconstruction, 19, 142
poverty, 119, 140
  alleviating, 3
  civil wars and, 33
  economic violence and, 22, 24
  eradication of, 101
  racism and, 25
  structural violence and, 89
poverty reduction strategy papers (PRSPs), 106
Princess Bride, The (movie), 58
principle of complementarity, 51–53
problem solving, 111
prosecutions, 1, 6, 7, 46, 50, 53
  in Argentina, 84
  of "big fish," 152
  in Chile, 85
  in Côte d'Ivoire, 80
  domestic, 50
  for embezzlement, 26
  hybrid tribunals for, 68
  international, 24, 43, 48, 51, 54–55, 62, 118

limited and selective, 34
local ownership of, 61
peace agreements and, 118, 119
preference, 10
in Rwanda, 79
for torture, rape and murder, 28
truth commissions and, 12, 31

racism, 20, 25, 28, 140
radical humility, 164–65
rape, 10–11, 19–20, 25, 28, 124
Reaganism, 3
reconciliation, vii–viii, 1, 14, 46, 50, 53, 56, 57, 64–65, 69, 71, 80, 81, 82, 87–88, 96–97, 104–05, 114, 120, 134–35, 143–44, 152
rectificatory justice, 10
refugees, 99, 102, 116
regional organizations, 108
Regulation 64 Panels (Kosovo), 48
Reiter, Andrew, 88
relativism, 72
religious extremism, x–xi, 78
reparations, vii–viii, 1, 19, 36, 42–43, 46, 85, 137, 152
reparative justice, 75, 89
repugnancy clause, 71
request for proposals (RFPs), 106
responsibility to protect (R2P), 52, 102, 106
restorative justice, 21–22, 43, 53, 82, 160–61. *See also* justice
retributive justice, 10, 21–22, 50, 53, 160–61. *See also* justice
Rettig Commission, 85
Richmond, Oliver, 138
Roberts, David, 145
Robins, Simon, 90
Roht-Arriaza, Naomi, 32
Rome Statute, 50, 51–52, 53
Roosevelt, Franklin, 44
root causes, 22, 24, 35, 90, 98, 104–05, 110, 121–35
Rousseff, Dilma, 86
rule of law, 2, 120, 121, 143–44, 149
Rumsfeld, Donald, 51
Russia, 24
Rwanda, 7, 47, 60, 62, 79–80, 87, 100, 146
  Gacaca process, 64–69, 70
  genocide, 64, 65–66
  international criminal tribunal, 7, 43, 45–46, 47–48, 67–68, 79, 81, 83, 120
  prison population, 64
Rwandan Patriotic Front (RPF), 68, 79

Sábato Commission (Comisión Nacional sobre la Desaparición de Personas, CONADEP), 6
Schmidt, Evelyne, 20

second-generation rights, 27
security-sector reform (SSR), 115, 130–32
self-determination, 59, 148, 149, 150
Senegal, 7, 79, 83
Serious Crimes Panels of the District Court of Dili, 48
sexual violence, 19–20
Shany, Yuval, 73
Shaw, Rosalind, 56–57
Sierra Leone, 7, 8, 24, 31, 33, 34, 36, 48, 62, 69, 100, 120, 135, 146, 152, 158
Sikkink, Kathryn, 7, 8, 14, 19–20, 50, 88
Simón case, 85
slavery, 142–43
social justice, 119, 150. *See also* justice
social services, 145
Somalia, 100
South Africa, 4, 6, 30, 51
South African Truth and Reconciliation Commission Act, 25
Soviet Union, 97, 111
Special Court for Sierra Leone (SCSL), 34, 43, 48, 61
Spencer, Herbert, 148
Spivak, Gayatri Chakravorty, 63
Sriram, Chandra, 124, 141
stage theory, 76
Stahn, Carsten, 59, 61, 62
Stanley, Ruth, 58
starvation, 21
statebuilding, 45–46, 103, 112
strategic essentialism, 63
structural adjustment programs (SAPs), 106
structural violence, 20, 21, 26, 29, 89
subsidiarity, 73
Sudan, 50, 100, 118
Sumner, William Graham, 148
sustainable development, 114
sustaining peace, 105, 120–21, 125
Syria, viii, 78, 98

Tadjbakhsh, Shahrbanou, 109
taxation, 10–11, 26, 28–29, 30, 148
Taylor, Charles, 48, 51
Teitel, Ruti, 3, 76, 119
Thatcherism, 3
The Gambia, 51
The Hague, 7, 45, 48, 50
Third World Approaches to International Law (TWAIL), 14, 138
third-wave transitions, 2, 89
Timor-Leste, 100
Tokyo War Crimes Tribunal, 2, 45
top-down, 11, 13, 66, 67–68, 117, 126–27, 133, 145

torture, 10–11, 19–20, 25, 28, 85, 124
traditional practices, 12, 42, 53, 150
transformative justice, 75
transition, 75–91, 137, 139, 153
  concept of, 82
  conceptualization of, 76–77, 88–90
  democratic, 4–5, 22, 76, 78, 87, 89, 90
  intelligibility of, 88–89
  as narrow liberal theology, 78–83
  paradigmatic, 5, 10–11, 28–29, 76, 77, 81, 82–83, 86–87, 88, 90, 95, 153–54
  relevance of, 86–91
  as window of opportunity, 83–86
transitional justice, vii–viii
  agenda for, 153–54
  as an apolitical toolbox, 5
  atrocity justice and, 4–5
  backward looking vs. forward looking projects, 119
  conflicts and, 23–26
  contested peripheries of the field, 13–16
  definitions of, 1
  democratization and, 4–5
  destination of, 28–29
  dilemmas of, 13
  dilution of, 32
  duration of, 28
  economic violence in, 29–34
    cost and complexity, 31
    political backlash, 30–31
  expansion and growth of, 89
  foundations, 137–54
  future of, 155–65
    emancipatory peacebuilding, 162–64
    extended concepts of peace/justice/violence, 156–58
    liberal localism, 159–60
    radical humility, 164–65
    retributive/restorative/distributive justice, 160–61
  global-local, 39–41, 42, 43–57, 63–69
  invisibility of economic concerns in, 23–26
  legitimacy of, 62
  mechanisms and interventions, 6
  mechanisms of, 82, 87, 88
  origins of, 1–16
    in 1980s and 1990s, 3–4
    experts and professionals, 10–13
    journey from exception to mainstream, 5–10
  paradigmatic transitions of, 5, 88, 95
  peace vs. justice debate, 118, 154
  periphery of, 5, 7, 22, 25–26, 106
  policy and practice, 35–37
  politics of, 37–38

transitional justice (cont.)
  promotion of injustice and, 82–83
  reasons for, 19–23
  toolbox, 19, 28–29, 42–43, 82, 118, 137
translocality, 63
tribunals
  ad hoc, 46–47, 48, 50
  distanced and isolated nature of, 45–46
  hybrid, 48, 49
  legitimacy of, 47–48
  time and resource management, 47–48
trickle-down peace, 112, 145
trusteeship, 99
Truth and Dignity Commission (Tunisia), 158
Truth and Reconciliation Commission (South Africa), 25
truth commissions, 12, 24, 31, 33, 35–36, 161
  aims of, 55
  assumptions of, 57
  as a global phenomenon, 56
  global-local balance in, 55–56
  location of, 55
truth-telling, 46, 56, 57, 137
truth versus justice, 6, 118
Tunisia, x–xi, 35, 158
Tutu, Desmond, 7

Uganda, 10, 50, 53, 80, 87, 118
Ulvin, Peter, 41–42
United Kingdom, 7
United Nations, vii–viii, 22, 39–41, 57, 96–97, 104, 106, 108, 115, 144, 155
United Nations Assistance Mission in Sierra Leone (UNAMSIL), 128
United Nations Charter, 120
United Nations Department of Peacekeeping Operations (DPKO), 100, 121–35
United Nations Department of Political Affairs (DPA), 100
United Nations Development Programme (UNDP), 100, 120
United Nations Disengagement Observer Force, 98
United Nations General Assembly (UNGA), 104, 125
United Nations Military Observer Group, 98
United Nations Mission in Côte d'Ivoire (UNOCI), 128
United Nations Mission in Liberia (UNMIL), 128
United Nations Mission in the Sudan (UNMIS), 128
United Nations Office of the High Commissioner for Human Rights (OHCHR), 56, 64–65, 100, 120

United Nations Office of the High Commissioner for Refugees (UNHCR), 100
United Nations Operation in Burundi (UNOB), 128
United Nations Peacebuilding Commission (PBC), 103–05, 132, 135
United Nations Peacekeeping Force, 98
United Nations Secretary-General (UNSG), 7–8, 35
United Nations Security Council Resolution, 46
United Nations Security Council (UNSC), 46, 50, 100, 104, 125, 128
United Nations Stabilization Mission in Haiti (MINUSTAH), 128
United States, 2, 20, 24, 51, 90, 132, 140
US Bureau of Crisis Prevention and Recovery (BCPR), 120
US Institute for Peace (USIP), 83
Universal Declaration of Human Rights (UDHR), 27
universal periodic review (UPR), 106
universalism, 69–70, 72, 148
Uruguay, 4
Uvin, Peter, 46

Valech Commission, 85
van Boven, Theo, 3
Vermeule, Adrian, 13
vetting, 1, 19, 26, 42–43, 46, 130–32, 137
victor's justice, 44, 45–46, 54–55, 80, 81, 109
Videla, Jorge Rafael, 84, 85
Viola, Roberto Eduardo, 84
violence
  conception of, 25
  cultural, 20
  direct, 20
  economic. See economic violence
  physical, 20–21, 22, 36–37
  structural, 20, 21, 26, 29, 89
  transitional justice and, 157
virtual peace, 110

Waldorf, Lars, 28
war crimes, 2, 20, 33, 44, 80–81, 83
Washington Consensus, 3
Westphalian, 97–98, 108
World Bank, 3, 124, 132
World War II, viii, 2, 44

Yugoslavia, 7

zone of confidence, 101

Lightning Source UK Ltd.
Milton Keynes UK
UKHW022027071121
393484UK00018B/283